IMPORTANT NOTICE

The massive Willow Fire of September 1999 burned over 63,000 acres on the north slope of the San Bernardinos and the high desert. It was the largest fire in the San Bernardino National Forest in 80 years. Eleven trips in *San Bernardino Mountain Trails* are partly or wholly burned over: trips 4, 9, 10, 12, 13, 14, 15, 16, 17, 18, and 19. Although they are still hikeable, you will be walking through large areas of charred forest and chaparral until the vegetation can grow back. We suggest you call the Arrowhead Ranger District (909) 337-2444 or the Big Bear Ranger District (909) 866-3437 before you attempt any of these trips.

San Bernardino Mountain Trails

100 HIKES
IN SOUTHERN CALIFORNIA

John W. Robinson

Wilderness Press
Berkeley

FIRST EDITION May 1972
SECOND EDITION April 1975
THIRD EDITION April 1979
FOURTH EDITION August 1986
Second printing March 1988
Third printing September 1989
Fourth printing November 1990
Fifth printing October 1992
Sixth printing January 1995
Seventh printing June 1997
Eighth printing November 1999

Photos by the author except as noted
Design by Thomas Winnett
Cover design by Larry B. Van Dyke
Cover photo © 1986 by Ed Cooper
Drawings by Lucille Winnett

Library of Congress Card Catalog Number 82-62811
International Standard Book Number 0-89997-023-0

Printed in the United States of America

Published by **Wilderness Press**
      1200 5th St.
      Berkeley, CA 94710
      (800) 443-7227
      FAX (510) 558-1696
      EMAIL mail@wildernesspress.com
      www.wildernesspress.com

      Contact us for a free catalog

Library Of Congress Cataloging-in-Publication Data

Robinson, John W.
  San Bernardino Mountain Trails
  Bibliography: p.
  Includes index.
  1. Hiking—California—San Bernardino Mountains—Guide-books.
2. Trails—California—San Bernardino Mountains—Guide-books.
3. San Bernardino Mountains (Calif.)—Description and travel—
Guide-books.
I. Title.
GV199.42.C22S257 1986   917,94'95   85-41027
ISBN 0-89997-063-X

ACKNOWLEDGMENTS

Many people provided invaluable help in this gathering of knowledge. First of all, I express gratitude to research institutions such as the Henry E. Huntington Library, the Bancroft Library, the San Bernardino County Museum, the San Bernardino County Library, the San Jacinto Museum, the Idyllwild Public Library, and the Palm Springs Desert Museum. For information on the San Bernardino Mountains, I owe most to the late George W. Beattie, historian-extraordinary who in his day probably knew more about San Bernardino County than anyone else. Pauliena La Fuze of Twin Peaks and Arda Haenszel of San Bernardino provided valuable pieces of information too. For material on the San Jacinto Mountains, my greatest source was Charles Van Fleet of San Jacinto, whose collection of historical information and photographs is second to none. Others who helped with these mountains were Harry C. James of Lake Fulmor, Richard Elliott of Idyllwild, Ernest Maxwell of the Idyllwild *Town Crier*, Jim Wellman of 101 Ranch, and Sam Fink of Santa Ana. Glen Dawson of Dawson's Book Shop, Los Angeles, provided valuable material on mountain history from his collection. Don McLain of Altadena, who mapped these mountains a half century ago, supplied information on place names. My friends in the Angeles Chapter of the Sierra Club introduced me to these mountains long ago and have often been my companions on hiking trips. Bill Kelsey of Long Beach provided valuable photographic help. To these, and to others who helped in lesser but still important ways, my heart-felt thanks.

J.W.R.

Keeping a guidebook up to date is a never-ending job. We have done our best to make the book as current as possible. Special thanks go to Ron Lawson of the Arrowhead Ranger District and Carol Hallacy and Judy Walton of the San Jacinto Ranger District, Russell Bell of Santa Monica, Jerry Keating of Placentia, and the late Charles Miller of Idyllwild, all of whom advised the author of trail changes and pointed out errors in previous editions.

J. W. R.
Fullerton, California
June 18, 1999

ABOUT THE AUTHOR

John W. Robinson has for more than 40 years explored, backpacked, and climbed thoughout the mountain west, from Alaska and Canada to Mexico. His first guidebook, *Camping and Climbing in Baja* (now out of print) was the standard guide to the Baja California mountains. His *Trails of the Angeles* remains the definitive hiking guide to southern California's San Gabriel Mountains. He authored or co-authored several of the Wilderness Press quadrangle guides to the High Sierra. His trilogy of *The San Gabriels*, *The San Bernardinos*, and *The San Jacintos* cover the history of southern California's three major mountain ranges. His articles have appeared in such periodicals as *Westways*, *Desert Magazine*, *The Southern California Quarterly*, *The Overland Journal*, and *Summit*. He is currently working on *Gateways to Southern California*, a history of the trails, highways, and railroads into the southern part of the state.

Table of Contents

Introduction

San Bernardino National Forest sprawls over a generous portion of Southern California's mountain landscape. It begins atop Old Baldy in the San Gabriel Mountains and ends on the desert-tempered slopes of Toro Peak and Martinez Mountain in the Santa Rosa Mountains — 100 miles in a great northwest-southeast arc. Within its bounds are all or part of four distinct mountain ranges — the eastern San Gabriels, the San Bernardinos, the San Jacintos, and the northern Santa Rosas (five ranges, if you consider Cahuilla Mountain to be separate from the San Jacintos).

Within the San Bernardino is all manner of mountain country. There are gentle flatlands and rolling hills, and there are sheer escarpments and rock-ribbed peaks that soar above everything else in Southern California. There are hot slopes smothered in thorny chaparral, and there are cool alpine forests of pine and fir. There are places where snow almost never falls, and there are spots where snowbanks linger half the year. There are sparkling mountain lakes and boggy meadows, quiet brooks and rushing streams. Often there are barrel cactuses and Joshua trees in close proximity to Jeffrey pines and incense cedars. Perhaps no other national forest in the United States contains such variety.

Man has made his indelible mark on much of this landscape. He has built a maze of roads, and he has erected a multitude of homes, resorts, and places of business high up in the forest country. Some areas — Crestline, Lake Arrowhead, Big Bear, Idyllwild — are so urbanized that they differ little from the cities below. About 15,000 people make their permanent home in the San Bernardino Mountains alone, and there are 16 post offices to serve them.

Yet there is wilderness here in these overused mountains, places where man — either by nature's design or his own foresight — has left the mountains to themselves. Here, deep in the forest, alongside an alder-canopied stream or high on a rocky crag, you can relax and contemplate and enjoy nature's solitude. You can breathe the restoring scents of forest and chaparral, and listen to the quiet sounds of the earth. You can come to understand the true value of wilderness to a civilization that too often places artificial values before real ones.

The largest wilderness regions in San Bernardino National Forest are the wild areas around San Gorgonio Mountain and San Jacinto Peak, set aside by man to remain forever in their natural, pristine state. Here is the highest mountain country in Southern California and, in the eyes of many, the most delightful. Besides these two official wild areas, there are many other parts of the mountains where, by reason of remoteness or difficulty of access, man's touch has been minimal. These are scattered throughout the mountains, some of them quite close to overused areas — the Pinnacles country north of Lake Arrowhead, lower Holcomb and Deep creeks, the bouldered slopes above Big Bear Lake, the Heart Bar country, Yucaipa Ridge, the palm-and-pinyon country on the desert slopes of the San Jacintos, the lonely Santa Rosas, to name the best.

This guidebook attempts to acquaint Southern Californians — and others — with the intimate parts of San Bernardino National Forest, the regions away from highway and byway where nature still reigns relatively undisturbed. The 100 hiking trips in this book take the reader and prospective hiker into almost every nook and cranny of the mountains. They vary from easy one-hour strolls to all-day and overnight rambles involving many miles of walking and much elevation change — excursions to satisfy the novice and challenge the veteran.

There is one overriding requirement — you must like to walk and be willing to forgo the comforts of civilization for periods ranging from a few short hours to several days.

Trails and fire roads crisscross much of San Bernardino National Forest, some well maintained and easy to follow, others almost-forgotten byways of the past, eroded and overgrown in spots. The great majority of trips in this guidebook are on maintained trails, and these should present no problems to the hiker. However, the writer has included a handful of cross-country scrambles and trailless peak climbs in areas well worth visiting but not served by standard routes. For these trips, directions have been presented in greater detail.

The writer has walked, recorded and researched all the trips in this guide. Every effort has been made to present the information as accurately and as explicitly as possible. Nevertheless, the prospective hiker should be aware that several factors — the rapid growth of chaparral, fire, flood, and the continual reworking of trails — may make some of this information out-of-date in a short time. Such changes will probably affect only a few of the trips described here, but if you are unfamiliar with the area in which you plan to hike, it is best to inquire at a ranger station before your trip.

The trail trips have been graded, based on the writer's evaluation, as "easy," "moderate" or "strenuous." An "easy" trip is usually four miles or less in horizontal distance, with less than 500′ elevation gain — suitable for beginners and children. A "moderate" trip — including the majority here — is a five-to-ten-mile hike, usually with less than 2500′ elevation difference. You should be in fair physical condition for these, and children under 12 might find the going difficult. "Strenuous" trips are all-day rambles involving many miles of hiking and much elevation gain and loss; they arc only for those in top physical condition and with hiking experience. The most important criteria for grading a trip are mileage covered, elevation gain and loss, and condition of the trail. Of less significance are accessibility of terrain, availability of water, exposure to sun, and ground cover. Obviously, some of the latter criteria depend on the weather and time of year: a 3-mile hike over open chaparral slopes can be miserable under the hot August sun but delightful in January's cool breeze and cloudiness.

A season recommendation is also included for each trip. This classification is particularly important in the lower, south- and west-facing parts of the mountains; due to fire danger these sections are closed from July 1 until the first appreciable rain in the fall.

This book is entitled *San Bernardino Mountain Trails* because the mountain regions covered are predominantly in San Bernardino National Forest. There are two exceptions. The western end of San Bernardino National Forest extends into the San Gabriel Mountains and this section is included in the companion volume *Trails of the Angeles*. To make up for this absence, the entire Santa Rosa Range is covered in this guide, even though San Bernardino National Forest encompasses only the northern half. So, the reader comes out even.

It is the writer's earnest desire that this guidebook will provide the prospective mountain visitor with the knowledge that can make an outing in the San Bernardinos, San Jacintos or Santa Rosas an enjoyable and meaningful experience. If you learn and heed forest regulations, follow route directions, become familiar with the area, have proper equipment, and use good sense, you will thoroughly appreciate your intimacy with the mountains. Never leave the trailhead without this preparation. The mountains are no place to travel alone, unbriefed, ill equipped or in poor condition. Enter their portals with the enthusiasm of adventure tempered with respect, forethought and common sense. The mountains belong to those who are wise as well as willing.

Hiking Hints

Some hikers have emerged from the mountains with the scent of laurel and pine on their clothing and with dust on their boots, tired but enriched — both physically and mentally — by their wilderness experience. Others have stumbled out of the mountains exhausted, footsore, sunburned, dehydrated, chilled, with clothing and skin torn by thorny chaparral, or soaked to the bone by unexpected downpour, sadder but wiser for their ordeal. Some have had to be carried out. And a few have not come out.

An outing in the mountains can be many things — fabulous, pleasant, unpleasant, harrowing or disastrous. How it turns out depends to a large degree on the hiker himself — his preparation, his clothing and equipment, his physical condition, and his good sense.

Below are some hints to make your mountain trip an enjoyable and rewarding experience.

Preparation

Choose a trip that suits your ability. If you have never hiked before, visit Little Bear Creek or South Fork Meadow — something in the "easy" category. As you gain experience and learn the feel of mountain travel, graduate to something in the "moderate" class. Do not undertake a "strenuous" outing until you are both experienced and in top physical condition.

Become familiar with the terrain and landscape features of the area you plan to visit by studying a good map beforehand. It may be advisable to check with the Forest Service before your trip, particularly if you plan to walk a trail not regularly maintained (such trails are so indicated in this guide). Most rangers on duty at the National Forest ranger stations are only too glad to help, and few people know the mountains better than they. Or contact San Bernardino National Forest headquarters at 1824 South Commercenter Circle, San Bernardino, CA 92408-3430 (phone (909) 383-5588).

If you plan to visit the San Gorgonio Wilderness, the San Jacinto Wilderness or Mount San Jacinto State Wilderness, you must obtain a Wilderness Permit first. The permit is free to anyone who will agree to follow some simple rules intended to protect the visitor as well as the wilderness. To obtain the permit, visit or write to one of the following ranger stations:

San Gorgonio Wilderness: Mill Creek Ranger Station, Route 1, Box 264, Mentone, CA 92359. Phone: (909) 794-1123

San Jacinto Wilderness: Idyllwild Ranger Station, Idyllwild, CA 92349. Phone: (909) 659-2117

Mount San Jacinto State Wilderness: P.O. Box 308, Idyllwild, CA 92349. Phone: (909) 659-2607

Some winter-season trips in this book start on private property. Landowners apparently have the right to block public access to the public property farther up the trail any time they wish. Be prepared to ask for permission, and have an alternative trip in mind in case you are refused.

Clothing

Mountain weather can vary considerably, even within a few hours. It is best to come prepared for both warm and cool temperatures with several layers of clothing — shirt, sweater and windbreaker, for example — that can be put on or peeled off as needed. This is particularly advisable if you plan to climb any of the high peaks.

Short pants may be satisfactory when walking a fire road or rambling through an open forest at middle elevations, but they are miserable for thrashing through chaparral. If any part of your trip is through this elfin forest, wear sturdy long pants — and expect to get them torn.

Choice of headgear depends on the hiker. If you sunburn easily, you will probably want a hat with generous brim. If the weather looks threatening, bring raingear.

Footgear

If the walk is short and on good trail, tennis shoes are adequate. But if the trip is long or over rough terrain, a pair of sturdy boots, preferably with lug soles, should be worn.

Properly fitting shoes and close-fitting, heavy-duty socks are essential to prevent blisters and sore feet. A mistake in footwear can ruin your trip. Break in new boots on short walks before you attempt a long hike. If you blister easily, carry moleskin, and use it at the first hint of oncoming trouble.

Equipment

A day hike in the mountains requires little in the way of equipment. It is surprising how many novices over-burden themselves with large packs, extra clothing, too much food, tin cans, hunting knives, and miscellaneous gadgets.

Still, there are essentials that all hikers should carry. These include a full canteen (unless the trail is close to a stream), a first-aid kit, an area map, and some food. If you are doing any cross-country hiking, a compass is advisable and a topographic map is virtually a requirement. You will probably want to bring a camera. To carry all this, a lightweight rucksack or "summit pack" is advisable, preferably with a waistband to better distribute the weight.

An overnight outing, of course, requires more (see *Backpacking* below).

Food

Trail menus vary considerably, and there is little agreement among experts about what foods are best. Sandwiches, cheese, fruit, nuts, cookies and candy are probably the most popular trail foods. A planned, balanced diet is necessary only on an outing of several days.

What you eat is not nearly so important as how much

you eat, and when. Small lunches plus snacks along the trail are best, because exertion after a feast causes competition for blood between stomach and hiking muscles, and leads to indigestion and weakness.

As important as food on a hike is liquid. Without enough water, exertion and heat dehydrate the body surprisingly soon and cause marked muscular weakness. Unless you are walking alongside a stream, bring a full canteen — two if the weather is hot and your walk is long.

Giardia has made its appearance here. All water should be boiled, treated or filtered first.

On the trail

Walking a mountain trail is not as simple as one might think. An enjoyable hike requires proper pace and rest stops, knowledge of the terrain, correct reading of trail signs and, above all, good judgment.

Unless you are training for the Olympics, a trail hike should not be a race to your destination and back. Start out slowly, easing your muscles into condition. Work up to the steady, rhythmic pace that suits you best. Your best trail speed is one at which you are working but not panting, and you feel you can continue almost indefinitely. When the trail steepens, shorten your steps but maintain your rhythm. Take short rests at moderate intervals, rather than stopping too frequently or too long at a time. If you are exceeding your ability, symptoms of exhaustion soon set in: sore or cramped leg muscles, profuse sweating, pounding pulse, headache, dizziness, redness of the face. Not only do these lessen your enjoyment, but a tired hiker is more accident-prone. The speedster who rushes up the trail, then collapses in a panting heap, is usually overtaken before long by the leisurely hiker. "Who goes into the mountains fast, comes out last," says an old proverb.

Stay on the trail. Short cuts not only break down the trail (see *Mountain Courtesy* below) but can lead you astray. Probably the greatest temptation is to cut switchbacks — but sometimes the last zigzag doesn't zag, and you find yourself stumbling down a steep talus slope to nowhere, or thrashing through thorny brush in the wrong direction. When you finally realize your mistake, you are faced with the unpleasant necessity of churning back up the loose talus or beating through an ocean of chaparral — a painful, time-consuming object lesson in mountain sense.

When you come to a marked trail junction, read the sign carefully. If a junction is unmarked, consult your map and observe the surrounding landmarks to keep yourself oriented. If the trail seems to disappear in brush or boulders, look ahead for the way you think it should go; most trails take the obvious route. Look for *ducks* (several stones piled atop one another) that indicate the route. If you still can't find the trail, and you are not experienced in cross-country travel, it is better to return the way you came than to risk getting lost.

Off the trail

Although trails crisscross San Bernardino National Forest, there are some places they don't go — the length of Deep Creek in the San Bernardinos, and up Cornell Peak in the San Jacintos, for example. To reach these objectives, you must leave the established footpath and travel cross country. Off-trail hiking, except for very short distances, is not for beginners. Attempt it only if you are an experienced hiker, and then never alone.

Cross-country hiking in the San Bernardinos and San Jacintos is practical only in parts of the mountains — at higher elevations, along ridgetops and along streambeds. In lower-elevation chaparral it is virtually impossible.

If you are planning a trip that is part cross-country, be sure you know the terrain, the landmarks, the ground cover and the distance. Obtain a topographic map of the area and plan your route beforehand. Before you leave road or trail, make a visual survey of the region, noting the locations of landmarks. Continue this careful observation as you hike; look back at landmarks you'll want to use on the return trip — it's surprising how different the country sometimes looks when you're going the other way.

Without question, the most unpleasant type of cross-country travel is bushwhacking — an ordeal you should avoid whenever possible. One mile through unyielding chaparral is as difficult and tiring as 6 or 8 miles on trail, and much rougher on your clothing. If you must bush-whack, seek out terrain where the elfin forest is less dense — along ridges, in gullies, over recently burned areas. Chaparral also is thinner on shady, north-facing slopes than on sun-drenched, south-facing slopes. When entering a brushy area, secure loose items of clothing and equipment. It's mighty tough to retrace your exact route to find a lost camera or canteen.

On slopes of loose talus or scree, tread lightly; even the most careful walker cannot avoid dislodging a few rocks or triggering a slide. Solid-looking boulders may be precariously balanced; you must be ever-ready to leap nimbly aside when a foothold gives way.

Stream crossing is an art thoroughly mastered by few, and rare is the hiker who has never dampened his boots. If you cannot find a dry crossing — a series of stepping-stones or a strategically located log — you must wade. It is better to wade the widest part of the stream, where the water is shallower and the current is slower. If the stream-bed rocks are smooth, wade across barefoot. If they are sharp-edged, remove your socks and wear your boots across. Then drain your boots, dry your feet, and replace socks and boots.

Hiking over snow can be a pleasure if the grade is gentle and the snow firm but not icy. It can be tedious if the sun has softened the snow so much that you break through at every step. And it can be extremely dangerous if the slope is steep and the snow icy, as it often is in higher elevations during late winter and spring. If you plan to snow-hike, a pair of lug-soled boots are a necessity, preferably treated with a waterproof wax and worn with gaiters (waterproof leggings covering the upper part of the boot and part of the pant leg) to keep your feet dry. An ice axe, and knowledge of how to use it, is a requirement for steep snow slopes. Serious climbing on snow and ice, requiring ice axe, crampons and rope, is only for skilled mountaineers. If you are interested, the Sierra Club offers a mountaineering course.

Rock climbers have graded mountain routes into six categories, ranging from Class 1 (hiking) to Class 6 (climbing a vertical or overhanging cliff). You won't find much above Class 1 or 2 in these mountains, but there are some peaks whose ascent by certain routes involves some steep rock-scrambling — categorized as Class 3. The Pinnacles and Cornell Peak are examples. Class 3 climbing requires great caution. Move slowly, and test every handhold and foothold before shifting your weight. Take extra care on the descent, for this is when most accidents occur. And you must wear lug-soled boots or climbing shoes for traction on rock. If you are interested in serious rock climbing, the Sierra Club Rock Climbing Section holds practice sessions during winter and spring. Tahquitz Rock above Idyllwild is a favorite practice area for advanced rock climbers.

Backpacking

San Bernardino National Forest offers superb opportunities for overnight backpack trips — particularly in the San Gorgonio and San Jacinto wilderness areas. The Forest Service maintains a number of overnight trail camps in these and other areas, many of them in delightful sylvan haunts away from the markings of civilization.

Most important is your choice of a pack itself. A wrong choice can cause an aching back and make backpacking a disagreeable experience. There are two main types of packs — the rucksack and the frame pack — and both have their advantages and their disadvantages. The rucksack, a rounded canvas bag that clings against the back or has a rudimentary frame, takes up less space and is superior for bushwhacking and steep cross-country scrambling. As long as your pack weight is below 20 or 25 pounds, a rucksack is usually big enough and relatively comfortable. For long trail trips or for comfort with heavy loads, it is hard to beat the rectangular aluminum-and-nylon frame pack, which has attained great popularity in recent years. Whichever type you use, a waistband is important to place most of the weight on the hips rather than the shoulders.

For a good night's rest, you need a good sleeping bag.

Down is the most efficient material for keeping you warm, but down bags are expensive. "All-feather" bags are about 80% as warm as down, and dacron bags about 66% as warm — per unit weight of filling. For summertime trips in elevations below 8,000 feet, chances are that nights in these mountains will be mild, and a cheaper bag will be adequate. If you're a winter or spring backpacker, or if you plan to camp at any of the high trail camps in the two wild areas, better go down. "Mummy" and rectangular shaped bags each have their adherents. Some people cannot tolerate the close fit of the mummy style, despite its superior thermal and weight characteristics.

Other backpacking essentials include warm clothing, raingear, plastic ground cloth, air mattress or foam pad, utensils, cooking gear, flashlight, first-aid kit, snakebite kit, matches and toilet paper. During rainy season (winter and spring) better tote a waterproof tent or — much less expensive — a plastic "tube tent" held up by nylon line.

Camping

You are required to obtain a campfire permit, obtainable at most ranger stations, if you plan to camp overnight in San Bernardino National Forest. If your trip is in the San Gorgonio Wilderness (Federal) or the San Jacinto State Wilderness, you must obtain a wilderness permit (which includes permission for a campfire). Camp only in established trail camps and build your fire only in campground stoves or fire rings; open fires are not allowed. If you are travelling in the San Jacinto Wilderness (Federal), camping rules have recently been changed. The Forest Service no longer maintains established trail camps. Instead, there are now camping zones, with yellow posts to indicate camping areas within each zone. At present, you do not need to obtain a wilderness permit to enter the new Santa Rosa Wilderness.

Emergencies

The Sierra Madre Search and Rescue Team, without doubt the top mountain-rescue organization in Southern California, says that in the great majority of mountain emergencies in which a hiker is lost or injured, 1) the victim went hiking alone, 2) he did not tell anyone where he was going or when he planned to return, and 3) he took a "short cut" off the established trail. If you do all three, and are a relatively inexperienced mountaineer, you are inviting trouble. However, even the experienced and careful hiker may have a crisis. Knowing what to do in an emergency may save your life.

The first rule for survival in any outdoor emergency — be it losing your way, injury, snakebite, storm or fire — is common sense: make a calm, reasoned judgment of the situation and act accordingly. The biggest threat to survival is panic. Panicky hikers have been known to throw away their supplies and wander aimlessly for miles. According to mountain-rescue experts, 8 of 10 survival-situation fatalities could have been prevented if the hiker had known survival techniques and had used common sense.

Getting lost is by far the most common crisis faced by hikers. If you ever face this prospect, awareness of several basic rules should spare you unnecessary strain, fatigue or injury, and maybe even your life. The minute you realize you are lost, stop and appraise the situation. If you are reasonably certain of your general location and have map and compass, try to retrace your steps, looking always for footprints and familiar landmarks. You may want to climb a nearby high point to survey the terrain for landmarks. Never take what you think is a "short cut" over unfamiliar terrain; you stand a chance of becoming hopelessly tangled in thorny chaparral or slipping down a steep slope. If you are uncertain of your whereabouts, stay put. Never try to find your way at night.

If you've told people where you were going (and never enter the mountains on foot without telling someone your planned itinerary), a search will be made, probably the next day. Try to stay warm by huddling against a tree or by using branches, bark or pine needles to build a primitive shelter. Don't search extensively for food; water is far more critical. To attract help from the air (search-and-rescue teams make much use of the helicopter nowadays) hang out bright-colored clothing or other objects, but do not under any circumstances start a fire — you could burn down the forest, endangering your life and the lives of many others. A common distress signal is three signs, visible or audible, repeated at intervals — for example, three bright objects placed in a row or three shouts. If you manage to find your way out on your own, immediately notify the Forest Service or Sheriff's Office so that the search can be ended.

The best way to avoid being trapped in a storm is to stay out of the mountains when the weather is threatening. If you are caught in a sudden blizzard at higher elevations, descend as rapidly as you can with safety, but don't start down unfamiliar slopes that might lead to dropoffs or to box canyons. Stay off ridges and open saddles, where wind velocity often becomes extreme. At lower elevations, your worry is water rather than snow or wind. Stay clear of canyon bottoms and gullies that may flash-flood. If you're on the trail, stay on it. If you try a short cut, your anxiety to get out, combined with the decreased visibility, could get you hopelessly lost. If you can't make it out, seek shelter in the hollow of a tree or under a rock overhang, away from the raging stream.

Fire in the Southern California mountains can be a fearful thing. Chaparral, especially when it's tinder-dry in late summer and fall, burns with unbelievable intensity, and wind can cause a brush fire to rampage at enormous speeds. If you see a fire in the mountains, even one that seems a safe distance away, get out fast and notify the Forest Service — the fire could be upon you before you realize it. If you are confronted by a close-at-hand brush fire, you must act fast. Determine the wind direction — fire moves much more rapidly downwind — and move laterally from that direction. Seek slopes and gullies where chaparral is sparse or absent — the fire may pass around these pockets. Or seek the refuge of a stream, preferably where brush does not crowd the banks. About 90% of Southern California forest and brush fires are caused by human carelessness, so make certain that no one in your party contributes to this tragic destruction.

MOUNTAIN COURTESY

Traveling a mountain trail, away from centers of civilization, is a unique experience in Southern California living. It brings intimate association with nature — communion with the earth, the forest, the chaparral, the wildlife, the clear sky. A great responsibility accompanies this experience — the obligation to keep the mountains as you find them. Being considerate of the wilderness rights of others will make the mountain adventures of those who follow equally rewarding.

As a mountain visitor, you should become familiar with the rules of wilderness courtesy outlined below.

Trails

Never cut switchbacks. It breaks down trails and hastens erosion. Take care not to dislodge rocks that might fall on hikers below you. Improve and preserve trails, as by clearing away loose rocks (carefully) and removing branches. Report any trail damage and broken or misplaced signs to a ranger.

Off Trail

Restrain the impulse to blaze trees or to build ducks where it's not essential. Let the next fellow find his way as you did.

Campgrounds

Spread your gear in an already-cleared area, and build your fire in a campground stove. Don't disarrange the camp by making hard-to-eradicate ramparts of rock for fireplaces or windbreaks. Rig tents and tarps with line tied to rocks or trees; never put nails in trees. For your campfire, use fallen wood or carry your own wood in; do not cut standing trees nor break off branches. Use the camp-

ground latrine. Place litter in the litter can or carry it out.
Leave the campground cleaner than you found it.

Fire

Fire is the greatest danger in the Southern California
mountains; act accordingly. Smoke only in cleared areas
along the trail where a Forest Service sign authorizes it.
Report a mountain fire immediately to the Forest Service.

Litter

Along the trail, place candy wrappers, raisin boxes,
orange peels, etc. in your pocket or pack for later disposal;
throw nothing on the trail. Pick up litter you find along the
trail or in camp. More than almost anything else, litter
detracts from the wilderness scene. Remember, you can
take it with you.

Noise

Boisterous conduct is out of harmony in a wilderness
experience. Be a considerate hiker and camper. Don't ruin
another's enjoyment of the mountains.

Good Samaritanship

Human life and well-being take precedence over everything else — in the mountains as elsewhere. If a hiker or
camper is in trouble, help in any way you can. Indifference
is a moral crime. Give comfort or first aid; then hurry to
a ranger station for help.

MAPS

When you are hiking, it is important to know where you
are in relation to roads, campgrounds, landmarks, etc. and
to know the lay of the land in general. For learning these
things there is no substitute for a good map. Unless your

trip is very short, and over a well-marked route, you should carry a map.

There are two types of maps readily available that will give you the picture you need of San Bernardino National Forest and its adjacent mountain areas. Each type has its advantages and its disadvantages.

1. The U.S. Forest Service provides recreation maps of the national forests for a small price ($2). New Forest Service topo maps of the San Gorgonino, San Jacinto, and Santa Rosa wildernesses are available at $2 a piece. The California Department of Parks and Recreation offers free state park maps. Three of these recreation maps cover most of the areas included in this guidebook: The San Bernardino Mountain Area map and the San Jacinto Mountain Area map, put out by the Forest Service, and the Mount San Jacinto State Wilderness map put out by the State of California. These maps show the highways, dirt roads, maintained trails, campgrounds, and major landmarks of the mountains. Their main advantages are that they give you an overall picture of the mountains and are fairly up-to-date, being revised frequently. These maps can be obtained at most ranger stations, or write to the forest or state park headquarters:

San Bernardino National Forest
1824 South Commercenter Circle
San Bernardino, CA 92408-3430
(909) 383-5588

Mount San Jacinto State Park
P.O. Box 308
Idyllwild, CA 92349
(909) 659-2607

2. If you do much hiking, particularly cross country, you will want to use topographic ("topo") maps, because they give accurate information about the topography and the ground cover (trees, bushes or neither). Topo maps are available in several sizes and scales. The San Bernardino, San Jacinto and Santa Rosa mountains are covered in two series: the 15′ quadrangle series and, for part of the area, the newer 7½′ quadrangle series. The 15′ series scale is

approximately 1" to a mile, the contour interval (elevation difference between contour lines) is 80 feet, and the area covered by each map is about 14 x 17 miles. The 7½' series scale is approximately 2½" to a mile, the contour interval is 40 feet, and the area covered by each map is about 7 x 9 miles. These maps show most maintained and many unmaintained trails, elevations, relief, watercourses, forest and brush cover, and works of man. Learning to "read" these maps takes some practice, but the savings in shoe leather and frayed temper make it a worthwhile undertaking. Almost all of the mountain areas described in this guidebook are now covered by the new 7½' series. Topo maps can be bought at many sporting goods and mountaineering-ski shops. Or write to the Geological Survey's Western Distribution Center:

U.S. Geological Survey
Federal Center
Denver, CO 80225

Or order direct from:

The Map Center
2440 Bancroft Way
Berkeley, CA 94704
(510) 841-6277

IMPORTANT NOTICE!

A *Forest Adventure Permit* is required for all vehicles parking in any of the four national forests of southern California — San Bernardino, Cleveland, Angeles, Los Padres. A one-day permit is $5; an annual permit is $30. Permits can be purchased at Forest Service stations and some mountain stores.

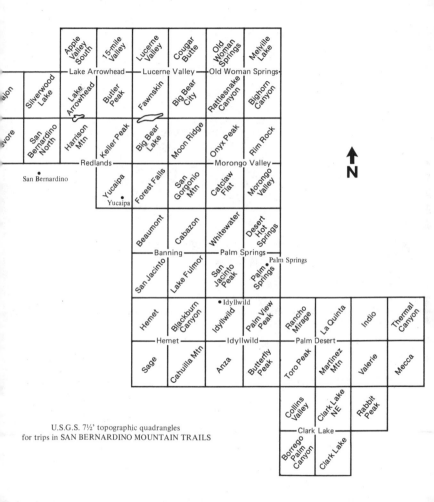

| Apple Valley South | 15-mile Valley | Lucerne Valley | Cougar Butte | Old Woman Springs | Melville Lake |

Silverwood Lake — Lake Arrowhead — Lucerne Valley — Old Woman Springs

| Lake Arrowhead | Butler Peak | Fawnskin | Big Bear City | Rattlesnake Canyon | Bighorn Canyon |

San Bernardino North — Harrison Mtn | Keller Peak | Big Bear Lake | Moon Ridge | Onyx Peak | Rim Rock

— Redlands — — Morongo Valley —

San Bernardino

| Yucaipa | Forest Falls | San Gorgonio Mtn | Catclaw Flat | Morongo Valley |

Yucaipa

| Beaumont | Cabazon | Whitewater | Desert Hot Springs |

— Banning — — Palm Springs —

Palm Springs

| San Jacinto | Lake Fulmor | San Jacinto Peak | Palm Springs |

Palm Springs

• Idyllwild

| Hemet | Blackburn Canyon | Idyllwild | Palm View Peak | Rancho Mirage | La Quinta | Indio | Thermal Canyon |

— Hemet — — Idyllwild — — Palm Desert —

| Sage | Cahuilla Mtn | Anza | Butterfly Peak | Toro Peak | Martinez Mtn | Valerie | Mecca |

| Collins Valley | Clark Lake NE | Rabbit Peak |

— Clark Lake —

| Borrego Palm Canyon | Clark Lake |

N

U.S.G.S. 7½′ topographic quadrangles
for trips in SAN BERNARDINO MOUNTAIN TRAILS

One Hundred Hikes

The hiking trips in this guide are arranged by geographical area, generally northwest to southeast, from Cajon Pass at the west end of the San Bernardinos to Rabbit Peak at the southern end of the Santa Rosas. Trips 1–62 are in the San Bernardino Mountains, with the largest concentration (38–52) in the San Gorgonio Wilderness. Trips 63–94 are in the San Jacinto Mountains, concentrated (67–85) in Mount San Jacinto State Park and the San Jacinto Wilderness. Trips 95–100 are in the Santa Rosa Mountains.

The guide is divided into three parts — The San Bernardinos, the San Jacintos and the Santa Rosas — with introductory information on each mountain range preceding the trips for that range.

Information about each trip is divided into three parts: TRIP, FEATURES and DESCRIPTION.

The TRIP section gives vital statistics: where the hike starts and ends; the walking mileage and elevation gain or loss; a rating of *easy, moderate* or *strenuous*; the best time of year to make the trip; and the appropriate USGS topographic map or maps, followed (in parentheses) by whether the maps are in the 7.5′ or 15′ series.

The FEATURES section tells something of what you will see on the trip, and gives information on the natural and human history of the area. It also contains suggestions for the particular trip, such as, wear lug-soled boots, or bring fishing rod.

The DESCRIPTION section details the driving and hiking route. The driving directions are kept to the necessary minimum, but the walking route is described in detail. (This book is for the hiker; if you want to explore the mountains by car, consult Russ Leadabrand's two fine guidebooks to the San Bernardinos and the San Jacintos.) Also, the hiking-route options that a trip offers are presented.

If you are a dedicated hiker who enjoys exploring the Southern California mountains on foot, the trips listed here are just a beginning. Many more than 100 hikes are possible, crisscrossed as these mountains are by roads, trails and cross-country routes. Furthermore, various combinations of routes described here are possible, particularly if you can arrange car shuttles. You could spend a decade rambling through these mountains and still not fully know them.

On the trail near Hidden Lake Divide

PART 1

The San Bernardino Mountains

The San Bernardino Mountains

From Cajon Pass and the slanted troughs of the great San Andreas Fault, the San Bernardinos rise, rather steeply at first, in chaparral-coated slopes, to the 5,000' summits of Cleghorn and Cajon mountains. Eastward from here, for thirty miles, the crest of the San Bernardinos is remarkably uniform. Undulating ridges and tapered hillocks conceal within their folds forested glens and sparkling blue lakes. This is the Crestline-Lake Arrowhead-Running Springs-Big Bear country, the part of the mountains best known to thousands of Southern Californians. Here, among the lakes and streams that form the headwaters of the Mojave River, are summer homes, winter resorts, commercial centers, schools, paved roads by the mile — and only bits and pieces of wilderness.

From Big Bear Lake, the San Bernardinos veer southward and, beyond the deep valley of the upper Santa Ana River, reach their majestic heights in the San Gorgonio Wilderness. Here the hiker and the lover of pristine mountain country can rejoice. Here, under granite spines hammered up against the sky, lodgepole and limber pines grow sturdy and weather-resistant, tumbling streams flow icy cold, and the thin air is crisp with the chill of elevation. Reigning over all is 11,502' San Gorgonio Mountain — or "Greyback" as it is known to thousands of hikers — the rooftop of Southern California. And man has possessed the foresight and initiative to forever preserve this high country in its primitive state.

South from Greyback, the mountains drop abruptly into the deep trench of Mill Creek, rise to rugged Yucaipa Ridge, and finally descend into the San Gorgonio Pass country.

Geologists place the San Bernardino Mountains, as well as the neighboring San Gabriels, in the Transverse Range province — a system of mountain chains that stretch west-to-east, athwart the general northwest-southeast structural grain of California. Like all the Tranverse ranges, the San Bernardinos were formed by intensive folding and fault-ing. The generally smooth summit region of the range — in marked contrast to the rough surface of the San Gabriels — reveals that the San Bernardinos were molded in com-paratively recent geologic time. A complex network of faults separates the San Bernardinos from the surrounding landscape. Most pronounced is the great San Andreas Fault, which runs obliquely from northwest to southeast and forms the southern edge of the range. Adjoining the San Andreas is the Mill Creek Fault, which slices through the southern part of the mountains and forms the deep trough of Mill Creek. On the north side of the range, the faultlines, not so clearly evident, appear to be a series of short fracture zones. The largest on this flank is the Helen-dale Fault, which runs from the Mojave Desert up Cush-enbury Canyon to the vicinity of Baldwin Lake. To the east is the Morongo Valley Fault. Other faults slice through the heart of the mountains. The surface rocks of the San Bernardinos are intermixed in great confusion, with granitic types and gneisses predominating, along with quartzites and crystallized limestone.

The forest-and-brush cover of the San Bernardinos shows marked contrast. On the south slopes of the range chaparral predominates. Covering most of the rolling crest of the mountains are lush stands of pine, cedar and fir. Above 10,000′ in the San Gorgonio Wilderness is boreal vegetation, sparse but hardy. Desert-facing slopes on the north and east are primarily pinyon-juniper woodland above and Lower Sonoran vegetation below.

"Nothing seems more hauntingly Californian than the sight and aroma of chaparral drenched in sunlight," wrote a prominent western naturalist. What is chaparral? It is defined as "a dominant, deep-rooted, shrubby vegetation, chiefly evergreen, with leathery, often hard-surfaced

leaves." The many-branched shrubs tend to look like miniature trees, and for this reason chaparral has been called
"elfin forest." These shrubs can adapt themselves to a wide
spectrum of soils, and can exist in terrain and climatic conditions that will support little else. The woodiness of trunks
and stems and the thick, small leaves allow chaparral to
conserve the moisture they absorb during the short rainy
season through the long, hot, rainless summer, so they are
ideally suited to Southern California hillsides. Shrubs col-
lectively called chaparral include dozens of species, and
many of them are present in the San Bernardinos. The most
abundant types here are chamise, scrub oak, manzanita,
California holly, and several forms of ceanothus. Hikers
generally try to avoid chaparral; indeed, anyone so unfor-
tunate as to become caught in its thorny maze will quickly
come to curse it. But those who pay a friendly visit to the
elfin forest instead of trying to thrash through it will come
to see chaparral in a more favorable light. In bloom, many
of the shrubs are sprinkled with colorful flowers. Yucca
bursting with fragrant, creamy-white blossoms, ceanothus
blooming misty blue or white, California laurel unfolding
masses of yellow flowers, wild lilac giving forth its sweet
aroma after a spring rain — these charms await the casual
visitor. Chaparral is also valuable as a soil cover; where it
has been burned off, rain rushes down the hillsides, causing severe erosion on the slopes and flooding in the canyons and lowlands.

Within the chaparral belt, in the watered canyons, is
an association of plants that naturalists call *streamside
woodland*. Lush, verdant growth is the chief characteristic
of this habitat. Many varieties of ferns and rushes, and a
profusion of flowering herbs grow rich under a green canopy of sycamore, white alder, willow, big-leaf maple, and
live oak. After one has slogged for several miles through
the elfin forest, reaching this streamside woodland is a
special treat — particularly on a warm summer day. The
streamside woodlands of Bear and Siberia Creeks are particularly delectable.

Amid this ocean of chaparral, nestled on sun-sheltered

slopes, are sometimes found islands of bigcone spruce, the lowest-growing conifer in the Southern California mountains. Easily identifiable by its long, horizontal branches and its sparse foliage, this adaptable tree is found from elevations as low as 2000' up into the main mountain forest at 6000' and 7000'.

The crest of the San Bernardinos from Crestline to Big Bear Lake is blessed by a forest as magnificent as any in Southern California. Here grow dense and stately stands of Jeffrey pine, ponderosa pine, sugar pine, Coulter pine, knobcone pine, white fir and incense-cedar. Adding a beautiful touch of color is the California black oak, its leaves sprouting pink in springtime, light green in summer, and turning a striking yellow in autumn. Beneath ponderosa pine and incense cedar, we often find Pacific dogwood, and no other forest flower equals the ethereal grace of the dogwood's white blossoms. Walking beneath the canopy of this mountain forest can be a refreshing and enriching experience.

High up in the San Gorgonio Wilderness — on the granite slopes of Greyback and Mount San Bernardino, in the Dry Lake basin — is what naturalists call boreal or subalpine forest. The predominant conifer here is lodgepole pine — tough, cold-resistant, standing erect where sheltered, or twisted and bent where exposed to nature's high-altitude fury. Limber pines, gnarled and ground-hugging, live a marginal existence on the loftiest ridges. The high-altitude chaparral — manzanita, snowbrush, bush chinquapin — is rich and green, and waist high. In season, alpine wildflowers burst forth in splashing colors. This is delightful hiking country, a touch of the High Sierra in Southern California. May it ever stay wild.

The backside of the San Bernardinos shows the strong influence of the desert. Here, just over the ridge from the main mountain forest, lying in the "rain shadow" of the range, are extensive stands of pinyon pine and western juniper. Lower down grows that shaggy monarch of the high desert, the Joshua tree. Hard-wooded mountain mahogany thrives on the higher desert-facing slopes. Along

Deep Creek and the West Fork of the Mojave grow Fremont cottonwood, desert willow and velvet ash. Mesquite and several varieties of sage are the dominant shrubs below 5000'. This desert slope of the San Bernardinos sees few hikers; this is a shame, for during the cooler months this is an enchanting landscape.

The wildlife of the San Bernardino Mountains is timid, and for the most part, scarce. Man has killed off or driven out many species that once roamed in abundance. Grizzly bears, which were thick in these mountains during pioneer times, have been gone for half a century. Black bears — misnamed, for most of them are brown — were once near extinction, but seem to be on the increase. Naturalists estimate that there are around 200–250 in the range. On desert-facing slopes live a handful of statuesque bighorn sheep, extremely shy, seldom seen. There are perhaps fifteen mountain lions in the San Bernardinos. Rare is the hiker who spies one of these big cats romping through the forest, although its large and unmistakable track is sometimes seen on the trail. The most abundant large mammal in the range is the California mule deer. Several thousand head roam the San Bernardinos from top to bottom, feeding on a great variety of plants and sometimes being fed upon by the mountain lion. Smaller mammals include the bobcat, ring-tailed cat, gray fox, coyote, opossum, raccoon, skunk, weasel, and a host of squirrels and chipmunks. The only creature considered dangerous to man in these mountains is the western rattlesnake, abundant below 6000', sometimes seen up to 8000'. However, most rattlers are not very aggressive and will crawl away if given half a chance.

These, then, are the San Bernardinos — overused yet possessing prime wilderness, smothered with elfin forest below and rich with conifers above, sea-influenced on one side and desert-facing on the other, the highest mountain country in Southern California and some of the most gentle. These are the aspects of the San Bernardinos that have lured visitors into the high country for decades. Come up and sample its delights.

Man in the San Bernardinos

I only went out for a walk and finally concluded to stay
out till sundown, for going out, I found, was really going
in.   — John Muir
who visited the San Bernardino Mountains in 1896.

Mountains have always held a special significance to man.
They have inspired in him awe and fear and wonder, and
filled him with curiosity and longing. They have affected
his climate and helped to shape his way of life. They have
afforded him livelihood, refuge, pleasure and peace. They
have been objects of cherishment and worship. In all,
mountains have been a great source of human fulfillment.

The San Bernardino Mountains have been important to
man since his ancestors first set foot in Southern California.
To primitive man, they were a source of food, water and
materials. Spaniards and Californios sought water and
timber. Anglo pioneers expanded the use of water and
timber, and added a feverish quest for gold. To modern
man, the mountains have provided homes, recreation, and
a place to find solitude and relaxation.

A complete history of the San Bernardino Mountains
would be a monumental work, involving many volumes,
covering all of man's varied and sometimes hectic activities in the range. Like the neighboring San Gabriels, the
proximity of the San Bernardinos to centers of civilization
has resulted in their being swarmed over, dug into, and
built upon to a degree equalled by few other mountain
ranges in the West. All we have space for here are the
highlights of this activity, a sketch that should give the

Left: John Browns toll road, 1879; Cajon Pass, lower toll gate.
W. A. Vale.

31

reader a general idea of what man has done to these mountains.

For untold centuries before the arrival of the white man, Indians lived in and below the San Bernardino Mountains. The mountains provided them acorns, pinyon nuts, berries and other wild fruits, together with such game as they killed with their bows and arrows or caught in their snares and traps. The mountains were thick with wildlife. The Indians avoided bears, but relished deer and rabbits, both for their food and their skins. In the mountains they gathered fibers for ropes and baskets, willow splints for arrow shafts, and greasewood for any number of uses.

To make their way through the mountains, the Indians forged a network of trails. Hunting trails, food-gathering trails, and trading trails crisscrossed much of the range. The most important of these trade routes was the ancient Mojave Trail, which led up the Mojave River into the mountains, up Sawpit Canyon to the crest of the range near today's Monument Peak, and down the south slope via the ridge just west of Devil Canyon. This famous pathway, along with another route through Cajon Pass, was used for centuries by desert Indians to trade with peoples living in the San Bernardino Valley and coastal plains.

The Spaniards gave the name *Serrano* — meaning "mountaineer"— to these hardy Indians of the San Bernardino Mountains. Most of the Serrano villages were located below the south slopes of the range, although some Indians apparently lived most of the year well up in the mountains. In the Big Bear region dwelled the Pervetum people, and around Little Bear Valley (now Lake Arrowhead) lived the Kaiwiems. South of the Santa Ana River were villages of the Wanakik or (Pass) Cahuillas, one of the three branches of this widespread Indian group. North and east of the mountains — in the desert and along the Colorado — lived the Mojave people.

The Spanish soldier Pedro Fages entered the scene in 1772 — the first white man known to have reached the mountains. Fages was pursuing army deserters from San Diego; he followed them as far as the Colorado Desert. Evidently the desire to do some more exploring seized him, for he turned north and skirted the San Jacinto Mountains by a route Anza was to travel two years later, entered the San Bernardino Valley, crossed the mountains in the vicinity of Cajon Pass, and made his way northwest along the south edge of the Mojave Desert to the Tehachapis, the southern San Joaquin Valley, San Luis Obispo, and eventually Monterey.

Fages was followed four years later by the intrepid missionary-explorer-martyr Fray Francisco Hermenegildo Garces, who crossed the San Bernardino Mountains on his way from the lower Colorado River to Mission San Gabriel in 1776. From his diary, it appears that he used the ancient Mojave Trail over the mountains, rather than Cajon Pass. (In 1931, the San Bernardino County Historical Society erected a monument to mark the point where Garces crossed the crest of the range.

In a notable 1806 expedition, Fray Jose Zalvidea started from Mission Santa Barbara, explored the southern San Joaquin Valley, crossed the Tehachapis to the desert, and skirted the northern foothills of the San Gabriel and San Bernardino Mountains. They entered the latter near the junction of Deep Creek and the Mojave's West Fork, then traversed through Summit Valley and Coyote Canyon into lower Cajon Canyon before continuing on to San Gabriel.

Four years later — on May 20, 1810, the feast day of Saint Bernardino of Siena, a Franciscan preacher of the 15th century — a party from Mission San Gabriel set up a temporary chapel in the valley south of the mountains.* From this came the name "San Bernardino." This original chapel was evidently short-lived, but in 1819 Spaniards came into the San Bernardino Valley to stay. An *asistencia* of Mission San Gabriel was established southeast of the present city of San Bernardino.

The Spaniards, and a short time later the Californios*,

---

*The establishing of this chapel in 1810 is disputed by historians. The original diary reporting its founding has long been lost.
*This term refers to Mexican Californians. In 1821 Mexico won independence from Spain and by 1823 had established hegemony over California.

soon were engaged in agriculture in the San Bernardino Valley. To bring water to the lands under cultivation, a *zanja* (irrigation ditch) was built from Mill Creek into the valley in 1820. This was the earliest known use of water from the San Bernardino Mountains for irrigation. Timber was taken out also by the Californios. In 1830 mountain hemlock was cut in Mill Creek for use in building the San Bernardino *asistencia* — the earliest known lumbering in the mountains. Other than taking out water and carrying on some small-scale lumbering, the Spaniards and Californios put the mountains to very little use.

Until the 1840s, only the foothills and low western regions of the San Bernardino Mountains were known to the white man; the higher country to the east was virtually unexplored. It remained for Benjamin D. Wilson to make known the area now occupied by Big Bear Lake. In the summer of 1845, Wilson, who owned part interest in the Jurupa Rancho (Riverside), led a troop of Mexican cavalry in search of cattle rustlers. Setting out toward the desert, where it was believed the rustlers had headed, Wilson divided his command. Most were sent through Cajon Pass, while Wilson took 22 troopers directly across the mountains. After two days of strenuous travel, Wilson's party reached a wooded valley and a small lake inhabited by scores of grizzly bears. The soldiers formed pairs, and they bagged and skinned eleven bears. Then they continued across the mountains, rejoined the main party, and surprised the rustlers along the Mojave River. Afterwards, Wilson and his 22 troopers returned home via the mountain lake. Here they lassoed eleven more bears, enough for each man to have a bearskin trophy as a remembrance of the trip. Wilson gave the name *Bear Lake* to the little body of water high in the mountains, and later the grassy basin south of the lake became known as Bear Valley. Years later the name of the body of water Wilson discovered was changed to Baldwin Lake, but the name he gave survives in Big Bear Lake, created when a dam was built at the lower end of Bear Valley in 1884.

The 1840s were watershed years in the history of the mountains. Already mentioned was Wilson's expedition, opening up a part of the range little known before. This was the decade that saw the last of the great Indian raids across the mountains, when Wak (or Walkara), a crafty Ute chieftan, led marauding bands through Cajon Pass and over the Mojave Trail, making off with livestock and striking fear in the hearts of rancheros as far as Claremont and Azusa. These raids caused authorities to station soldiers near Cajon Pass. The attacks continued into the 1850s, but on a diminished scale. Late in the decade California became part of the United States, and with the coming of the Anglos, the mountains began to receive much more attention.

During these years, the mountains became known by the name they hold today — the San Bernardinos. Thomas Coulter, in his *Notes on Upper California: A Journey from Monterey to the Colorado River in 1832*, published by the Royal Geographical Society of London in 1835, refers to the "great snowy peak of San Bernardino." Coulter, an Irish botanist, is remembered in the name of the Coulter pine. Charles Wilkes' map of 1841 labeled San Bernardino Peak "Mt. Bernardino," and by 1849 most maps showing the mountains used this name or "San Bernardino."

It was the Mormons, who lived in the San Bernardino Valley from 1851 until 1857, who really opened up the mountains. The Mormon settlers needed lumber for building their town of San Bernardino, and what better place to get this lumber than from the rich stands of pine and cedar in the nearby mountains? Their first efforts were directed toward Mill Creek; here Daniel Sexton built the sawmill in 1852 that gave Mill Creek its name. A second mill was built farther up the creek the following year, known as Mormon Mill. Stumps discovered years later revealed that lumbering was undertaken as far up-canyon as the site of present-day Fallsvale, well up under the shoulder of San Gorgonio Mountain.

Mill Creek met the Mormons' lumber needs for several months, but soon their eyes turned to the much richer stands of timber on the mountain crest to the north. But first a road would have to be built up the steep south slopes of the range. This was accomplished through back-

breaking efforts in 1853, by "every man leaving his family
in camp and freely laboring and camping upon the road
incessantly until finished." This first road onto the crest of
the San Bernardinos climbed directly up Hot Springs (later
Waterman) Canyon and gave access to Seely and Huston
Flats, then heavily timbered. Charles Crisman built the
first sawmill here within ten days of the road's completion,
dragging up an engine and boiler for this small, portable
operation. The first major sawmill on the mountain crest
was erected by the brothers David and Wellington Seely
in the summer of 1853; they used waterpower from the
creek flowing through Seely Flat. Oxen hauled the cut
wood down to San Bernardino. By the middle of 1854 the
Mormons had six mills operating in the San Bernardino
Mountains — four on the mountain crest and two on Mill
Creek. Most of the lumber was used in San Bernardino,
but some was hauled as far away as Los Angeles.

The Mormons returned to Utah in 1857, but the mountain sawmills remained, and more were built in ensuing
years. Strawberry Valley, Grass Valley, Little Bear Valley
(later Lake Arrowhead), Hook Creek, Twin Peaks, Green
Valley, Snow Valley, Big Bear, Holcomb Valley and Barton
Flats all were the scene of lumbering operations, some of
them continuing into recent years. Most ambitious were
the activities of the Brookings Lumber Company at Fred-
alba, near today's Running Springs, in operation from 1898
until 1910. Robert Brookings built a narrow gauge logging
railroad network that gave access to most of the timber
between Heaps Peak and Arrowbear Lake — quite an
expanse of mountain country. Remnants of this turn-of-
the-century operation are still visible today.

Timber was the first magnet that lured man into the San
Bernardino Mountains; gold was the second. The precious
metal was reportedly found in the mountains as early as
1857 and there was some prospecting activity in 1859, but
not until William F. Holcomb made his famous discovery
in Holcomb Valley in 1860 was there a real gold rush. The
story goes that Holcomb and a companion named Ben
Chouteau, members of a prospecting party in Bear Valley,
crossed the ridge that separates the waters of the Santa

Ana River from those of the Mojave River during a hunting trip, and shot two bears. Next day they returned to secure the animals, and in addition to obtaining bear meat they discovered something much more thrilling — gold! Within a week the entire Holcomb party had moved into the gold-laden basin — later known as Holcomb Valley — and were feverishly digging for placer gold. The news of the discovery spread to San Bernardino, and by early July Holcomb Valley was swarming with prospectors, who were making $5 to $10 a day. A boom town sprung up in short order; the miners named it Belleville, in honor of little Belle Van Dusen, whose mother had furnished a flag for a patriotic occasion. More gold was discovered across the ridge in Bear Valley, and by the fall of 1860 the entire mountain region was overrun with gold seekers.

The original route to the mines was by wagon road from San Bernardino to the mouth of Santa Ana Canyon, then by steep pack trail up the Santa Ana River to Seven Oaks and over the ridge into Bear Valley. Bringing in provisions by this route was difficult and expensive, so the miners subscribed $1500 which they gave to a Mr. Van Dusen to build a new wagon road. Van Dusen wisely decided that the south slope of the range below Bear Valley was too steep and rugged for such a road; instead he built his road northwesterly from Holcomb Valley down to the Mojave River, then southwest to near the head of Cajon Pass, where it met the toll road through the pass into the San Bernardino Valley just completed by John Brown. By this roundabout route, all types of supplies were transported to the mines.

Through most of the 1860s, mining activities involving hundreds of men continued in Holcomb and Bear valleys. At one time the population in Holcomb Valley alone is said to have reached 2000. These were years of stormy excitement and controversy. Ruffians and outlaws came in large numbers, and during the Civil War, Southern sympathizers were vocal and active. As many as 40 men and probably many more met violent deaths during this frenzied period. But gradually the placer gold gave out and the miners drifted away to new diggings elsewhere in the west.

By 1870 Belleville was a ghost town and Holcomb Valley's hectic era was history.

Although the placer gold was gone, many quartz-gold prospects remained, hidden in canyons and hillsides throughout the Holcomb Valley-Bear Valley area. The last three decades of the 1800s saw the development of many of these hard-rock prospects — the Osborne Mine northeast of Holcomb Valley, the Ozier on John Bull Flat, the Rose Mine southeast of Baldwin Lake, the Santa Fe group in Blackhawk Canyon, and, most productive of all, Lucky Baldwin's Doble Mine on Gold Mountain. Gold was mined and milled at these and other prospects well into this century.

Water was the third lure that brought modern man into the San Bernardino Mountains. The streams gushing down from the high country had been utilized for domestic purposes and irrigation since man had first made his home in the San Bernardino Valley. But most of the water was wasted, flowing out to sea during the wetter months, and not available during the hot months when many of the streams dried up. The possibility of using Bear Valley as a storage reservoir was brought to public attention in 1880, when a state engineer's survey said the basin was one of the best sites for such a reservoir in Southern California. In 1883 the founders of the new colony of Redlands incorporated the Bear Valley Land and Water Company, intent upon impounding water in a mountain reservoir for use on the newly developed valley land. A single-arch stone-and-cement dam was completed at a cost of $75,000 the following year; thus was born Big Bear Lake. Although the mountain lake was now reality and the dam (to the surprise of many engineers) held, the water company was flooded with a mass of litigation over water rights that lasted for decades. In 1910–11 a second, stronger dam was constructed just below the original one; this is the dam the highway crosses today, holding back a lake eight miles long, containing 72,000 acre-feet of water.

Lake Arrowhead was formed in much the same way. In 1891 a group of Ohio businessmen organized the Arrowhead Reservoir Company, and two years later began construction of a dam across Little Bear Creek. The dam was completed in 1908, and tunnels were dug to divert the waters from their natural flow (northward) to the San Bernardino Valley. But a mass of litigation was involved here too. The state supreme court doomed the irrigation project by ruling that water could not be diverted from one watershed to another. But Little Bear Lake remained, to be renamed Lake Arrowhead in 1922.

During this era a number of toll roads were built into the mountains. The first ones were the Daley Road up Twin Creek Canyon, built in 1859, and the Cajon Pass Toll Road constructed by John Brown two years later. During the 1890s four new ones appeared – the Bear Valley, City Creek Canyon, Devils Canyon, and Arrowhead Reservoir Company toll roads. On the desert side the Johnson and Cushenbury grades were gouged out and another route opened into the high country. Then came the most famous road of all, the Rim of the World Highway, 101 miles long, completed in 1915.

With the roads came people, and with people arose the fourth lure of the mountains, recreation. At first there were cabins, then hotels and stores and saloons. Gus Knight Jr. built the first mountain resort at Big Bear Lake in the 1890s. Pine Knot was the first lakeside community here. Down in the canyon of the Santa Ana River was Seven Oaks, a popular tent camp in the '90s. In the 1920s Lake Arrowhead became a resort community, and subdivision for residential purposes began. Then came the development of Crestline, Lake Gregory, Running Springs, Green Valley, and many more centers of civilization in the high country. The mountains were being overrun by man.

Fortunately, mankind includes those who work to protect and preserve as well as those who might pillage and destroy. By 1890 it was evident to many farsighted people that the San Bernardino Mountains needed federal protection. Even those with myopic vision could see that reckless cutting of timber was destroying the mountain watershed. As a result of strong pressure from conservation-minded citizens, President Benjamin Harrison signed an act creating the San Bernardino Forest Reserve, on Febru-

ary 25, 1893. In 1898 the first rangers were assigned to the
reserve and a patrol system established. Unfortunately,
large areas of the high country were already in private
ownership and outside the jurisdiction of the Forest Service. But the lands within the forest reserve were zealously
guarded, and, starting about 1902, burned areas were re-
forested. In 1908 the San Bernardino Forest Reserve was
joined with the Angeles and the designation was changed
from forest reserve to national forest. This union lasted
until 1925, when San Bernardino National Forest again
became a separate entity. In 1931 the highest and most
primitive part of the mountains was set aside as the San
Gorgonio Wild Area, to be forever preserved in its natural
state.

Today, the San Bernardinos receive annually about
seven million visitors, making them one of the most heavily
used mountain regions in the nation. With this many
people motoring, sightseeing, picnicking, camping, horseback riding, boating, skiing and hiking in the mountains,
nature is hard-pressed to hold its own.

Even areas considered inviolate face pressures generated
by the people explosion. During the early 1960s, commercial skiing interests waged a determined and almost successful effort to "open up" the heart of the San Gorgonio
Wilderness to roads, resorts and ski lifts. Conservationists,
led by the Defenders of the San Gorgonio Wilderness,
barely won that battle. Now the problem is not skiers but
hikers — too many of them swarming over wilderness trails
and into campgrounds. To save the wilderness from the
perils of overuse, the Forest Service in 1971 instituted the
Wilderness Permit system. Eventually, perhaps within
another year or two, Wilderness Permits will be rationed,
and a limit placed on the number of people who can enter
a wilderness area at one time.

Regardless of the history, the future of these mountains
rests with the people who frequent them. They are the
ultimate guardians of God's handiwork.

TRIP: Cajon Pass to Cleghorn Mountain

1   **½ mile** round trip; **300′** elevation gain
Classification: **Easy**
Season: **Nov.-May**
Topo map: *Cajon* (7½′)

FEATURES

Cajon Pass, the deep cleft separating the San Gabriel from the San Bernardino mountains, is an historic gateway from the Mojave Desert to the Southern California coastal lowlands. Indians, explorers, trappers, traders and settlers were the pioneers who journeyed through the Cajon, and today the pass is the route of major highway and railroad arteries. Geologists say Cajon Pass was formed as a result of an overlapping of the east end of the San Gabriel Mountains with the west end of the San Bernardinos, caused by the earth-twisting movements of the San Andreas Fault, which cuts right through Cajon Canyon.

This trip takes you up the west end of the San Bernardinos for a bird's-eye panorama of this gateway to the Southland, with the abrupt northeast face of the San Gabriel Mountains as an imposing backdrop. Few other vantage points offer such a view of this historic cut in the mountains. The trip is through rather scraggly chaparral, on fire road and firebreak all the way, so it is best done on a cool winter or spring day, when the chaparral is blooming and fragrant, and the air is crisp and clean-washed.

The Cleghorn Ridge Road (2N47) has been upgraded and is now a popular route for recreational vehicles, especially on weekends. With a 4WD vehicle, you can now drive to a point just ¼ mile from Cleghorn Mountain's summit, which has turned this once-long hike into a short walk. In winter, with snow on the road, this trip becomes a longer hike.

Cleghorn Mountain — and Cleghorn Ridge, Cleghorn Pass and Cleghorn Canyon — were named for Matthew Cleghorn and his son John, who leased this western tip of the San Bernardinos for timber-cutting back in the 1870s. They must have been thorough; there is little timber left here today.

DESCRIPTION

From Interstate 15 (freeway), 17 miles up from San Bernardino, turn right (northeast) onto Cedar Springs Road (Highway 138). After 4 miles you reach the road leading left to Summit Railroad Station (the point of the real Cajon Pass); just beyond, on your right (south) a sign indicates *Elliott Ranch*. Turn and follow this dirt road southwest, going straight ahead where a road drops left, to a second junction just beyond a cement-block structure, 1.5 miles from Highway 138. If you have a standard, low-slung vehicle, or if snow is on the road, you must start walking here, going left (east) up Cleghorn Ridge Road (2N47), 8 miles round trip. With a 4WD vehicle, turn left at the second junction and drive up 2N47 just 3.7 miles to a clearing immediately west of Cleghorn's rounded summit. Park here and walk up the steep jeep track, then left through the brush to the top, ¼ mile.

From the summit, look northwest at the jumbled ridge-line that forms the summit of the Cajon. First you see the Santa Fe Railroad tracks, built in 1885, passing Summit Station — the low point of the pass. 1½ miles beyond (north of) Summit Station is a shallow defile which was the route of the historic Old Spanish Trail, used by explorers, hunters, trappers, traders and soldiers since the 1770s. Today only a seldom-used dirt road crosses here. Two miles beyond the old Spanish route, winding up the hillside and most obvious of all, is Interstate 15 freeway, crossing the divide at Cajon Summit. Farther west from Interstate 15 you can see the old highway crossing, the remains of Sanford's old wagon road put through in 1855, and State Highway 138 leading to Palmdale. Perhaps no other pass in the west has been so cut up by man: and you see it all from Cleghorn Mountain.

Return the way you came. An alternate route, requiring a car shuttle, is to drop southeast down the firebreak to the fire road at Cleghorn Pass (see trip 2).

TRIP: Forest Road 2N49 to Cajon Mountain Lookout

2

5 miles round trip; **300'** elevation loss and gain
Classification: **Moderate**
Season: **Nov.-May**
Topo map: *Cajon* (7½')

FEATURES

Cajon Mountain (5310') towers over the lower end of the Cajon Pass area, and its summit offers a sweeping panorama of the great fault-carved passage through the mountains. From here you can see the San Andreas Fault, its strange slanting ridges and twisted rock formations all bearing in a northwest-southeast direction. Directly below is the Blue Cut, where Cajon Canyon narrows to a gorge and crosses the fault. The view beyond is equally grand, with Mt. San Antonio (Old Baldy) and the cluster of high peaks at the east end of the San Gabriels looming massive and grayish.

This trip is all on fire road, shaded part of the way by California black oak, big cone spruce and sugar pine. In the winter and early spring, the eastern peaks of the San Gabriels are dazzling in their mantle of whiteness, and the foothills are velvet-green.

DESCRIPTION

From Interstate 15 (freeway), 17 miles up from San Bernardino, turn right (northeast) onto Cedar Springs Road (Highway 138). Follow this road northeast, east through Summit Valley, and south along the West Fork of the Mojave River to Cleghorn Road, 11 miles. Turn right (west) and follow this dirt fire road (2N49) up to Cleghorn Pass, then southeast up to a junction with Cajon Mountain Road, on your right (west), 6.5 miles from Highway 138. Park outside the locked gate.

Proceed past the locked gate, following Cajon Mountain Road through an open forest of black oak, big-cone Douglas-fir, and sugar pine, as it descends to a saddle, then climbs to the summit of Cajon Mountain and its fire-lookout tower, 2.5 miles.

Enjoy the superb panorama, then return the same way.

TRIP: Forest Road 2N49 to Sugarpine Mountain

3   **1 mile** round trip; **300′** elevation gain
         Classification: **Easy**
         Season: **All year,** except when 2N49 closed
         because of fire danger
         Topo map: *Cajon* (7½′)

FEATURES

Sugarpine Mountain is one of the high points along the
long front ridge of the San Bernardinos, offering a fine vista
over the San Bernardino Valley. The mountain was logged
over years ago, so the name is deceiving—there are few
sugar pines left here.

This easy walk climbs through open stands of black oak,
big-cone Douglas-fir and sugar pine to the view-rich
summit on the crest of the western San Bernardinos. If it
has recently snowed and you cannot drive all the way up
2N49, your walk is longer but no less pleasant.

Like all trips in this west-end country, it is best done in
winter or spring.

DESCRIPTION

From Highway 138, drive up Cleghorn Road (2N49) as
described in Trip 2. Continue up 2N49 as it reaches the
crest and turns east to a clearing just west of Sugarpine
Mountain, 9.7 miles from Highway 138. Park here.

Walk east up 2N49 about 100 yards to an unmarked
access trail that climbs east to the summit, ½ mile.

Return the same way.

TRIP: Bowen Ranch to Deep Creek Hot Springs

4   **3 miles** round trip; **700′** elevation loss and gain
Classification: **Easy**
Season: **All year**
Topo map: *Lake Arrowhead* (15′)

FEATURES

Deep Creek, on the north slope of the mountains, boasts the only genuine hot springs in the San Bernardinos. As many as 20 hikers bathe in the three warm pools beside the cold creek on winter weekends. **Warning:** Three cases of amebic meningoencephalitis, apparently caused by bathing at Deep Creek, were reported in 1978. There have been no reported cases since then. Overnight camping is disallowed at the hot springs, but you may camp at Bowen Ranch.

DESCRIPTION

From Interstate 15, 6 miles north of Cajon Pass, turn right (east) at the Hesperia turn-off. Proceed through Hesperia on Main Street, then bear left (east) on Rock Springs Road where Main Street curves south. Cross the dry bed of the Mojave River and follow Rock Springs Road east to its end, 10.2 miles from the freeway. Go left (north) .5 mile, then right (east) on Roundup Way. Follow the latter 4.4 miles, then turn right (south) onto Bowen Ranch Road. Proceed up the latter, going right at a junction at 2.5 miles, to Bowen Ranch, 5.8 miles from Roundup Way. You must stop at the ranch house, register, and pay a fee ($3). Camping is allowed ½ mile beyond the ranch house.

The trail begins at road's end atop a hill. You descend south, pass through a gate when you enter Forest Service land, and veer left, then right down a wash. You traverse a ridge, then drop steeply down to Deep Creek, 1.5 miles from the start. The hot springs are across the creek and just downstream.

The hottest pool is enclosed in rocks 20 feet above the creek. Luke-warm pools are below, separated from the creek by a man-made rock barrier.

Return the way you came. Remember, it's all uphill on the way back.

TRIP: Sawpit Canyon to Monument Peak

5   4 **miles** round trip; **700′** elevation gain

     Classification: **Easy**

     Season: **Nov.-May** (fire closure 7/1 to winter rain)

     Topo maps: *Cedar Springs, San Bernardino North* (7½′)

FEATURES

March 21, 1776 . . . Leaving the river I set forth southwestward, and having gone two leagues through a canada and some hills, I arrived at a rancheria of five huts on the bank of the river. I continued on a course to the south and entered into a canada of much wood, grass and water; I saw many cottonwoods, alders, oaks, very tall firs, and beautiful junipers; and having gone one league I arrived at a rancheria of about eighty souls . . . I was received with great joy . . .

March 22, 1776 . . . I went three leagues and passed over the sierra by the southsouthwest. The woods that I saw yesterday reach to the summit of the sierra, whence I saw clearly the sea, the Rio de Santa Ana, and the valley of San Joseph.* Its descent is little wooded. At a little distance from its foot I found another rancheria where the Indians received me very joyfully.

These are excerpts from the diary of Father Garces, first white man to cross the San Bernardino Mountains. His route was via the ancient Mojave Indian Trail that climbed from the West Fork of the Mojave River up Sawpit Canyon to the crest, then descended the ridge between Cable and Devil canyons to the valley. Over this historic pathway tramped Indians, Franciscan padres, Spanish soldiers, and probably Jedediah Smith, in 1826, the first Anglo to reach California overland. Later came loggers and a toll road. Today a fire road ascends Sawpit Canyon and a monument honoring Father Garces, placed by the San Bernardino County Historical Society in 1931, graces the summit of Monument Peak.

This is a short trip, following closely the route of the old

*San Jacinto Valley

Mojave Trail. The forest in Sawpit Canyon — once extensively logged — has grown back, and it is a beautiful walk through sugar pine, incense cedar and black oak to the small stone monument and the sweeping vista on the summit. For those with an historical curiosity, it is well worth the two or three hours of leisurely effort.

DESCRIPTION

From the Rim of the World Highway, 12½ miles up from Highland Avenue in San Bernardino, take the Crestline off-ramp and drive 4 miles northwest to Cedarpines Park. From the village center, turn right on Crest Forest Drive ⅔ mile, then left on Sawpit Canyon Road 1⅔ miles to a dirt road branching left next to a power line. Follow this dirt road ¼ mile to a junction with Forest Road 2N43. Turn left (southwest) up the latter and park outside the gate.

Walk southwest up the fire road, under shady stands of pine, cedar and oak, to a ridgetop junction with fire road 2N49, 2 miles. Walk 100 feet west on 2N49, then climb 50 yards south to the Garces Monument. The summit of Monument Peak is ⅓ mile to the southeast, an easy scramble.

You can also drive within 50 yards of the Garces Monument on Forest Road 2N49, 11.6 miles up from Highway 138 (see Trip 2), or steeply up 2N49 from the south, 5 miles from the head of Palm Avenue.

Note: Sawpit Canyon Road (2N43) crosses a section of private property and public access is a matter of dispute between the owner and the Forest Service. The owner wants to deny public access and has, in the past, put up *no trespassing* signs. You would be wise to consult with the Arrowhead Ranger Station in Skyforest before attempting the trip. An alternative is to drive 2N49, open to the public except in time of high fire danger or heavy snow.

TRIP: Highway 138 to Seeley Creek, Heart Rock

6   **2 miles** round trip; **300'** elevation loss and gain
     Classification: **Easy**
     Season: **All year**
     Topo map: *San Bernardino North* (7½')

FEATURES

Seeley Creek descends the north slope of the San Bernardinos, from its source west of Crestline to Miller Canyon, and eventually into the Mojave River. This short, delightful forest walk follows a one-mile stretch of the bubbling creek under a canopy of very tall Jeffrey pines, incense-cedars and black oaks. You end up alongside two limpid pools with a natural waterslide between. Nearby is Heart Rock, with a heart-shaped hole in the middle through which water sometimes splashes. For an introduction to the San Bernardinos, you can do no better than this magnificent forest stroll.

DESCRIPTION

From Crestline, take State Highway 138 northwest, down to the Camp Seeley entrance road, 1.5 miles. Turn left, then left again just outside the gate to Camp Seeley, and follow the narrow paved road to a parking area on your right, marked with a metal pole with 4W07 (the trail number) on it, .4 mile from the highway.

Walk down the broad trail as it descends north, through a shady forest of Jeffrey pine and incense-cedar, just above the creek. After ¾ mile, your pathway climbs a slight rise and forks. To your right, a short walk gets you to a viewpoint directly above Seeley Creek, where you look down on Heart Rock with its hole in the middle. Return to the main trail and follow it steeply down to the creek. Here, deep in the forest, are two pools with the natural waterslide between.

Return the same way.

TRIP: Rim of the World Highway to Marshall Peak

7   4 **miles** round trip; **400′** elevation gain

Classification: **Easy**

Season: **Nov.-May** (fire closure 7/1 to winter rain)

Topo map: *San Bernardino North* (7½′)

FEATURES

After a storm, when the sky is washed clean and the high mountains are glistening in their snow mantle, walk the short distance to Marshall Peak for an inspiring panorama. Overlooking the wrinkled foothills of the San Bernardinos, Marshall Peak offers a superb panorama of the valley, with the east-end high country of the San Gabriels, the San Gorgonio Wilderness, and the distant San Jacintos looming as lofty backdrops.

This trip, through chaparral all the way and mostly on fire road, ends with a short scramble up a firebreak to the rounded summit.

DESCRIPTION

From the Rim of the World Highway, 9½ miles up from Highland Avenue in San Bernardino, turn left at the entrance to fire road 2N40. Park outside the locked gate without blocking the entrance.

Follow the fire road south along the ridge, traversing around the east slope of two small bumps, to its intersection with the Cloudland Forest fire road, 1¾ miles. Then scramble southwest 300 yards up the firebreak to the top.

Return the same way. An option is to descend the Cloudland Forest fire road southeast to its junction with the Rim of the World Highway just above Inspiration Point, 3 miles. This would require a 5-mile car shuttle.

TRIP: **Rim of the World Highway to Arrowhead Peak,**
the Arrowhead

8

6 miles round trip; **1400′ loss** and gain
Classification: **Moderate**
Season: **all year**
Top map: *San Bernardino North* (7½)

FEATURES

Above San Bernardino, as if branded onto the mountain-side, is a near-perfect figure of an arrowhead pointing downward. Even more amazing, this nature-patterned landmark points directly to hot springs bubbling out of the mountain. Although not as distinct as it once was, the Arrowhead can still be readily observed by anyone start-ing up the Rim of the World Highway from San Bernar-dino.

Naturalists have studied this unique monument to dis-cover how it was formed. They have found that, 18 inches under the surface of the Arrowhead, there is granite, so that only shallow-rooted mountain sage and a few other bedrock species of a light grey-green color can grow here. The soil outside the Arrowhead is deeper, and it sustains greasewood and other darker shrubs. Hence the distinct color difference, forming the outline of the downward-pointing symbol.

The Arrowhead is the subject of a host of Indian leg-ends, and a few from more modern times. No other natu-ral landmark in the San Bernardino Mountains has in the past been so regarded with awe and wonder. The most repeated tale is the Cahuilla legend: Long ago the Cah-uillas dwelt in lands far to the east. Although of a peace-loving disposition, they were constantly harassed by war-like neighbors. At last they could no longer endure their persecutions, so they called upon the God of Peace to help them find a new home where they could dwell in solitude. Being a gentle people, they were looked upon with favor by the Great Spirit. They were told to travel westward and watch for a fiery arrow in the sky, which would direct them to their new homeland. The Cahuillas started on their journey, and one moonless night there shot across the heavens a blazing arrow. The arrow finally came down upon a mountainside where the shaft was consumed by fire but the head embedded itself on the slope. The Indians aroused themselves from their camp and journeyed hastily to the still-glowing arrowhead. Here they lived happily ever after.

Directly below the Arrowhead are boiling hot springs, long used to bring relief to victims of rheumatism and other similar afflictions. Dr. David N. Smith was first to develop those hot springs; in 1863 he built a few cabins here and two years later he erected a hotel. This hotel was later destroyed by fire, as were two successors, the last one in 1937. Today the hotel and grounds are international headquarters for the Campus Crusade for Christ.

Unfortunately Campus Crusade for Christ has closed the lower end of the Arrowhead Trail. So you must do this trip from above, hiking down from the Rim of the World Highway, enjoying far-reaching views of the abrupt south front of the range. You're walking through chaparral all the way, so do it on a cool day.

DESCRIPTION

From San Bernardino, drive up Waterman Avenue, which becomes the Rim of the World Highway (State Route 18). 14 miles up, 1.6 miles beyond the Crestline junction, park in a prominent clearing to the right of the highway.

Walk past the gate and follow the trail, eroded and overgrown in places (its an old fireroad), as it switchbacks down to a saddle north of Arrowhead Peak. Your trail then climbs along the west shoulder of a ridge, high above Waterman Canyon, drops again, then climbs over the summit of Arrowhead Peak (4237'). Here your views are magnificent, over the abrupt south rampart of the mountains, down across the often mist-shrouded San Bernardino Valley, and eastward to snow-streaked San Bernardino Peak and the Yucaipa Ridge.

Hikers who want a moderate, view-rich walk should

turn back here. If you desire a close-up view of the Arrowhead and don't mind a long uphill trudge on the return, continue down the trail, which drops steeply in places, to the top of the Arrowhead, a mile farther. Remember, the lower end of the trail is closed, so after you've examined this unique geological feature, return back up the way you came.

The Arrowhead   *George Beattie*

TRIP: Rock Camp to Willow Creek, Deep Creek

9 14 miles round trip; 2300' elevation loss and gain
Classification: **Strenuous**
Season: **Sep.-June**
Topo maps: *Lake Arrowhead* (15'), *Lake Arrowhead* (7½')

FEATURES:

The first 2 miles of this trip are open to off-road vehicles, so make certain you don't try it during an off-road vehicle race (often held on summer and fall Sundays). The long section down Willow Creek follows a poorly developed trail, almost nonexistent in several places. Hiking experience and knowledge of map reading are prerequisites for making this trip successfully.

DESCRIPTION

From State Route 173, 5 miles north of Lake Arrowhead, turn right on the dirt road leading to Rock Camp Ranger Station (closed). Drive 100 yards beyond the buildings to the parking area adjacent to the sign reading *Metate Trail.*

Pass through the gate and follow the Metate Trail, well-worn by off-road vehicle tracks, northeastward down to a junction with the North Shore Trail, coming in to your right, 1.5 miles. Follow your Metate Trail northward to a junction with Forest Road 3N34, .5 mile. Turn right and follow 3N34 down across Willow Creek. 50 yards east of Willow Creek, look for an indistinct trail leading left, down the east slope of the Willow Creek drainage. Here you leave off-road vehicles and civilization behind and enter a wilderness. Your trail, faint in some places, distinct in others, descends northward, staying well above the churning waters of Willow Creek, winding up and down and around several side canyons. You reach a junction with the Pacific Coast Trail, on the south slope of Deep Creek Canyon, .4 miles from 3N34. Turn left and follow the PCT downstream 2 miles to Deep Creek Hot Springs. Return the way you came, or descend the PCT to Mojave Forks Dam with a car shuttle (see Trip 4).

TRIP: Highway 173 to the Pinnacles

10 **6 miles** round trip; **1000'** elevation gain
Classification: **Moderate**
Season: **Nov.-May** (fire closure 7/1 to winter rain)
Topo map: *Lake Arrowhead* (15')

FEATURES

The Pinnacles are an imposing stack of jumbo,
weathered granite boulders cutting high over the badlands
terrain on the desert-facing slope of the San Bernardinos.

The Forest Service has begun but not completed work
on a new trail from State Highway 173, immediately south
of the Arrowhead Rifle Range, to the summit of the
Pinnacles. As of this writing (July 1992) the trail route has
been marked with small rock ducks, but only the lower section has been cleared. Consult the Arrowhead Ranger
Station (714-337-2444) for the latest information.

DESCRIPTION

From Lake Arrowhead, drive north on Highway 173 to
the Arrowhead Rifle Range, 5 miles. Park off the highway
on the right (east) side.

Your trail begins at an opening in the fence, bounded by
two wooden posts, just before (south of) the entrance to
the rifle range. Follow the new trail as it leads northwest
and ascends a boulder-strewn ridge. The route soon
becomes difficult to follow; you must continue northwest
through scrawny chaparral and around large boulders,
looking for ducks, to the foot of the main ridge.

Climb the left (south) side of the boulder-stacked ridge,
going around the left side of the high point you see (class 3
climbing—use caution). At the top of the ridge, you will see
the summit about ¼ mile beyond; work your way over and
around the boulders to it.

Descend the same way, making certain your general
direction is southeast. (Climbers have descended the
wrong way, taking hours to go through this badlands country back to camp.)

TRIP: Lake Arrowhead North Shore Campgr
11
to Little Bear Creek
5 miles round trip; **600′** elevation loss and gain
Classification: **Easy**
Season: **All year**
Topo map: *Lake Arrowhead* (15′)

FEATURES

The canyon of Little Bear Creek — just east of Lake Arrowhead — is a delight to visit. A small stream glides and dances over water-tempered boulders, shaded by magnificent Jeffrey and sugar pines and incense cedars. Ferns and grasses grow lush along the banks. Civilization — just over the ridge — seems far away. This is a place to while away the hours in serene contemplation, a place to saunter and pause rather than stride.

The trip descends from North Shore Campground, just east of Lake Arrowhead, to visit this verdant sanctuary. You stroll through wilderness as woodsy and charming as any in the Lake Arrowhead country.

DESCRIPTION

From State Highway 173, ½ mile north of Lake Arrowhead, turn right (east) onto Hospital Road. Follow the latter ¼ mile to campground entrance, opposite the hospital. If you park in the campground you must pay the day-use fee. You can park free outside the campground, but not in the hospital parking lot without permission.

Your trail begins at the far right end of the campground, marked with sign reading *Trail 3W12*. Follow the trail downhill, crossing a dirt road, into the shady recess of Little Bear Creek. The path follows the left (north) bank of the trickling creek, climbs 100′ over a ridge to shortcut a horseshoe bend, and continues alongside the stream to Hook Creek Road (3N15), 2½ miles from the start.

You can return uphill the way you came, or have someone pick you up at your meeting with the Hook Creek road.

TRIP:
12
Hook Creek Road to Deep Creek
5 miles round trip, **500'** elevation loss and gain
Classification: **Moderate**
Season: **All year**
Topo map: *Lake Arrowhead* (7.5')

FEATURES

Deep Creek cuts an impressive swath through the north-slope country of the San Bernardinos. The creek and its numerous tributaries drain most of the mountain region from Lake Arrowhead almost to Big Bear. Although not so named, Deep Creek is really the east fork of the Mojave River. Its abundant waters flow year-round, sometimes becoming a raging torrent in stormy times.

About midway between its headwaters and its junction with the West Fork of the Mojave, Deep Creek runs through rugged, rock-ribbed terrain. Its waters tumble and cascade among huge boulders, here and there pausing briefly in limpid pools. This is the Devils Hole country; the Devils Hole itself is in a narrow chasm just east of the creek.

This is a trip for those who like to explore deep canyons and rushing creeks. It's easy walking on the slopes above Deep Creek on a new section of the Pacific Crest Trail. Bring your fishing rod, for trout linger in some of the pools.

DESCRIPTION

From Cedar Glen, east of Lake Arrowhead, drive northeast down Hook Creek Road (3N15), going left at a junction (3N34.2) in 3 miles, to Little Bear Creek. Drive across the creek and in 80 yards turn right onto a poor dirt road. If you have a standard car park on your right 100 yards down this road and walk the remaining ½ mile. With a 4WD vehicle, descend the road, very steep in spots, recrossing Little Bear Creek, to a parking area just above Deep Creek.

Take the trail that leaves the north end of the parking area. You ford Little Bear Creek and reach the Pacific Crest Trail in ¼ mile. Follow the PCT north as it climbs and then contours above Deep Creek, shaded by numerous live oaks. You then descend gently, matching the gradient of Deep Creek, and pass the confluence of Holcomb Creek, its waters churning in from the east. Continuing north on the PCT, you descend open slopes 150 feet above Deep Creek Narrows. Looking up a tributary creek to the east, you can see the tangled jumble known as Devils Hole (not for hikers). Your trail swings northwest, passing above some sandy flats ideal for sunbathing, and intersects the steep jeep trail coming down from Bacon Flats, 2½ miles from the start. Leave the PCT here and descend the jeep trail 100 yards to Deep Creek. There is a large pool here deep enough for swimming.

Return the way you came. An option requiring a long car shuttle is to continue north and then northwest on the PCT to Deep Creek Hot Springs and on to the Mojave Forks Dam, 9 miles (see Trip 4).

Deep Creek

TRIP: Hook Creek to Deep Creek, Holcomb Creek,
13 Coxey Road
12¾ miles one way; **2200′** elevation gain
Classification: **Strenuous** (1 day), **Moderate** (2 days)
Season: **April-October**
Topo maps: *Lake Arrowhead* (15′), *Lake Arrowhead* (7.5′), *Butler Peak* (7.5′)

FEATURES

This is the longest hiking trip in the western half of the San Bernardinos. For 12¾ miles you walk through silent forests of pine, cedar and oak, cross sparkling streams of cold water, and contour rocky slopes—quite an experience in this generally overused part of the range.

Most of the way you follow lower Holcomb Creek, either alongside the alder-shaded stream or a short distance above it. A third of the way, on a shady streamside bench, is Holcomb Crossing Trail Camp, the recommended overnight stop for those doing the trip in two days. A car shuttle between Hook Creek Road and Coxey Road is required.

DESCRIPTION

Driving directions same as for Trip 12.

Take the distinct but unmarked trail down to Deep Creek, then go north along the west bank to a junction with the Pacific Crest Trail, ¼ mile. Turn right (east) onto the PCT, cross Deep Creek on a new steel bridge, and climb four oak-shaded switchbacks. Your trail continues to climb through chaparral, scrub oak, and scattered Jeffrey pines, with far-reaching views back over the Deep Creek drainage. In 2½ miles you cross a ridge and begin a gentle descent into the Holcomb Creek watershed. You drop close to the creek, then contour about 100 feet above the south bank to a junction with the Crab Flats Trail (see Trip 15). About 300 yards beyond is Holcomb Crossing Trail Camp, on a Jeffrey-pine-shaded bench alongside the creek, with firepits and a toilet, 4½ miles from the start.

Just east of the trail camp your trail makes a bouldery crossing of Holcomb Creek, then passes a junction with the

Cox Creek Trail (see Trip 19). You climb the slope to pass some rocky narrows, then descend back to Holcomb Creek at a cedar-shaded bench, 0.7 mile from the trail camp. Here you pass a junction with the Cienega Redonda Trail, branching northeast to Big Pine Flat. You continue east up Holcomb Creek, climb 100 feet on a chaparral slope, and then return to the creek to a junction with the Crab Flats Road (3N16). Now you climb gradually eastward along the north slope above Holcomb Creek, through chaparral and open groves of ponderosa pine and oak, turn northeast, and finally drop back alongside the alder-shaded creek. Your trail continues northeast close to the creek, paralleling Forest Road 3N93 on the opposite bank. You pass several jeep tracks and reach a junction with Coxey Road (3N14). Here your transportation should be waiting. (To reach trip's end at the junction of Holcomb Creek and Coxey Road [3N14], drive 4 miles northwest from Fawnskin, on 3N14.)

A longer option, recommended for 3 or 4 days, is to continue eastward on the Pacific Crest Trail to its crossing of either Van Dusen Road 3N09, (11 additional miles) or to Doble on the Gold Mountain Road 3N08 (17½ additional miles).

TRIP: Crab Flats to Crab Creek, Deep Creek, Fisher-
14 mans Public Campground
4 miles round trip; 500' elevation loss and gain
Classification: **Moderate**
Season: **All Year**
Topo maps: *Lake Arrowhead* and *Redlands* (15')

FEATURES

This trip drops from the rolling high country north of
Green Valley into the upper reaches of Deep Creek. The
trail is well maintained; the views are far-reaching; the
forest is rich with Jeffrey and Coulter pines and several
varieties of oak. Along Deep Creek is Fishermans Public
Campground, popular with trout fisherman. Bring your
fishing rod.

DESCRIPTION

From the Rim of the World Highway (State 18), 2 miles
past Running Springs, turn left (north) onto Green Valley
Road. After 3 miles — just before you reach Green Valley
— turn left again onto Forest Service road 3N16. Follow
this road 3 miles north to Crab Flats. Turn left (west) at
the campground entrance and proceed 1 mile to the Crab
Flats Trail, indicated by a sign.

Follow the trail as it contours west around a ridge, with
fine views over the Deep Creek drainage and the north-
slope country. After ¼ mile the trail begins a descent into
Deep Creek, crossing the small stream of Crab Creek after
1½ miles, and reaching bottom at Fishermans Public
Campground, 2 miles from the start.

After trying your luck as an angler, return back up the
same way.

A winding dirt road comes down to Fishermans Camp
from Cedar Glen, 8 miles west. This road is private property, owned by the Los Angeles Council of the Boy Scouts
of America, and is closed to public travel. Hikers are allowed to use this road with permission, which allows for
a superb shuttle overnight trip from Crab Flats to Cedar
Glen. Contact the L. A. Area Council, 2333 Scout Way,
Los Angeles, CA 90026.

TRIP: Crab Flats to Holcomb Creek, Holcomb Crossing

15 Trail Camp

4 miles round trip; **600'** elevation loss and gain

Classification: **Moderate**

Season: **March-October**

Topo map: *Lake Arrowhead* (15')

FEATURES

This is the easy way to reach the woodsy haunt of lower Holcomb Creek. You drop right down from Crab Flats to intersect the Pacific Crest Trail just west of Holcomb Crossing Trail Camp.

The trip is a living demonstration of how the forest changes with access to moisture and heat. Most of the way down from Crab Flats you are in what botanists call *transition zone* — Jeffrey pines, California black and canyon live oak, a scattering of Coulter and sugar pine and incense cedar — trees that require a moderate amount of moisture and coolness. Directly across the canyon is *upper Sonoran* vegetation — pinyon pine and juniper — trees that grow in warm, semi-arid conditions such as found on this south-facing slope. And along Holcomb Creek are the lush trees of *streamside woodland* — white alder, willow and cottonwood — growing amid a verdant tangle of ferns, grasses and flowering herbs.

DESCRIPTION

Drive to Crab Flats Public Campground (see trip 14 for directions). Turn left (west) at the campground entrance and proceed ¼ mile to the beginning of the Holcomb Creek Trail, marked by a wooden sign. Park in the clearing to the right of the road.

You will notice a dirt road branching off to the northwest—don't take it. The trail starts down to the right of this road (northeast), winds downward through the open forest, crosses a small creek (often dry), rises 100' to top a low ridge, and drops steeply down to intersect the Pacific Crest Trail at 2 miles. Turn right (east); in 300 yards you drop alongside Holcomb Creek and reach Holcomb

Crossing Trail Camp, located on a pine-canopied stream-side bench (firepits and toilet).

You have several options on this trip: (1) return to Crab Flats the way you came; (2) follow the PCT west to Forest Road 3N34, then southeast back to Crab Flats; (3) follow the PCT east to Coxey Road (see trip 13); or (4) follow the Cox Creek Trail north to Hawes Ranch (see trip 19).

The last three require a car shuttle. Any way you do it, you are certain to enjoy this bit of canyon wilderness smack in the middle of the overdeveloped western half of the San Bernardinos.

TRIP: Coxey Meadow to Coxey Creek, Deep Creek

16 6 miles one way; 1400' elevation loss
Classification: **Moderate**
Season: **November-May**
Topo map: *Lake Arrowhead* (15')

FEATURES

This trip crosses the pinyon-pine and juniper country of the semi-arid north side of the San Bernardinos. You descend westward along Coxey Creek (Mill Creek on topo map) for 3½ miles, then cross open ridges for 2½ miles down to Deep Creek. Although both the Forest Service map and the topographic map show a trail, actually you follow rough jeep tracks all the way. Do it in springtime, when Coxey Creek is running strong, and the aroma of damp sage and pinyon pine permeates the air.

DESCRIPTION

From the Rim of the World Highway (State 18), 2 miles past Running Springs, turn left (north) onto Green Valley Road. After 3 miles — just before you reach Green Valley — turn left again onto Forest Service road 3N16. Follow this northeast 12 miles to Big Pine Flat, then turn left (west) on 3N14 and follow it 5 miles to Coxey Meadow. Here a small sign *2W01* points west along jeep tracks. Park off the road.

Walk west along the jeep tracks that follow the north bank of Coxey Creek, usually alongside the stream, occasionally climbing to get past narrows. In 3½ miles you pass Forest Road 3N59, cross Coxey Creek, and climb southward over a ridge. Another ½ mile and you begin the descent into the canyon of Deep Creek, 2 miles farther on.

You reach Deep Creek opposite the road down coming from Bacon Flats. Here, if you're doing the trip one way as recommended, your transportation should be waiting (see trip 12 for driving directions to Deep Creek).

TRIP: Hawes Ranch to Barrel Spring, Muddy Spring

17   6 miles round trip; 1100' elevation gain
Classification: **Moderate**
Season: **November-May**
Topo map: *Lake Arrowhead* (15')

FEATURES

There are many running springs and water seepages in the San Bernardino Mountains, and most of them can be reached by road. This trip visits two little springs that can be reached only by walking. The springs themselves are not much to see, but the trail walk through stands of Jeffrey pine and pinyon, high on the ridgeside with sweeping views over lower Holcomb Creek and Deep Creek, is pleasant. From the high point of the trail you can see Lake Arrowhead sparkling in the distance. This is lonely mountain country, seldom visited; you should have the trail all to yourself.

DESCRIPTION

From the Rim of the World Highway (State Route 18), 2 miles past Running Springs, turn left (north) onto Green Valley Road. After 3 miles — just before you reach Green Valley — turn left again onto Forest road 3N16. Follow this northeast 12 miles to Big Pine Flat, then turn left (west) on 3N14 and follow it 3½ miles to Little Pine Flat. Then again turn left (south) onto Hawes Ranch Road and follow it 1⅔ miles to its end just beyond the ranch.

About 50 yards west of the *Holcomb Creek Trail* sign (see trip 19) is a wooden sign indicating *Muddy Spring 3 miles.* Follow the trail — not a dirt road that soon ends — up the shallow gully westward, along a trickling creek, through a beautiful Jeffrey pine forest. In 1 mile you reach the saddle in the ridge between Little Shay and Shay mountains, from where Lake Arrowhead appears far to the southwest. The trail now drops down and follows the south slope of the ridge through pinyon pines. In ¼ mile you come to the small seepage of Barrel Spring, just below the trail (water enough to drink during wet months).

The trail then continues west, dropping 100′ or more before climbing back up to the ridgetop, then descending northwest to Muddy Spring, overlooking Deep Creek basin, 1¾ miles from Barrel Spring. The water here also flows enough to use only during times of abundant rainfall.

Return the same way.

TRIP: Hawes Ranch to Shay Mountain

18   4 **miles** round trip; 1100′ elevation gain
        Classification: **Moderate**
        Season: **November-May**
        Topo map: *Lake Arrowhead* (15′)

FEATURES

The long hogback of Shay Mountain (6730′) looms high
over the northside country of the San Bernardinos. From
its broad summit one has panoramic views reaching from
Lake Arrowhead almost to Big Bear and stretching far
out over the Mojave Desert.

This trip is half on trail, half cross-country scramble. But
the scrambling is easy climbing over pinyon-dotted slopes.
Do it in spring, when the northside country is damp and
aromatic, and the high peaks to the southeast are glistening in their snowy mantle.

There have been lots of Shays in the history of the San
Bernardinos. The particular Shay after whom the moun-
tain is named is said to be an early-day ranger at the old
Coxey Ranger Station, Art Shay.

DESCRIPTION

Drive to the roadhead below Hawes Ranch (see trip
17 for directions).

Proceed westward up the Muddy Spring Trail (see trip
17) 1 mile to the ridgetop saddle. Then leave the trail and
walk northwest along the upward slope, through open
stands of pinyon pine, to the nearly-bare summit, 1 more
mile. If you return to the trail saddle unfulfilled, scramble
up the other direction (southeast) ¾ mile to the top of
Little Shay Mountain (6656′).

TRIP:
19
Hawes Ranch to Cox Creek, Holcomb Creek, Holcomb Crossing Camp
6 miles round trip; **600′** elevation loss and gain
Classification: **Moderate**
Season: **All year**
Topo map: *Lake Arrowhead* (15′)

FEATURES

This is another route into the beautiful lower reaches of Holcomb Creek. You approach from the north, dropping down Cox Creek, then descending ridges and slopes into Holcomb Creek to Holcomb Crossing Trail Camp. Along Cox Creek are Jeffrey pines, but on the ridges and slopes you go through a semi-arid forest of pinyon pine and western juniper. In all but the hottest months, this is a very pleasant trail trip, with options when you reach Holcomb Crossing.

DESCRIPTION

Drive to the roadhead below Hawes Ranch (see trip 17 for directions).

A wooden sign pointing south along Cox Creek indicates *Holcomb Creek 3 miles.* For 1 mile the trail follows the creek, through a magnificent forest of Jeffrey pine. Then the trail climbs to near the top of the ridge immediately east of the creek and follows this pinyon-covered ridge down to a little open valley on the north side of Holcomb Creek. On the north bank of the creek you intersect the Pacific Crest Trail (see trip 13). Turn right (west), cross the creek via boulders, and in 100 yards reach shady Holcomb Crossing Trail Camp.

You can return the way you came or, with a car shuttle, take the Pacific Crest Trail in either direction (see trip 13), or, 300 yards west of the trail camp, find the trail that heads southwest to Crab Flats (see trip 15).

TRIP: Snow Valley to Little Green Valley, Green Valley
20 Public Camp
4 miles one way; **700′** elevation gain
Classification: **Moderate**
Season: **April-November**
Topo map: *Keller Peak* (7½′)

FEATURES

Before the loggers and subdividers arrived on the scene,
the top of the San Bernardinos from Crestline to Big Bear
were heavily clothed in tall timber. Today, stands of magnificent pine, cedar and oak, undisturbed by man, are rare
and widely scattered. One place where you can still find
them, rich and tall and verdant, is on the ridges north of
Snow Valley. This is a beautiful walk through the realm
of these forest monarchs, on good trail or fire road all the
way, and sometimes besides a trickling stream. Do it on a
day when you have plenty of time, so that you can saunter,
pause and fully soak up nature's handiwork.

DESCRIPTION

Drive up State Route 18 to Snow Valley, 5 miles east of
Running Springs. As you reach Snow Valley, a dirt road
forks left (north) to some cabins; turn off the highway and
park in the clearing on the left where you see the *Green
Valley Trail* sign. (If you reach Snow Valley picnic area,
you've driven 100 yards too far east.)

Follow the trail as it leads northwest, crosses a small
brook, and gently climbs the slope. You pass several logging roads during the first ½ mile, the result of recent
selective tree-cutting. In 1 mile you climb the forested ridge
and reach Little Green Valley. Here you pass a boys' camp
and reach a dirt road leading northwest to Green Valley
Lake. Follow the dirt road across a ridge and down into
the basin of Green Valley Lake, passing just behind the
campground, to Meadow Lane, 4 miles from the start.

If you have employed a car shuttle to Green Valley
Public Campground, your trip is over. Otherwise return
the way you came.

TRIP:

21

Rim of the World Highway to Bear Creek, Siberia Creek, Siberia Creek Trail Camp
8½ miles round trip; **2000′** elevation loss and gain
Classification: **Moderate**
Season: **All year**
Topo map: *Keller Peak* (7½′)

FEATURES

A fire raged through the Bear Creek drainage a few years ago, destroying much of the beauty of the mountain slopes. Fortunately, it spared most of the canyon bottom and its lush streamside growth. Here, bigcone spruce, white alder and canyon live oak protect the bubbling creek and its grassy banks from the sun's harshness.

Merging with Bear Creek just across from where the trail reaches canyon bottom is beautiful, woodsy Siberia Creek, probably the most delightful sylvan recess in the San Bernardinos outside of the San Gorgonio Wilderness. Its little singing stream, shaded by an over-arching canopy of green, is a favorite of hikers, campers and fishermen alike. Here, smack in the middle of the overused San Bernardinos, nature reveals her quiet, pristine best.

This trip leaves the Rim of the World Highway (State 18), drops down chaparral-clad slopes into Bear Creek, then continues into the deep, verdant oasis of Siberia Creek—miraculously untouched by the holocaust that ravaged the slopes just above. Here, just above the junction with Bear Creek, the Forest Service has placed Siberia Creek Trail Camp—stoves, tables and toilet. Bring your fishing rod; rainbow trout swim in nearby Bear Creek.

DESCRIPTION

Drive 5½ miles east of Running Springs (½ mile past Snow Valley) on State Route 18 to where a wooden sign reads *Camp Creek Trail.* Turn right and follow the dirt road, going left at a fork, to a small parking area on a ridgetop, ½ mile from the highway. A sign here reads *Bear Creek 4.*

Take the trail eastward, over the ridge, under scattered Jeffrey pines. In ½ mile you reach the 1970 burn, and the forest changes to chaparral, with a few blackened stumps jutting skyward. The trail now zigzags steeply down the brushy slopes to the welcome shade and cool water of Bear Creek, 4 miles. You cross Bear Creek, enter the mouth of Siberia Creek, and reach Siberia Creek Trail Camp, located on an alder- and oak-shaded bench just north of the stream.

Return the same way. Or, with car shuttle, take the trail northeast into the Bluff Lake country (see trip 30), or the trail south to Seven Pines (see trip 33).

Siberia Creek

TRIP: Holcomb Valley Road to Delamar Mountain
22 **5 miles** round trip; **1000′** elevation gain
Classification: **Moderate**
Season: **April-November**
Topo map: *Fawnskin* (7.5′)

FEATURES

8357′ Delamar Mountain stands tall on the divide separating the Holcomb Creek drainage from Big Bear Lake. From its rocky, forested summit, you are rewarded with a superb panorama of the central San Bernardinos, with sparkling-blue Big Bear Lake immediately to the south and Holcomb Valley's historic gold country right below to the north.

This trip follows a fairly new stretch of the Pacific Crest Trail for two miles, then climbs the east ridge of Delamar Mountain through an open forest of Jeffrey pine and white fir. Since part of it is trailless, wear lug-soled boots.

DESCRIPTION

From Highway 38, 1.4 miles east of Fawnskin, turn north onto Holcomb Valley Road (2N09). In 2.3 miles, almost at the summit of the divide, look for the marked crossing of the Pacific Crest Trail. Park here.

Walk west on the Pacific Crest Trail, ascending gradually along the south side of the Big Bear-Holcomb Valley divide. You pass through an open forest of conifer and oak, with numerous views south to Big Bear Lake. In 1.5 miles you cross to the shadier north slope of the ridge and then contour northwest another ½ mile. At the point where the PCT begins a steady descent, leave the trail and climb westward on an easy cross-country ascent to Delamar Mountain's forested east ridge. In ½ mile of trailless walking you reach the pile of rocks that is the summit (8398′). For the best view southward over Big Bear Lake, scramble about 100 yards south to a slightly lower summit.

Return the same way, or continue westward on the PCT to Forest Road 3N12, which you reach at a point 3½ miles north of Fawnskin. A car shuttle is required for this option.

TRIP: State Highway 38 to Bertha Peak

23 **6 miles** round trip; **1400′** elevation gain
Classification: **Moderate**
Season: **April-November**
Topo map: *Fawnskin* (7.5′)

FEATURES

Like neighboring Delamar Mountain, 8201′ Bertha Peak rises high on the forested ridge between Holcomb Valley and Big Bear Lake. From its rounded summit, you get a striking perspective over the gentle valley-and-ridge country of the central San Bernardinos.

This trip takes the Cougar Crest Trail from Highway 38, on the north shore of Big Bear Lake, to the Pacific Crest Trail, then ascends a steep dirt track to the electronic relay station on the summit. It is a pleasant walk through an open forest of pinyon pine and juniper, climaxed by a panoramic view well worth the effort. Do it on a clear day, when almost the entire San Bernardinos sprawl below you, and the great Greyback-Mt. San Bernardino ridge looms high and stark on the southeast skyline.

DESCRIPTION

From Fawnskin, drive east on State Route 38 2.3 miles to a parking area on the north side of the highway with the sign *Cougar Crest Trail.* (If you reach the Big Bear Ranger Station, you've driven ½ mile too far.) Park here.

Walk up the Cougar Crest Trail, through an open forest of pinyon pine, juniper, and scattered Jeffrey pines. For the first mile you're on a maze of old mining roads, but you should have no trouble following the beaten trail route. Beyond, you're on new trail as you wind upward toward Bertha Peak's west ridge. Panoramic views open over the Big Bear Lake country as you gain elevation, and in 2 miles you intersect the PCT. Turn right (east) and follow the PCT to a junction with a dirt road on the ridgecrest, ½ mile. Walk up this dirt road, very steep in places, through pinyon pines and some rather large western junipers, to the summit relay station.

After taking in the 360-degree panorama, return the way you came.

TRIP: Doble Mine (ruins) to Gold Mountain

24   4 miles round trip; 1000' elevation gain
Classification: **Moderate**
Season: **April-November**
Topo map: *Lucerne Valley* (15')

FEATURES

The eastern and northern flanks of the San Bernardino
Mountains are honeycombed with abandoned gold prospects. No other mountain region in Southern California has
seen so much mining excitement spread over so many
years — from the 1850s well into this century.

Of all the lode-mining operations in the range, none was
as storied nor as famous as Lucky Baldwin's Gold Mountain (or Doble) Mine high on the mountainside overlooking Baldwin Lake. The rich quartz ledges were discovered
in 1873 by prospectors Barney and Charley Carter. Their
discovery turned out to be a mountain of gold ore, and
the rush was on. Elias J. "Lucky" Baldwin bought "Carter's
Quartz Hill" for $6,000,000 and by 1875 he had constructed
a 40-stamp mill to process the ore and employed 180 men.
Baldwin was not as "lucky" in this venture as he was in
others, and it is doubtful that he ever saw a full return on
his investment. During the early 1900s the mine was
worked by several lessees, the most recent operation being
in the late 1940s. The end finally came in 1951, when the
equipment was removed and the property abandoned.

The site of the large mill and cyanide-processing plant
can still be seen on the northeast slopes of Gold Mountain.
This trip visits these storied ruins and climbs the pinyon-
covered ridge of Gold Mountain for a panoramic view en-
compassing most of the old mining areas. For those with
vivid imaginations, it is possible to look down over Doble
Mine, Holcomb Valley, Arrastre Flat, and Van Dusen
Canyon and visualize the feverish excitement and hectic
activity that once occurred here. This trip is for those with
such imaginations.

DESCRIPTION

From State Route 18 where it makes its loop around the
north end of Baldwin Lake, turn left (north) onto Holcomb
Valley Road (3N08). Drive up this dirt road 1¾ miles to the
site of Doble Mine. Park in the clearing across from the old
wooden "hopper."

Before starting out on foot, look south along the mountainside, toward Baldwin Lake; the foundations and diggings you see are all that remain of this most famous lode
mine in the San Bernardinos.

Walk up the dirt road about 200 yards, then start up the
gentle, pinyon- and juniper-covered northeast ridge of
Gold Mountain. The climb is trailless but easy going.
Proceed around the right (north) side of a false summit to a
junction with the Pacific Crest Trail, 1 mile. Continue up
the broad pinyon-clad ridge to the 8227-foot summit of
Gold Mountain for far-reaching views over this mine-
poxed northeastern corner of the San Bernardinos.

Return the same way. An attractive option requiring a
short car shuttle (1¼ miles) is to descend via the PCT. You
will get a good panorama of Baldwin Lake's usually dry
playa where Budd Doble, Lucky Baldwin's son-in-law,
once trained race horses. The PCT reaches Road 3N08 just
above the ghost town of Doble.

Doble Mine   *Huntington Library*

TRIP: Cactus Flat to Silver Peak (Blackhawk Mountain)

25
4 miles round trip; 750′ elevation gain
Classification: **Moderate**
Season: **All year**
Topo map: *Lucerne Valley* (15′)

FEATURES

The desert-tempered north slope of the San Bernardinos holds delightful surprises. When winter's snowy mantle grips the higher parts of the range, this land of pinyon, juniper and Joshua tree is warm and inviting. This trip samples this semi-arid terrain. You climb the grayish hogback of Silver Peak — partly on old mining road, partly by cross-country scrambling — for a far-reaching view over the Mojave Desert and its islands of treeless, steep-sided tawny mountain ranges.

Blackhawk Mountain (the summit of which is called Silver Peak) was once the scene of gold and silver mining activities. Abandoned diggings and shafts dot the slopes on all sides. The greatest activity was in Blackhawk Canyon, down the north side of the mountain. Gold deposits were discovered here in 1887 and developed soon afterward by the Blackhawk Mining Company, financed by English capital. Tunnels were dug and a 10-stamp mill erected, but high operating costs forced suspension of the venture within a few years. In 1921 the mines were reopened by the Arlington Mining Corporation, and they were worked continuously until 1940, yielding a reported $300,000. Since 1940 they have been idle.

Cactus Flat, where the hike begins, commemorates "Cactus Jim" Johnson, builder of the Johnson Grade road up Cushenbury Canyon to Baldwin Lake. Old Cactus Jim selected his own burial site here, where his grave is now located and marked with a small sign.

DESCRIPTION

From the north shore of Big Bear Lake, proceed east on State Route 18 to Cactus Flat, 8½ miles past the junction of Highways 18 and 38. Just north of the 61.78 mileage sign (and south of the 62.03 sign) turn east onto a dirt road. Follow this side road ¼ mile to the first dirt road on the left; turn left and continue ⅛ mile to a small parking area where the road turns left. Park here.

Follow this dirt road down into a gully, then turn left and hike up the gully to its end at another dirt road (old mining roads crisscross the mountain). Proceed right and follow this dirt road to its end at a large graded area. Turn up the canyon (north), roughly following the cables to the top of the ridge. Climb up the spur ridge to the main ridge, where you will intersect another dirt road. Turn right (east) and follow the road up the main ridge to the 6757-foot summit.

Return the same way, avoiding the private property area on the southwest flank of the mountain, where exploratory mining work is being done.

Champion Joshua tree

TRIP: Forest Road 3NO3 to Champion Joshua Tree

26

2 miles round trip; 100' elevation gain
Classification: **Easy**
Season: **October-May**
Topo map: *Old Woman Springs* (15')

FEATURES

In the broad, desert-draining canyon of Arrastre Creek and its east fork, on the north slope of the San Bernardinos, is one of the most magnificent Joshua tree forests in the world. The shaggy Joshua tree is the oddest of all plants in these mountains. This weird giant of the lily family has bayonetlike leaves and a trunk with no annual rings and, therefore, no way to tell how old it is. In the springtime, clusters of greenish white, bell-shaped flowers with a rather unpleasant odor appear. Indians relished the roasted flower buds, and obtained a dye from the tree's red roots. Mormon settlers gave the tree its name; they saw a likeness to Joshua praying in the wilderness with his arms uplifted to the heavens. The tree owes its continued existence to the little Pronuba moth. The Joshua relies on the moth for pollination, and the moth larvae rely on the Joshua for food. Each depends on the other for its survival.

The largest Joshua tree in the world — discovered in 1967 and named "The Champion" — grows here at the foot of Granite Peak. This overgrown, shaggy monarch of the high desert is 14' 11" in circumference and over 32' high.

This trip is a short stroll through a forest of pinyon pine, western juniper and Joshua tree to the world champion. It follows jeep tracks all the way.

DESCRIPTION

Drive 3½ miles northeast of Baldwin Lake on State Route 18. Turn right (southeast) onto Smarts Ranch Road (dirt) and follow it 5⅓ miles up the valley of Arrastre Creek. About ¼ mile past the creek crossing, you reach unmarked jeep tracks leading left (north). Park here off the road (4-wheel vehicles can drive to the tree).

Walk along the jeep tracks, heading northeast, through an open forest of pinyon, juniper and Joshua. After ½ mile you enter groves of king-sized Joshuas. In 1 mile, just under the rocky slopes of Granite Peak, you reach the world champion, on your right just before the end of the jeep tracks. You should have no trouble identifying the tree, as it dwarfs the other large Joshuas around it. (Unfortunately, it can also be identified by the beer cans and litter spread around it by some visitors.)

Return the way you came.

marmot

TRIP: State Highway 38 to Grays Peak

27 **6 miles** round trip; **1200′** elevation gain
Classification: **Moderate**
Season: **April-November**
Topo map: *Fawnskin* (7.5′)

FEATURES

Forested 7952-foot Grays Peak looms close over the western end of Big Bear Lake. The peak is named for Gray's Landing on the north shore of the lake, founded by Alex Gray in 1918 and still used by anglers.

This is an easy-graded, very pleasant walk through stands of Jeffrey pine, black oak, and white fir, partly on a newly constructed trail, partly on fire road.

DESCRIPTION

Follow State Highway 38 along the north shore of Big Bear Lake to the Grays Peak parking area, 2.8 miles east of Big Bear Dam, or 0.3 mile south of Fawnskin. There are restrooms and picnic tables here, and many spaces for parking.

The signed trailhead is at the north edge of the picnic-parking area. Follow the pathway as it gently climbs through open forest to intersect a dirt fire road, ½ mile. Turn right onto the road, going straight ahead at a road junction, to a signed junction with the Grays Peak Trail, another ½ mile. Turn left and follow the trail as it climbs, contours, and climbs again, circling around to the south flank of the peak. The trail ends 100 feet below the top; work your way through buckthorn thickets and downed trees to the summit. Views are limited by the forest cover, but you can make out shimmering Big Bear Lake to the south, and the rugged lower Holcomb Creek country to the north.

Return the way you came.

TRIP: Highway 18 to Castle Rock

28 2 miles round trip; **700′** elevation gain
Classification: **Moderate**
Season: **April-October**
Topo map: *Big Bear Lake* (7.5′)

FEATURES

South from Big Bear Lake, rising from the heavily forested ridge that divides the Big Bear basin from the canyon of the Santa Ana River, are a number of granite knobs
and boulder outcroppings. Most impressive of these is a
weather-eroded, knobby gendarme known as Castle Rock.

Castle Rock has long attracted attention because of its
sentrylike position above the lower end of the lake and its
unusual shape. Such qualities impress the imaginations of
men, and from these imaginations legends arise that per-
sist through the ages. The legend of Castle Rock is one of
the most famous of those known to Indians who once made
the San Bernardinos their home.

This trip climbs steeply up the forested mountainside
to this rock rooted in legend. You follow a trail to the foot
of the rock; then it is a Class 3 scramble to the summit.
Wear lug-soled boots. Do it when a breeze freshens the
mountains; perhaps you will be able to hear the soft wail
of the forlorn Indian princess who waited for her husband
on Castle Rock.

DESCRIPTION

From State Route 18 1 mile east of Big Bear Dam or 3
miles west of Big Bear Lake Village, the marked trail
starts up a forested gully. Park 50 yards east of the trailhead in a clearing across the highway (on the north side).

The trail climbs steeply up the left (east) side of the
gully through a magnificent forest of ponderosa pine,
white fir and incense cedar, passing jumbo granite boulders. In about ¾ mile the trail reaches a saddle and starts
to descend. Castle Rock is the large outcropping immediately east of this saddle. Leave the trail here. The easiest
way up the rock (Class 3) is to contour about 50 feet

around the north and west sides of the outcropping, then climb up an indentation to the summit. There is one spot about half way up where a belay may be warranted for the unsteady.

Descend the same way.

Champion Lodgepole pine (see next page)

TRIP: Forest Road 2N11 to Champion Lodgepole Pine

29

1 mile round trip; 50' elevation loss and gain
Classification: **Easy**
Season: **April-October**
Topo map: *Big Bear Lake* (7.5')

FEATURES

Lodgepole pines seldom grow taller than 70 feet, and in Southern California they are seldom seen below 8000'. An exception to these rules occurs in the vicinity of Bluff Lake, a shallow body of water surrounded by lush forest and meadow country, 3 miles south of Big Bear Lake. Here, at 7500', grow the largest lodgepole pines in the world. The world champion, discovered in 1963, is a mammoth, double-topped tree standing 110' tall with a circumference of 20'. Its age is estimated at 400 years, meaning that the tree's life has spanned California's history since shortly after Cabrillo's epic voyage of discovery in 1542.

Lodgepole — also known as tamarack — pines are readily identified by their thin, scaly bark and their paired needles (the only pine in these mountains with two needles per bundle). They are usually found only in high subalpine forests, just below timberline. This trip is a very short stroll through lush forest and grassland to the world champion.

DESCRIPTION

From the west end of Big Bear Lake Village, turn south onto either Mill Creek Road or Tulip Lane (they intersect). In about ½ mile you reach a sideroad branching southwest to Clarks Summit (a sign says 3 miles). Follow this road to its intersection with Forest Road 2N11; turn right (southwest) and follow *Champion Lodgepole* signs to road's end, 7 miles from Big Bear Lake Village.

Follow Trail 1W04 west ⅓ mile alongside a trickling stream to a junction. Then go right (north) 100 yards to Champion Lodgepole, near the east end of a meadow. Stay outside the wooden fence built by the Forest Service to protect the tree.

Return the same way.

TRIP: Forest Road 2N11 to Siberia Creek, Siberia Creek

30

Trail Camp

12 miles round trip; **2500′** elevation loss and gain
Classification: **Strenuous**
Season: **All year**
Topo maps: *Big Bear Lake, Keller Peak* (both 7.5′)

FEATURES

Siberia Creek begins in the shallow pond known as Bluff
Lake, on the high tableland between Big Bear Lake and
the valley of the Santa Ana River. It flows southwest across
this lushly forested tableland, through magnificent stands
of white fir, ponderosa and lodgepole pine, and emerald-
green meadows of tall grass, ferns and flowering herbs.
Then it abruptly drops down a boulder-filled gorge, finally
to empty its spent waters into Bear Creek. Here, set amid
alders, oaks and spruces, is Siberia Creek Trail Camp
(stoves, tables and toilet).

A trail recently constructed descends most of the length
of Siberia Creek — from the west end of Forest Road 2N11
two miles south of Bluff Lake all the way down to Siberia
Creek Trail Camp, where it joins the trail up to the Rim
of the World Highway (see trip 21). This trip follows this
new trail — first across the verdant tableland, then down
around the steep slopes of Lookout Point to avoid the difficult gorge, and into lower Siberia Creek and its small trail
camp. From here, options are available with a car shuttle
(see below).

DESCRIPTION

Follow driving directions of trip 29.

From the end of Forest Road 2N11, follow Trail 1W04
⅓ mile west, alongside a small creek, to the junction with
the champion lodgepole pine trail (see trip 29). Continue
straight ahead, alongside lush meadowland and through
open forest. In ¾ mile you cross Siberia Creek and follow
its north bank downstream; ¼ mile farther you recross the
creek. Here the tableland ends and the stream abruptly

drops into a boulder-stacked gorge. Follow the trail as it contours out onto the open-forested slopes of Lookout Mountain, drops to a saddle, and zigzags down the steep ridge westward to a junction with the Seven Pines Trail (see Trip 33), 5 miles from the start. Turn right (north) and follow the latter one mile down to Siberia Creek Trail Camp, located alongside the stream to your left, just before Siberia Creek meets Bear Creek.

Return the same way, all uphill now. Or, with a car shuttle, ascend the Green Valley Trail to the Rim of the World Highway (see trip 21) or the Seven Pines Trail to Seven Pines (see trip 33). Any way you do it, plan to spend the night at Siberia Creek Trail Camp.

TRIP: Aspen Glen Picnic Ground to Grand View Point

31   **6 miles** round trip; **1200′** elevation gain
Classification: **Moderate**
Season: **May-October**
Topo map: *Big Bear Lake* (7.5′)

FEATURES

This trip climbs from the new Aspen Glen Picnic Ground to the summit of the high ridge that separates Bear Valley from the basin of the Santa Ana River. En route you are rewarded with occasional views over Big Bear Lake and its crowded resort complex, and from aptly named Grand View Point you look across the deep trench of the Santa Ana to the lofty peaks and ridges of the San Gorgonio Wilderness. You're on trail or fire road all the way to Grand View Point. On weekends this trail is popular with horseback riders.

DESCRIPTION

From State Route 18, near the west end of Big Bear Lake Village, turn right (southwest) onto Mill Creek Road and drive ⅓ mile to the new Aspen Glen Picnic Ground, on your left.

Your trail starts at the extreme east end of the parking area, just above the road. In 50 yards go left at a fork and follow the trail over a rise and down into a willow-choked draw. Turn right at a second trail junction and follow the broad path as it ascends the draw, then climbs above it, under a shady canopy of Jeffrey pine, black oak and white fir. You climb to a spur road (2N93Y), then follow this road up to a junction with Forest Road 2N10 at the top of the ridge. Cross the road and follow the marked trail ¼ mile southeast to the open summit of Grand View Point for a panorama of the eastern San Bernardinos that is truly grand.

Return the same way, or cut the trip in half by having transportation awaiting you on Forest Road 2N10.

TRIP: Green Canyon to Sugarloaf Mountain

32

8 **miles** round trip; **2000′** elevation gain
Classification: **Moderate**
Season: **May-October**
Topo map: *Moonridge* (7.5′)

FEATURES

Sugarloaf Mountain — as the name implies — is a massive rounded lump on the main divide between the Big Bear country and the canyon of the Santa Ana River. From its 9952′ forested summit, you are treated to an all-encompassing vista over the whole eastern half of the San Bernardinos. It is the highest peak in the range outside of the San Gorgonio Wilderness.

For a mountain almost 10,000 feet high, Sugarloaf displays a surprising variety of flora. The usual Jeffrey pine, sugar pine, white fir and incense cedar are found along the summit ridge and in sheltered recesses. Near the summit are some teepee-like western junipers. Pinyon pine, juniper and mountain mahogany abound on the middle slopes, and purple sage and skeleton weed are prevalent in the sparsely forested sections. The rare black swallowtail butterfly, *Papilio Bairdi,* can be seen on the summit in late August and early September.

This trail trip ascends beautifully forested Green Canyon to the top of the ridge, then follows the ridge westward to the summit. It is an ideal jaunt for a warm summer day, when the cool breezes along the ridgetop offer refreshing relief from the sweltering valley below.

DESCRIPTION

Drive east, then south on State Route 38 from Big Bear City. About 3 miles from town, turn right onto Forest Road 2N93. Follow 2N93, passing two roads that turn off to our left, as it curves left and climbs along the mountainside to the Green Creek crossing, 1⅓ miles from Highway 38. Just across the creek, turn right (south) onto an unmarked dirt road and follow it about ¼ mile to a shaded parking area.

it about ¼ mile to a shaded parking area.

Walk up the steep dirt road that turns to jeep tracks in a short distance, following alongside trickling Green Creek. In 2 miles you reach the saddle atop the ridge, a trail junction. Turn right (west) and follow the ridgetop trail to the forested summit, 2 more miles.

Return the same way. An option, requiring a car shuttle, is to descend to the saddle junction, then turn south and descend the trail to the Wildhorse Creek roadhead (see trip 34). Another option is to descend west from the summit along the ridge, where you soon pick up a poor ridgetop trail descending to Forest Road 2N21, 3 miles.

Sugarloaf Mountain

TRIP: Seven Pines to Siberia Creek Trail Camp

33

8 miles round trip; **600'** elevation gain
Classification: **Moderate**
Season: **All year**
Topo map: *Big Bear Lake* (7.5')

FEATURES

This is the back-door approach to Siberia Creek, coming
in from the valley of the Santa Ana River. It was once a
pleasant hike through overarching oaks and spruces, but
a major conflagration a few years ago destroyed most of
the forest cover. Today you walk across open slopes spotted with charred stumps, completely at the mercy of the
sun. For this reason, it is best done on a cool winter or
spring day when the other approaches — via the Rim of
the World Highway (trip 21) and Bluff Lake (trip 30) —
are snowed in. Fortunately, Siberia Creek was spared from
the holocaust and is as delightful as ever.

DESCRIPTION

From Redlands drive 19 miles east on State Highway
38 to Angelus Oaks. Just beyond, turn left (north) and
descend Middle Control Road (1N06) to Santa Ana River
Road (1N09), 3½ miles. Turn left (west) on the latter and
follow it ¼ mile to a junction with Clark Grade Road
(1N54). Turn right and ascend Clark Grade 1½ miles to a
junction with Forest Road 1N64. Turn left (west) and
follow the latter 1.6 miles to Seven Pines Trailhead,
marked by a wooden sign. Park just beyond.

Follow the trail, overgrown with brush and downed
trees in many places, as it climbs and contours northwest
above Bear Creek. In 3 obstacle-filled miles you intersect
the new trail coming down from Bluff Lake (see Trip 30).
Continue north 1 mile, dropping to Siberia Creek Trail
Camp and its welcome shade and water.

Return the same way. Or you have the options mentioned above (see trips 21 and 30), both requiring a car
shuttle.

TRIP: Highway 38 to Wildhorse Creek, Wildhorse
Creek Trail Camp

34

8 miles round trip; **1400'** elevation gain
Classification: **Moderate**
Season: **April-October**
Topo map: *Moonridge* (7.5')

FEATURES

The fault-carved canyon of Wildhorse Creek descends
in an almost straight line from high on the Sugarloaf Ridge
to the Santa Ana River. Near the head of the canyon is
Wildhorse Spring, feeding the creek that runs full in spring
but fades to a lazy trickle by late summer. The creek and
the protective shade of the canyon walls nourish a lush
forest of Jeffrey pine, white fir, incense cedar and several
varieties of oak. For the most part, this forest is confined to
the canyon bottom, and it stands in marked contrast to the
sparse growth of scattered Jeffreys and semi-arid brush
that dot the slopes above.

This trip follows a newly built trail up over chaparral-
coated ridges and down into upper Wildhorse Creek,
superseding the old trail that follows the length of the
creek. For an overnight stay there is Wildhorse Creek Trail
Camp, nestled amid tall Jeffrey pines and white firs alongside the trickling creek. If you like solitude and nature's
peace, this is the trip for you. In summer, when a multitude
of hikers tramp through nearby San Gorgonio Wilderness,
Wildhorse Canyon is usually left alone. The author likes it
best in April or early May, when the air is crisp, Wildhorse
Creek runs full, and Old Greyback sparkles under its
snowy mantle.

DESCRIPTION

From Redlands drive east on State Route 38 for 32 miles,
5 miles past Barton Flats, to the signed turnoff of the Wildhorse Trail, on your left just 0.2 mile *before* the Heart Bar
Campground road. Turn left (north) and drive about 100
yards up a dirt road to a parking area.

Follow the trail, which for the first mile is an old jeep
track, up through an open forest of Jeffrey and pinyon pine
and juniper. From the end of the jeep track, your trail

winds steadily upward, over and around several ridges, leaving the forest behind. As you climb higher, snow-streaked Greyback ridge begins to emerge from behind the forested slope of Grinnell Mountain, and views open up down the broad canyon of the upper Santa Ana River. After 3 miles you finally round the last ridge and then descend into the forested canyon of Wildhorse Creek. Another short mile brings you to Wildhorse Creek Trail Camp, located on a bench above the stream, shaded by tall Jeffrey pines. A stove, a toilet and several flat sleeping areas are here. The creek usually runs all year, although fading to a trickle by late summer.

Across the creek is a junction with the old Wildhorse Creek Trail. A mile up the creek trail is Wildhorse Meadows, Forest Road 2N93, and the Sugarloaf Trail (see trip 35), an option requiring a car shuttle. Or you can descend the Wildhorse Creek Trail, no longer maintained but readily passable, to Highway 38 1 mile east of South Fork Campground.

"The Tarn," located at 10,560 feet just southeast of the summit of San Gorgonio Mountain. When melting snow fills it each spring, it becomes the highest lake in southern California.

Bob Tosh

TRIP: Wildhorse Meadows to Sugarloaf Mountain

35

7 miles roundtrip; **1300′** elevation gain
Classification: **Moderate**
Season: **May-October**
Topo map: *Moonridge* (7.5′)

FEATURES

This is the shortest and easiest way to climb Sugarloaf Mountain, but it involves a drive over a narrow and in some places rocky dirt road. You climb from Wildhorse Meadows up to the saddle east of Sugarloaf, then follow the ridgetop to the summit, on trail all the way. (For more on Sugarloaf Mountain, see trip 32.)

DESCRIPTION

From Redlands drive east 34 miles on State Route 38 through Barton Flats to the beginning of Forest Road 2N93 (2¼ miles past the entrance to Heart Bar Campground). The road is easy to pass by, so keep a sharp eye out for it on your left (north). Drive up Forest Road 2N93 to Wildhorse Meadows, 5.3 miles. Continue up 2N93 0.7 mile beyond the meadow, to where you see a locked gate blocking a steep jeep road on your left. Park here.

Pass the locked gate and walk west, up the jeep road, to the top of the ridge. Here the road divides into several indistinct jeep paths. Continue west, atop the ridge, then drop to a 4-way trail junction. A sign indicates *Sugarloaf Trail* leading west. Follow this good trail as it climbs, contours, drops, and climbs again to the forested 9952′ summit of Sugarloaf Peak, 3½ miles from the start.

Return the same way. Or, with a car shuttle, descend Green Canyon to Forest Road 2N93, 4 miles north of where you left it (trip 32).

TRIP: Forest Road 1N05 to Fish Creek, Aspen Grove,
36 Lower Fish Creek Meadows
5 miles round trip; **650'** elevation gain
Classification: **Easy**
Season: **June-October**
Topo map: *Moonridge* (7.5')

FEATURES

Fish Creek rises high on the massive slopes of Grinnell Mountain and Ten Thousand Foot Ridge, and cuts a deep swath before joining the Santa Ana River 2 miles east of Barton Flats. This all-year stream is shaded most of the way by a mixed forest of conifers and the largest grove of aspens in the San Bernardino Mountains. Verdant grasses carpet the creekside, particularly at Lower Fish Creek Meadow, an oval clearing where the canyon elbows from northeast to northwest. A wilderness permit is needed.

This pleasant streamside trip follows the canyon through its middle reaches, the most delightful portion, where aspens quake in the cool mountain breeze and monkey flowers add a dash of color in early summer. In early autumn, the tremulous aspen leaves turn a brilliant golden yellow, in sharp contrast with the surrounding forest.

DESCRIPTION

From Redlands drive east on State Route 38 for 32 miles, 5 miles past Barton Flats, to the entrance road to Heart Bar Campground (1N02). Turn right on 1N02, passing the campground entrance (on your right in .2 mile), to a junction in 1.2 miles. Go right, up 1N05 to the signed *Aspen Grove Trail* parking area, 2.6 miles from the highway.

Follow the old dirt road that leads southeast down to Fish Creek, 250 yards. You cross the creek and immediately reach the San Gorgonio Wilderness boundary (permit required). There are a few aspens here, but to see more of these lovely trees, take the side trail that goes right (northwest) ½ mile to Aspen Grove. (The grove is not what it used to be; many of the trees are down.) The main trail passes the wilderness boundary sign and follows a sloping bench paralleling the creek on its west side. You climb gently through a beautiful forest of white fir, interspaced here and there with tall Jeffrey pines and incense cedar. You pass the small clearing known as Monkey Flower Flat, then climb over a low ridge before dropping down to the creek. In 1½ miles your trail crosses Fish Creek to the east bank and, ¾ mile beyond, reaches the grassy clearing of Lower Fish Creek Meadow and a junction with the Upper Fish Creek Trail (see Trip 44).

Return the same way. An option, requiring a car shuttle, is to go left at the junction to the Upper Fish Creek roadhead, ⅓ mile (Trip 44).

Tree-ring study on limber pines, high on San Gorgonio Mountain. Bore samples reveal that some of these pines are 2000 years old.   *Bob Tosh*

TRIP: Ponderosa Nature Trail

37

1 mile round trip; 150' elevation gain
Classification: **Easy**
Season: **May-October**
Topo map: *Big Bear Lake* (7.5')

FEATURES

In recent years the Forest Service has constructed and
maintained a number of "nature trails" in San Bernardino
National Forest. These trails are designed to inform the
visitor of the natural history of the San Bernardinos, pointing out the flora, the fauna, and landscape features. Walking these nature trails, seeing first-hand the various species
and features, is the best way to learn nature's story in
the mountains.

This short loop trail offers a fitting introduction to the
nearby San Gorgonio Wilderness. In a one-mile, circle walk
around a hillside and through the forest, you pass examples
of most of the flora found in the lower half of the Wilderness. Signs are posted every few hundred feet or so, describing what you see. This is a hike you should stroll rather than stride; go slowly, digest nature's secrets, and you
will more fully enjoy your next trip into the San Gorgonio
Wilderness.

DESCRIPTION

From Redlands drive 25 miles east on State Route 38
to the beginning of the Ponderosa Nature Trail, marked
by a large wooden sign on the left (north) side of the road
(just before the Jenks Lake turnoff). Park in the adjacent
clearing.

The well-graded trail climbs north along the slope, passing and describing various forms of vegetation, turns west
and zigzags down into a forested shallow, then ascends
southeasterly back to the parking area.

If you return to your car unfulfilled, cross the highway
and sample the short Whispering Pines Nature Trail.

TRIP: Jenks Lake Road to South Fork Meadows

38 8 miles round trip; **1600'** elevation gain
Classification: **Moderate**
Season: **May-October**
Topo map: *Moonridge* (7.5')

FEATURES

There is only one designated wilderness area in the San Bernardino Mountains. But for multitudes of hikers, it is the grandest in all of Southern California. This is the 35,000-acre San Gorgonio Wilderness, a high mountain wonderland of granite peaks, forests of pine and fir, lush subalpine meadows, sparkling streams and placid lakes, and abundant wildlife. Man has wisely seen fit to set aside this region and preserve it forever in its pristine state. Here, under an evergreen canopy, alongside a singing stream or limpid pool, or high on a wind-washed ridge, you can find solitude and freedom, away from the civilization so near yet seemingly a world away. The nourishment afforded by true wilderness should redeem and revitalize you.

The old trailhead at Poopout Hill is no longer open; you must now begin your hike from the Jenks Lake Road. This adds 2¼ miles each way (4½ miles round trip) and a thousand feet of elevation gain to your walk. The trail change was made to protect the South Fork Meadows area from further desecration. Past overuse has severely damaged its wilderness value. With access now more difficult, verdant South Fork (also called Slushy) Meadows, where a multitude of springs form the headwaters of the santa Ana River, should regain its former glory.

Casual hikers going only 2¼ miles to the wilderness boundary do not need a permit. If you're proceeding beyond, to South Fork Meadows, you will need a wilderness permit, available at the Mill Creek Ranger Station, on Highway 38 a mile below the mouth of Mill Creek Canyon.

DESCRIPTION

From Redlands drive 25 miles east on State Highway 38 to the Jenks Lake Road turnoff. Turn right (southeast) and follow Jenks Lake Road 2.5 miles to the new, well-marked trailhead. There is a large paved parking area with restrooms on your left.

Follow the well-built, easy-graded trail as it winds up through stands of Jeffrey pine and white fir, passing the broad expanse of Horse Meadow, to the wilderness boundary, 2¼ miles and 1000 feet of elevation gain. You contour eastward along the richly forested hillside, and after another mile begin to hear the rushing waters of the Santa Ana's South Fork down to your left. The trail climbs 200 feet in the last ¼ mile and reaches South Fork Meadows, a sloping glen shaded by pine and fir, with lush ferns and grasses sprouting along the several converging streams and in the marshy cienegas.

Due to overuse, overnight camping in the South Fork Meadows area has been suspended indefinitely. Picnicking and day use are still allowed. Please take out everything you bring in.

Trails lead southwest to Dollar Lake (see Trip 39) and southeast to Dry Lake (Trip 40) and on to the summit of San Gorgonio Mountain (Trips 41 and 42). But this particular trail walk ends here at South Fork Meadows; so after enjoying your stay, return the way you came.

TRIP: Jenks Lake Road to South Fork Meadows, Dollar Lake

39 **12 miles** round trip; **2400'** elevation gain
Classification: *Moderate* (2 days). **Strenuous** (1)

Season: **June-October**
Topo map: *Moonridge* (7.5')

FEATURES

High under the north face of the Greyback-San Bernardino Peak ridge, tucked snuggly against rockbound slopes, is the tiny jewel called Dollar Lake. The little circular lake was so named because, when viewed from above on a sunny day, it shines like a silver dollar. Surrounding the lake is a healthy forest of lodgepole pine and white fir. In the trees, along the west shore, is Dollar Lake Trail camp, one of the most popular and heavily used in the San Gorgonio Wilderness.

This trip follows the well-traveled pathway from Jenks Lake Road to Dollar Lake, where you may picnic but not camp. Overnight camping is allowed at Dollar Lake Forks, just northwest of the lake. A wilderness permit is required.

DESCRIPTION

From Redlands drive to the Jenks Lake Road Trailhead (see trip 38).

Follow the excellent trail from Jenks Lake Road to South Forks Meadows, 4 miles (see trip 38). The trail then skirts the west edge of the meadow for 100 yards and begins switchbacking up the ridge. You start out in a forest of ponderosa pine and white fir, but as you climb above 8800' lodgepoles begin to predominate. The trail then rounds the ridge and climbs along the west slope of the big draw leading to Dollar Lake Saddle, passing a grassy cienega, and entering an area of waist-high manzanita. About 1¾ miles above South Fork Meadows, you reach a junction; go left, dropping into the bowl above Dollar Lake. In 200 yards you reach another junction; again go left, and follow the trail down to the lake, ¼ mile. The new trail camp is located ¼ mile above (northwest of) the lake, adjacent to the junction of the Dollar Lake Saddle and Dollar Lake Trails.

Return the way you came. An alternative is to take the old, unmaintained trail that drops directly down the draw to South Fork Meadows: a shortcut, but overgrown and hard to locate in spots. Another option is to climb San Gorgonio Mountain from here, making it an easy two-day trip rather than a strenuous one-day scramble (see trip 41).

Above timberline on the San Gorgonio Trail

TRIP: Jenks Lake Road to South Fork Meadows, Dry
40 Lake, Lodgepole Spring Trail Camp
12½ miles round trip; **2300′** elevation gain
Classification: **Moderate** (2 days), **Strenuous** (1
day)
Season: **June-October**
Topo map: *Moonridge* (7.5′)

FEATURES

Dry Lake sits in a great amphitheater, surrounded on
three sides by the lofty horseshoe crest of Grinnell, Lake,
San Gorgonio and Jepson peaks. The lake is shallow, and
in seasons of light precipitation, it dries up by midsummer
— hence the name. But in early summer, after abundant
rainfall, Dry Lake is full to the brim, and it beautifully
mirrors the high granite ridges that soar above it. The
forest cover on the surrounding slopes is almost exclusively lodgepole pine, with low clumps of chinquapin here
and there. Dominated by the steep, grey-granite face of
San Gorgonio, which is often snow-lined into midsummer,
this delectable mountain basin approaches true alpine
conditions and bears a striking resemblance to the High
Sierra.

An excellent, easy-graded trail climbs from South Fork
Meadows into Dry Lake basin, where two trail camps have
been placed by the Forest Service — one just above the
north shore of the lake, the other ¼ mile beyond at Lodgepole Spring. For those who desire a small taste of the
Sierra Nevada close to home, this is an ideal trip. Bring
warm clothing and a good sleeping bag if you are going
to stay overnight: nights can be nippy at 9000 feet.

DESCRIPTION

Follow driving directions of trip 38.

Follow the trail from Jenks Lake Road to South Fork
Meadows, 4 miles (see trip 38). Leave the main trail here,
which continues up to Dollar Lake and Dollar Lake Saddle
(see trip 39), and cross to the southeast side of the
meadows on any one of several beaten paths (a sign points
to Dry Lake). Pick up the Dry Lake trail just past South

Fork Meadows Trail Camp and follow it southeast into a draw. After about 100 yards, the trail turns left (northeast) and crosses the small stream coming down from Dry Lake basin. It then switchbacks up the mountainside through open stands of ponderosa and Jeffrey pine and white fir. After gaining 400', the switchbacks end and your trail contours along the slope until it rejoins the floor of the draw. A short distance up the draw it reaches Dry Lake—1¾ miles from South Fork Meadows. Here is a trail junction: right to Mine Shaft Saddle and San Gorgonio Mountain (see trip 42), left to the two trail camps. You go left. In ⅛ mile the trail reaches Dry Lake Trail Camp, located in a grassy area surrounded by lodgepoles just above the northeast shore of the lake. ¼ mile farther, just inside the draw southeast of Dry Lake, is Lodgepole Spring Trail Camp, with water trickling from the small spring.

Return the way you came. Options include going on up San Gorgonio Mountain (trip 42) and returning via Dollar Lake Saddle (trip 41), making a grand loop trip around the eastern part of the Wilderness, or taking the new trail across the ridge to Fish Creek (trip 44). Any way you do it, you will enjoy this alpine section of the highest wilderness in Southern California.

Dry Lake

TRIP: Jenks Lake Road to South Fork Meadows, Dollar
41 Lake Saddle, San Gorgonio Mountain
21½ miles round trip; **4700′** elevation gain
Classification: **Very Strenuous** (1 day), **Moderate** (2 days)
Season: **June-October**
Topo maps: *Moonridge, San Gorgonio Mtn.* (both 7.5′)

FEATURES

San Gorgonio Mountain crowns all of Southern California. No other peak south of the Sierra Nevada rises high enough to challenge its 11502′ elevation. Gleaming white in winter snows and somber grey during summer months, its massive granite bulk can be seen for a hundred miles in many directions.

The great hogback mountain is the culminating hump of the 10000′-plus, 7-mile long, sky-piercing ridge that dominates the San Gorgonio Wilderness. Gravelly, boulder-strewn slopes and broad, shallow draws slant downward from the summit crest, dropping far into shadowy canyons. Snow patches linger well into the summer months. The air is crisp with the chill of elevation. The sky is deep blue, free of the urban-generated murkiness that clogs lower elevations.

Although a familiar sight to millions living below, only the hiker or horseback rider can really know the charm of this alpine island in the sky. What look like barren, lifeless slopes from the distance are spotted with hardy, weather-resistant life forms. Wind-buffeted dwarf lodgepoles and limber pines hug the ground between boulders. Small clumps of high altitude chinquapin sprout in protected hollows. Diminutive alpine wildflowers bloom colorfully in midsummer – most common are pink-flowered locoweed, alpine buttercup and silver mat. Golden-mantle ground squirrels and grayish lodgepole chipmunks dart among the elfin trees. Red-tailed hawks and Clark's nutcrackers are occasionally seen flying above. Just east of the summit, on desert-facing slopes, dwell a handful of Nelson bighorn sheep.

The mountain received its name from Rancho San Gorgonio, the easternmost cattle ranch of Mission San Gabriel, established sometime before 1824 (located in today's San Gorgonio Pass). The rancho, in turn, was named for Saint Gorgonius, an obscure Christian martyr of the 3rd century, A.D., whose feast day is September 9th. But for many years, the mountain was known by other titles. The Cahuilla Indians called it "Kwiria-Kaich," meaning "bald" or "smooth". Lieutenant Robert S. Williamson's Pacific Railroad Survey party of 1853 were the first to describe the mountain and called the whole ridge "Mount San Bernardino". In 1878 the U.S. Army's Wheeler Survey saw in the great grey hogback a resemblance to a grizzly bear at rest and labelled it "Grizzly Peak" on their map. From the 1870s on, many San Bernardino Valley residents knew the mountain as "Greyback", a name that persists today. Not until E.T. Perkins, topographer for the United States Geological Survey, surveyed the mountain in 1899 and placed the name "San Gorgonio Mountain" on the government topographical sheet did the latter become commonly accepted as the correct title for the peak.

The earliest known ascent of San Gorgonio Mountain was made by W.O. Goodyear of the California Mining Bureau and Mark Thomas of San Bernardino on June 2, 1872. Their route was up the south slope of the mountain from Mill Creek Canyon. Goodyear toted a mercury barometer to the summit and calculated its elevation at 11600' — not a bad estimate considering his primitive instrument.

Since then, thousands have made the ascent in all kinds of weather conditions. Charles Francis Saunders, in his classic *Southern Sierras of California,* described a terrifying climb amid lightning, thunder and dashing rain in 1904, in which one was killed and another dazed by a lightning bolt. Because of the elevation and unstable winds, this type of weather occasionally occurs in the summertime. But most often the weather is clear and cool during the summer months, a welcome relief from the sweltering valley far below.

This is a trip every Southern California hiker should make at least once. The trail is in excellent condition, the high-altitude atmosphere is invigorating, the alpine life forms offer a striking change from the usual southern California pattern, and the view from the top encompasses a 360-degree panorama from the Mexican border to the southern Sierra Nevada, from the Pacific to the farthest reaches of the Mojave Desert.

You have a number of options. You can do it up and back in one strenuous day. You can make it an overnight backpack by staying at one of several inviting trail camps. Or, with a car shuttle, you can go up this way and descend by another route. All of these options are outlined below.

DESCRIPTION

Follow driving directions of trip 38.

Follow the trail from Jenks Lake Road to South Fork Meadows, 4 miles (see trip 38). The trail then climbs above the west edge of the meadow and begins switchbacking up the ridge. You start out in a forest of ponderosa pine and white fir, but as you rise above 8800′ lodgepoles begin to predominate. The trail then rounds the ridge and climbs along the west slope of the big draw leading to Dollar Lake Saddle, passing a grassy cienega and an area of waist-high manzanita. Just beyond, you pass the junction of the trail going down to Dollar Lake.

Continue up the trail to Dollar Lake Saddle (10,000′), 3 miles from South Fork Meadows. Two small trail camps are just west of the saddle: Red Rock Flat (no water) and, ½ mile farther west, just south of the main divide trail, High Meadow Springs (always water), both shaded by lodgepole pines. If you are doing the trip in two days, stay overnight at one of these trail camps. Trails lead northwest along San Bernardino Peak Divide (see trip 47), southwest down Falls Creek to Mill Creek Canyon (see trip 50), and southeast to San Gorgonio Mountain. You turn left and take the latter trail. The pathway leads through a silent, stony forest of lodgepoles around the west and south slopes of Charlton Peak. In ½ miles you reach the steep sidetrail up to Charlton's summit (Charlton Peak is named for Rushton

Charlton, supervisor of Angeles National Forest from 1907 to 1925, when the San Bernardinos were part of the Angeles). ½ mile beyond, the trail reaches the saddle between Charlton and Jepson peaks, where you can look down into Dry Lake basin. Here is Dry Lake View Trail Camp, a small overnight stop amid stunted lodgepoles and granite boulders, waterless. The trail now climbs the treeless west slope of Jepson Peak (named for Willis Linn Jepson, 1867–1946, University of California botanist who made a botanical survey of the San Bernardino Mountains in the early 1900s and wrote *Trees of California* and *A Manual of Flowering Plants*), contours high on the south side through dwarfed and windbent lodgepoles, and reaches a junction with the Vivian Creek Trail (see trip 52). Continue upward and eastward. About ¼ mile farther is a second junction, this one with the Sky High Trail leading down around the east slope of the mountain to Mine Shaft Saddle (see trip 42). The trail now crosses nearly bare slopes, passes the top of Big Draw, crosses a slight rise, and climbs to the boulder-stacked summit of San Gorgonio Mountain, 10¾ miles from the start. Adjacent is Summit Trail Camp—no trees, no water, exposed to the elements, but a favorite of hardy backpackers who relish the mountaintop sunrise and don't mind below-freezing temperatures (a Southern California counterpart of sleeping on Mt. Whitney's summit).

After taking in the all-encompassing view, return the way you came. Or you have several options. You can descend by the Sky High Trail to Mine Shaft Saddle and Dry Lake, and back to Jenks Lake Road, a 21½-mile round trip (see trip 42). With car shuttles, you can descend the Vivian Creek Trail or the Falls Creek Trail into Mill Creek Canyon (see trips 50, 52). Or—very strenuous—you can follow the ridge line trail westward over San Bernardino Peak and down to Angelus Oaks, a 23¾-mile round trip (see trip 47). Any way you decide to do the trip, you will thoroughly appreciate this sky-reaching part of Southern California.

TRIP: Jenks Lake Road to South Fork Meadows, Dry

42

Lake, Mine Shaft Saddle, San Gorgonio Mountain
22½ miles round drip; **4700′** elevation gain
Classification: **Strenuous** (1 day), **Moderate** (2 days)
Season: **June-October**
Topo maps: *Moonridge, San Gorgonio Mtn.* (7.5′)

FEATURES

The Sky High Trail, zigzagging up the northeast and east slopes of San Gorgonio Mountain from Mine Shaft Saddle, was constructed about six years ago. It offers a new way to climb the mountain and when combined with the standard trail route from Dollar Saddle, makes for an ideal loop trip. You can go up one way and down the other, covering a good part of the unspoiled alpine country in the eastern half of the San Gorgonio Wilderness. The main attraction of the Sky High Trail is the superb view down over the Coachella Valley; on a clear day you can see to the Salton Sea and beyond. Be in top shape for this one, particularly if you plan to hike it in one day. It is more enjoyable as an overnight backpack, camping at Dry Lake or at one of the timberline trail camps.

DESCRIPTION

Follow driving direction of trip 38.

Follow the trail from Jenks Lake Road to South Fork Meadows, 4 miles (see trip 38); then the trail to Dry Lake, 1¾ more miles (see trip 40). If you plan to make this a two-day trip, you may want to camp overnight at Dry Lake, the last available water. Where the trail from South Fork Meadows reaches Dry Lake's outlet is a junction. Go right (south). The trail follows the west shore of the little lake, enters a draw, and climbs up the ridge south of the lake, through a forest of almost exclusively lodgepole pine with clumps of chinquapin for ground cover. In 2 miles it reaches Mine Shaft Saddle, on the divide between Dry Lake basin and the desert-draining North Fork of the Whitewater River. Here is a primitive trail camp, no water. Just beyond is a trail junction: left goes down to North Fork

Meadows (see trip 43), and Fish Creek Meadows (trip 44); right is the Sky High Trail to San Gorgonio Mountain. Go right (southeast); a sign indicates *San Gorgonio 3½ miles.* The trail climbs eastward through granite boulder fields and a lodgepole forest, then makes 8 switchbacks up the northeast slope of the mountain. You pass the wreckage of a DC-3 that splattered against the mountainside in 1953. Finally, after gaining a thousand feet, the trail rounds the east ridge of San Gorgonio and climbs westward up the south slope. Good views are obtained down into the rugged Whitewater country and beyond to the desert. About 3¼ miles from Mine Shaft Saddle, the trail intersects the main pathway from Dollar Saddle. Turn right (east) and climb ¼ mile to the summit.

If you are doing the loop trip, descend via the Dollar Saddle-South Fork Meadows route (see trip 41). Or return the way you came. Other options include descending into Mill Creek Canyon via either the Vivian Creek (see trip 52) or the Falls Creek trail (see trip 50). Or, very long, follow the crest trail west to San Bernardino Peak and down to Angelus Oaks (see trip 47).

Atop Greyback, 1913   *San Bernardino County Museum*

TRIP:

43

Jenks Lake Road to South Fork Meadows, Dry Lake, Mine Shaft Saddle, North Fork Meadows

19½ miles round trip; **3100′** elevation gain, **1500′** loss

Classification: **Moderate** (2 days)

Season: **June-October**

Topo maps: *Moonridge, San Gorgonio Mtn.* (both 7.5′)

FEATURES

The eastern end of the San Gorgonio Wilderness drops steeply toward the desert. Draining the 10,000′ and 11,000′ peaks of this eastern high country are the three forks of the Whitewater River, tumbling streams that through the ages have carved deep, V-shaped gorges from the high mountains down into arid Coachella Valley, where the spent waters sink into the desert sands and the river becomes a broad, gravely wash. This lower part of the river is the Whitewater known to most people, drab and unimpressive. But the high Whitewater reveals a different character; it is a rugged, isolated wilderness, even today seldom trod by man. Here dwell Nelson bighorn sheep, the largest herds of these noble animals in the San Bernardino Mountains.

Very few trails enter the Whitewater country. One that samples a small bit of it is the overgrown pathway from Mine Shaft Saddle down into the headwaters of the North Fork to North Fork Meadows. Here, alongside the verdant meadow, with Jeffrey pines as a backdrop, the Forest Service has constructed Big Tree Trail Camp. This small campsite, easternmost in the San Gorgonio Wilderness, is well off the beaten track of most hikers. If you relish solitude and quiet beauty on your wilderness outings, this place should be one of your favorites.

Experienced mountaineers have descended the Whitewater all the way to the desert roadend. It is a difficult, trailless venture. Don't do it unless you have done ample cross-country mountaineering, and then never attempt it alone.

DESCRIPTION

Follow driving directions of trip 38.

Follow the trail from Jenks Lake Road to South Fork Meadows, 1¾ miles (see trip 38); then the trail to Dry Lake, 1¾ more miles (see trip 40). At the outlet of Dry Lake is a junction; go right (south) and follow the trail up to Mine Shaft Saddle, 2 miles (see trip 42). Here is another junction; right up San Gorgonio Mountain (trip 42), left down into the North Fork of the Whitewater River. Go left (east). The trail gradually descends through a lodgepole forest. In ¼ mile you pass a trail leading left (northeast) to Fish Creek (see trip 44); continue straight ahead. Down to your right in Mine Shaft Flats, the scene of an unsuccessful turn-of-the-century mining operation. Just beyond, the trail drops more steeply and leaves the lodgepole forest. You must now fight your way through buckthorn thickets down to the upper edge of North Fork Meadow, 2 miles from Mineshaft Saddle. Here the trail disappears completely and you must thrash through thick brush across the meadow to Big Tree Trail Camp, located under several large pines on the north edge of the meadow. Water runs year-round in the creek, but no wood fires are allowed.

It is easier to approach Big Tree Trail Camp via the unofficial Big Tree track that runs along the northeast side of the creek. This track leaves the official trail below Mineshaft Flat at the head of the ravine that lies on the northeast side of the smaller, upper meadow. It is very hard to find at this point. Work your way down the scree very carefully. You will pick out the track where the terrain levels out. It takes you straight to Big Tree and allows you to circumvent most of the buckthorn that is fast eradicating the regular trail.

The trail ends at Big Tree Trail Camp. Beyond, the Whitewater is wild, and strictly for experienced cross-country backpackers.

Return the way you came. Options include returning over San Gorgonio Mountain (see trips 41 and 42) or via the new Fish Creek Trail (see trip 44). The latter requires a car shuttle.

TRIP: Forest Road 1N05 to Upper Fish Creek, Fish

44 Creek Trail Camp, Fish Creek Saddle, Mine Shaft Saddle

10 miles round trip; **1900′** elevation gain

Classification: **Moderate**

Season: **June-October**

Topo maps: *Moonridge, San Gorgonio Mtn.* (both 7.5′)

FEATURES

This new trail trip enters the "back door" of the San Gorgonio Wilderness, climbing up Fish Creek and over Fish Creek Divide into the northeastern corner of the wild area. Because the trail is new and the driving access is difficult, few hikers use this route. But the forest of pine and fir is rich and green, the waters of Fish Creek are cold and sweet, and the high mountain air is thin and invigorating. For those who wish to linger awhile in upper Fish Creek, there is Fish Creek Trail Camp, with primitive facilities. With a car shuttle, many enjoyable options are available (see below).

DESCRIPTION

From Redlands drive east on State Highway 38 32 miles (5 miles past Barton Flats) to the entrance road to Heart Bar Campground (1N02). Turn right on 1N02, passing the campground entrance (on your right in .2 mile), to a junction in 1.2 miles. Go right, up 1N05, bearing right at all road forks, to the signed *Fish Creek Trail* parking area, 7.4 miles from the highway.

Walk westward on the well-defined trail (avoiding several other less defined paths that lead in other directions), gradually descending, to a new junction with the upper terminus of the Aspen Grove Trail, to your right (see Trip 36). Continue straight ahead as your trail curves southwest into upper Fish Creek. Down to your right, as you near the creek, is a small, inviting trail camp shaded by Jeffrey pine and white fir. The trail then passes through an area of verdant growth, crosses two small side creeks, and climbs along the left (southeast) slope above the main creek, through a rich forest of Jeffrey pine and white fir. After several switchbacks to gain elevation, the pathway contours over into the main draw and reaches Fish Creek Trail Camp, 1¾ miles. The camp consists of several cleared flats amid rocky terrain, shaded by white fir. Water flows year-round in the stream just west of camp.

Beyond the camp, the trail starts climbing the broad slopes of Grinnell Mountain. As it rises above 9000′, the view opens to the north and east, over the rugged east-end country of the San Bernardinos and out into the desert. Lodgepole pines begin to predominate. After four long switchbacks, you reach Fish Creek Saddle, on the high divide between Fish Creek and the South Fork of the Santa Ana, 4 miles from the start. A ½-mile side trip north along the crest gets you to Grinnell Mountain for far-ranging views over the eastern part of the wilderness. (Grinnell Mountain is named for Joseph Grinnell 1877–1924, University of California zoologist who made animal studies in the eastern San Bernardino Mountains during 1905–07.) From the saddle, the trail contours across the west slopes of Lake Peak, through a forest exclusively lodgepole, to Dry Lake Saddle, 1 mile. Here a side-trail leads right (north) down to Lodgepole Spring and Dry Lake (see trip 40). Continue straight ahead; in 50 yards you intersect the Mine Shaft Saddle-North Fork Meadows trail. Go right (west) ¼ mile to Mine Shaft Saddle.

Here a number of options present themselves. You can return the way you came. You can take the Sky High Trail to the summit of San Gorgonio (see trip 42). You can descend to Dry Lake and on out to Jenks Lake Road, requiring a car shuttle (see trip 40). You can go down the North Fork of the Whitewater to North Fork Trail Camp (see trip 43). With several days available for your outing, you can use this Fish Creek access to visit just about any part of the San Gorgonio Wilderness you desire.

TRIP: Forsee Creek Ridge Trail to Jackstraw Springs, Trail Fork Springs, San Bernardino Peak Divide, Dollar Lake Saddle, Southfork Meadows, Jenks Lake Road

45

17¼ miles round trip; **3700′** elevation gain
Classification: **Mod.** (2 days), **strenuous** (1 day)
Season: **June-October**
Topo map: *Big Bear Lake, Moonridge* (both 7.5′)

FEATURES

There are numerous opportunities for loop trips in the San Gorgonio Wilderness, laced as the region is with trails. This trip climbs the steep, heavily wooded north slope of San Bernardino Peak Divide via the Forsee Creek Trail, follows the divide trail east to Dollar Lake Saddle, and descends via South Fork Meadows to Jenks Lake Road. En route are several inviting trail camps for overnight stay, and three springs with icy-cold water. You pass through some lush forest country and are rewarded with far-ranging views from high on the 10,000-foot divide. This is one of the best circle trips in the Wilderness. A 5-mile car shuttle is necessary.

DESCRIPTION

From Redlands drive east 25 miles on State Route 38 to the Jenks Lake turn-off, just before Barton Flats. Turn right (southeast). After ⅓ mile turn right again onto a dirt road where a sign reads FORSEE CREEK TRAIL. Drive ½ mile to the large parking area at the trailhead.

The trail leads uphill through a forest of Jeffrey pine, incense cedar, black oak, and white fir. In ¼ mile you reach a trail junction; the fork to the right leads west to Johns Meadow Trail Camp, 2.7 miles. Continue straight ahead. In 1 mile you cross little Stetson Creek, trickling water until late summer. A mile farther up, the trail crosses a sloping bench, resplendent with grasses and ferns, spotted with Indian paintbrush and lupine. Beyond, the lodgepole pines begin to appear. Vistas open as the trail rounds the east side of the ridge. As you rise above 8600 feet, lodgepole becomes the predominant forest tree. Four miles up, a sign points right 100 yards to Jackstraw Springs Trail Camp, wood, water, little flats for sleeping. The trail now climbs the slope east of Forsee Creek and in 2 more miles reaches a junction with the lower branch of the San Bernardino Peak Divide Trail, traversing the mountain crest east and west. Just to the right (west) is Trail Fork Springs. Trail Fork Springs Camp (primitive facilities) is on the lodgepole-shaded bench to your left.

Turn left (east); in ¼ mile you reach a junction with the upper branch of the divide trail, which traverses close under Anderson Peak (named for Lou Anderson, district ranger at Barton Flats during the 1920's). Continue east through a parklike lodgepole forest, around the rocky north slope of Shields Peak (named for Leila Shields, manager of Camp Radford in the 1920's), and down to Shields Flat. There is a waterless campsite here, 80 yards south of the trail. Your trail climbs over a slight rise and drops to a junction with the side trail to High Meadow Spring. The spring and its cozy trail camp are ¼ mile down the slope to your right (south). Water is always available here.

The trail turns southeast and descends 400 feet to Dollar Lake Saddle, ¾ mile. Here is a 4-way trail junction and, just to the west, Red Rock Flat Trail Camp (no water). Trails lead southeast to San Gorgonio Mountain (see trip 41), southwest down Falls Creek to Mill Creek (see trip 50), and northeast to South Fork Meadows and Jenks Lake Road. Take the latter (see trips 38 and 41 for description).

There are numerous ways to vary this loop trip. From Trail Fork Springs, you can turn west along the divide, cross San Bernardino Peak, and descend to Angelus Oaks (see trip 47). From Dollar Lake Saddle, you can almost double the length of the loop by continuing on to San Gorgonio Mountain (trip 41), then descending the Sky High Trail to Mine Shaft Saddle, and on down past Dry Lake and South Fork Meadows to Jenks Lake Road (see trip 42). With a long car shuttle, you can descend the Falls Creek trail into Mill Creek Canyon (see trip 50).

TRIP:
46
Camp Angelus to Manzanita Springs, Limber Pine Springs, Initial Base Line Monument, San Bernardino Peak

16 miles round trip; **4600′** elevation gain
Classification: **Strenuous** (1 day), **mod.** (2 days)
Season: **June-October**
Topo map: *Big Bear Lake* (7.5′)

FEATURES

The men were exhausted. All day they had struggled up the rugged, trailless, brush-infested north slope of San Bernardino Peak, all the way from the canyon of the Santa Ana River. The important work they had been assigned to do would have to wait until the next day.

The men were Colonel Henry Washington of the United States Army, under contract with the U.S. Surveyor General's Office; Mr. Gray, deputy surveyor; and 11 workmen. The date was November 7, 1852. Colonel Washington had been assigned the difficult task of establishing an initial point and erecting a monument from which an east-west base line and a north-south meridian could be surveyed. Then land surveys for all of Southern California would be undertaken, based on Washington's pioneering calculations.

After thoroughly checking the rugged terrain around the peak, Colonel Washington selected a point overlooking the San Bernardidno Valley about ½ mile west of the summit. Here he and his men erected an elaborate wooden monument 23′ 9″ in height. 11 bearings were taken to define the location of the monument, and here the surveyors ran into trouble. They found it impossible to obtain true fixes on distant triangulation marks because of shimmering heat waves from the valley. To overcome this problem, huge fires were lit atop San Bernardino Peak and at the other triangulation points, and the surveys were made at night.

Upon the completion of this initial triangulation, Washington and his party commenced surveying Southern California. All land surveys in this part of the state have subsequently been based on Colonel Washington's base line.

Today, 120 years later, the wooden base and supporting rock cairn of Colonel Washington's monument remain intact, a few yards above the San Bernardino Peak Trail.

This trail trip visits this historic spot en route from Angelus Oaks to the summit of San Bernardino Peak. You pass through beautiful subalpine country in this western end of the San Gorgonio Wilderness. If the day is clear, views are breath-taking, extending over the foothills and across the vast San Bernardino Valley to the distant San Gabriel Mountains. Two delightful trail camps—Columbine Springs and Limber Pine Springs—offer opportunities for overnight stays. Both have water nearby. It's a long uphill climb, but one you shouldn't miss. Best do it on a cool early-summer or late-fall weekend; long stretches of the trail traverse open manzanita slopes, and are unpleasant walking on a hot day.

DESCRIPTION

From Redlands drive 19 miles east on State Route 38 to Angelus Oaks. Where a sign says *San Bernardino Peak Trail* turn right (south). Follow the dirt road ¼ mile to the parking area.

A sign at the east end of the parking area marks the beginning of the trail: *San Bernardino Peak* — 8. The trail starts up through a forest of Jeffrey and sugar pine, white fir and several species of oak. Soon you are switchbacking up a steep slope. In 2 miles you reach the boundary of the San Gorgonio Wilderness, marked by a wooden sign. A short distance beyond, the switchbacks taper off and you climb more gently through open stands of Jeffrey pine. As you near the top of a long 8000' ridge, the Jeffreys become less numerous and the trail slices through oceans of manzanita. 4 miles from the start is Manzanita Springs just off the trail to the right (south). A side trail leads south down to Manzanita Springs, trickling water in early season but often dry by late summer, and continues ¼ mile to Columbine Springs Trail Camp, water until midsummer, sometimes later. The main trail climbs up a slope covered with manzanita, snow brush and chinquapin, and in 2 miles reaches Limber Pine Springs Trail Camp. This camp site, located on a bench shaded by lodgepole pines, is the largest trail camp in the western half of the Wilderness and is a favorite of Boy Scout groups. Water is available from Limber Pine Springs, ¼ mile up the trail. From the springs, the trail turns south and climbs steadily to the top of the high ridge leading west from San Bernardino Peak. In 1½ miles you reach the west ridge of San Bernardino Peak and climb eastward. Just 100 yards beyond, 50 feet to the right and above the trail is Colonel Washington's initial base-line monument. The trail climbs eastward along the ridge and in ½ mile passes just north of the summit of San Bernardino Peak. A side trail ascends 150 yards to the 10624' high point.

After fully enjoying the tremendous view and signing the summit register, return the way you came. An option is to continue eastward along the San Bernardino Peak Divide Trail (see trip 47), then descending to Jenks Lake Road or Mill Creek Canyon.

Colonel Washington's Monument

TRIP: Angelus Oaks to Limber Pine Springs, San
Bernardino Peak, San Bernardino Peak Divide

47 Trail to Dollar Lake Saddle, San Gorgonio Mountain, down to Mine Shaft Saddle, Dry Lake, South Fork Meadows, Jenks Lake Road

28¼ miles round trip; **6200'** elevation gain
Classification: **Mod.** (3 days), **strenuous** (2 days)
Season: **June-October**
Topo maps: *Big Bear Lake, Moonridge, San Gorgonio Mtn.* (all 7.5')

FEATURES

This long trail trip traverses the entire San Bernardino Peak-San Gorgonio Mountain ridge from west to east, covering a generous part of the San Gorgonio Wilderness. It is for experienced backpackers who relish long stretches of high-altitude walking. This is the rooftop of Southern California, the largest piece of subalpine wilderness south of the Sierra Nevada, delightful summer hiking country, cool and refreshing. But the climb to this sky island is tough, involving over a mile of elevation gain. Be in good condition before you try this one.

DESCRIPTION

From Redlands drive 19 miles east on State Route 38 to Angelus Oaks. Turn right (south) where a sign says *San Bernardino Peak Trail.* Follow the dirt road ¼ mile to the parking area. The trip ends at Jenks Lake Road, so shuttle another car there (see trip 38).

Follow the trail to San Bernardino Peak, 8 miles (see trip 46). (If you are doing the trip in the recommended 3 days, a first-night stop at Limber Pine Springs Trail Camp is suggested.) From San Bernardino Peak, the San Bernardino Peak Divide Trail leads east along or just north of the ridgetop, through an open forest of lodgepole pine. You drop 200' to a saddle, then climb up the slopes of San Bernardino East Peak, passing just north of the summit. A side trail leads 100 feet to the top. About ¼ mile beyond you pass the unmarked junction of the Momyer Creek

Trail coming up from Mill Creek Canyon (see trip 48). In another ½ mile is a trail fork: left to Trail Fork Springs and a junction with the Forsee Creek Trail (see trip 45), right for a traverse close under the slopes of Anderson Peak. The two forks rejoin after a mile. Almost pure stands of lodge-pole pine cover the ridge from San Bernardino Peak eastward to the upper slopes of San Gorgonio. These hardy veterans of high elevations lack the sylvan greenery and underbrush of lower levels, forming a strange, open, stone-floored forest. Among them a profound silence reigns, occasionally broken by the rat-tat-tat of white-headed woodpeckers and the shrill chatter of chickadees, while toward evening the vesper-like antiphony of hermit thrushes is often heard.

The trail rounds the rocky slope of Shields Peak, drops to Shields Flat, crosses a rise and reaches the High Meadow Springs Trail junction. The springs and trail camp are ¼ mile to your right (south). The water here is the last before the climb of San Gorgonio, so fill canteens. (If you're doing the 3-day trip, a 2nd night stay here is suggested.) The trail then descends to the 4-way junction at Dollar Lake Saddle, ¾ mile. Continue southeastward along the divide trail, rounding the south slopes of Charlton Peak to Dry Lake View Trail Camp, no water, then up around the bare slopes of Jepson Peak and on to the rocky summit of San Gorgonio, 4 miles (see trip 41 for detailed description).

You have now traversed the great San Bernardino Peak-San Gorgonio Mountain ridge. After taking in the summit view that encompasses half of Southern California, retrace your steps ¼ mile to the Sky High Trail junction. Turn left (southeast) and follow the Sky High Trail down to Mine Shaft Saddle, then on down past Dry Lake and South Fork Meadows to trip's end at Jenks Lake Road. This 28¼ mile sky-high ramble is the longest in the wilderness, but the spectacular subalpine country you traverse makes the trip well worth the effort.

TRIP: Mill Creek Canyon to San Bernardino Peak Divide

48 14 **miles** round trip; 5400′ elevation gain

Classification: **Strenuous**

Season: **June-October**

Topo maps: *Forest Falls, Big Bear Lake* (both 7.5′)

FEATURES

From the fault-line gorge of Mill Creek Canyon, San Bernardino Peak Divide rises precipitously over a mile above. This is one of the highest and steepest mountain walls in the San Bernardinos. Climbing directly up this towering slope in seemingly endless switchbacks is the Momyer Creek Trail, gaining 5000′ in 7 miles. The trip presents a living demonstration of how the forest changes with altitude: first through brush and oak, then through belts of Jeffrey and ponderosa pine and white fir, then across manzanita slopes, and finally into the realm of lodgepole pine. There is no dependable water en route, unless you make the 2-mile round trip to Alger Creek. This is a trip for the well-conditioned hiker. Do it on a cool day, and get an early start, for much of the trail is open to the sun. You will probably have the trail to yourself; few hikers use this tough route to the high country.

DESCRIPTION

From Redlands drive 14 miles east on State Route 38 to its junction with Forest Home Road. Turn right and continue east up Mill Creek Canyon to the large parking area for the Momyer Creek and Falls Creek trails, on your left 100 yards before the fire station, 3 miles.

Follow the trail down into the broad shoulder wash of Mill Creek. Go left at a hard-to-spot junction and traverse directly across the boulder maze to the north bank. Here the newly built trail turns left (west) and climbs the open slope to a junction with the old beginning of the Momyer Creek Trail coming up from Torrey Pines Road. Turn right and follow the footpath as it switchbacks steeply up the divide between Momyer Creek and Alger Creek, through chaparral and scrub oak. Soon you are climbing through a patchy forest of oak and Jeffrey pine. In 2½ miles you reach a junction: a trail right goes 1 mile to Alger Creek Trail Camp (see trip 49); you go left. Long switchbacks continue and the forest becomes richer — mostly Jeffrey and ponderosa pine and white fir. In 4½ miles the trail steepens and you cross slopes blanketed with manzanita, and some patches of snow brush and chinquapin. You cross over the sharp south ridge of San Bernardino East Peak, pass more manzanita, and finally enter an open lodgepole forest. One final switchback gets you to the top of the divide ½ mile east of San Bernardino East Peak, where you meet the San Bernardino Peak Divide Trail (see trip 47), 7 miles from the start.

You now have a number of options. You can return the same way. You can follow the divide trail west over San Bernardino Peak and down to Angelus Oaks (see trip 46). You can take the divide trail east to Dollar Lake Saddle (see trip 47), then down the Falls Creek Trail (see trip 50) to Mill Creek Canyon, reaching the latter ½ mile east of the Momyer Creek Trail roadhead, making a 19-mile loop trip without a car shuttle. These are the most practical options; others will reveal themselves if you study the map.

Old Greyback from Lost Creek Trail

TRIP: Mill Creek Canyon to Alger Creek Trail Camp
49 6½ miles round trip; 1400′ elevation gain
Classification: **Moderate**
Season: **June-October**
Topo map: *Forest Falls* (7.5′)

FEATURES

Alger Creek rises high on San Bernardino Peak Divide
and flows steeply down the south slope into Mill Creek
Canyon. Deeply recessed into the mountainside, shaded
by rich stands of pine, fir, cedar and alder, the little creek
seldom suffers the full glare of sunlight. It is a delightful
place to relax and keep cool and enjoy nature's sylvan
charms on a hot summer day. The Forest Service has built a
beautiful trail camp on a bench shaded by tall incense
cedars, just above the churning waters of Alder Creek.

This formerly was a loop trip, until a property owner's
complaint cowed the Forest Service into closing the lower
portion of the Falls Creek Trail — in spite of the fact that
the trail, built by John W. Dobbs in 1898, has been a public thoroughfare for 80 years. Now you must go and return
via the Momyer Creek Trail.

DESCRIPTION

Follow the driving directions of Trip 48.

Follow the trail down into the broad boulder wash of
Mill Creek. The path across the creek is washed away
almost every spring, so there's no use trying to follow it.
Instead, traverse directly across the boulder maze to the
north bank, where you will pick up a recently constructed
trail that climbs north onto a low bench. Here your trail
turns left (west) and climbs the chaparral-blanketed slope
to a junction with the old beginning of the Momyer Creek
Trail coming up from Torrey Pines Road. Turn right and
follow the well-defined footpath as it switchbacks steeply
up the divide between Momyer Creek and Alger Creek,
through chaparral and scrub oak. Soon you are climbing
through a patchy forest of oak and Jeffrey pine.

In 3 miles you reach the marked (as of July 1987) junction with the Alger Creek Trail, branching right (northeast). Turn right and follow this lateral trail, following the line of John Dobbs' old flume, before dropping to Alder Creek Trail Camp, 1 mile. The cedar-shaded trail camp is to your right, just above the tumultuous creek.

Your trail continues 100 yards to the creek, fords it, and continues on to Falls Creek (see Trip 50). But you enjoy the delightful wilderness setting of Alder Creek, then return the way you came.

Bighorn sheep on ridge east of San Gorgonio Summit. 30-40 of these timid animals live in the Wilderness Area.

Bob Tosh

TRIP: Mill Creek Canyon to Dobbs Cabin Trail Camp,
Saxton Trail Camp, Dollar Lake Saddle

50

20 miles round trip; **4500′** elevation gain
Classification: **Mod.** (2 days), **strenuous** (1 day)
Season: **June-October**
Topo maps: *Forest Falls, San Gorgonio Mtn.*
(both 7.5′)

FEATURES

The Falls Creek Trail, climbing from Mill Creek Canyon to Dollar Lake Saddle atop the main divide, is one of
the historic pathways in the San Gorgonio Wilderness.
The lower part of it was constructed by John W. Dobbs in
1898, in order to tap the water of Falls Creek and build a
flume for a hydroelectric plant in lower Mill Creek. Unfortunately the Forest Service has closed the lower portion
of the trail because of an objection by a property owner
in Mill Creek Canyon. Now the only legitimate route into
Falls Creek from below is via the Momyer Creek Trail
and the Alger Creek Lateral Trail, a roundabout way
adding six miles to the round trip. Nevertheless, this trip
is an inviting one, reaching into the geographical center
of the Wilderness and giving access to three beautiful
trail camps — Alger Creek, Dobbs Cabin and Saxton. You
can stay the night at one of these trail camps and return the
same way, or you can use the route as a springboard for any
of several Wilderness loop trips, the best of which are
mentioned on the next page.

DESCRIPTION

Follow the driving directions of trip 48.

Follow trip 49 to Alger Creek Trail Camp. Cross the
creek and continue east on the Alger Creek Lateral Trail
as it climbs, then contours around the steep mountainside
to a junction with the Falls Creek Trail, 1 mile. Turn left
(northeast) onto the latter. In 100 yards you pass the San
Gorgonio Wilderness boundary sign, then climb east

through a lush forest of Jeffrey pine and white fir to the ridge just west of Falls Creek. Here is another trail junction. To visit Dobbs Cabin Trail Camp, go right and steeply down to Falls Creek, ¼ mile. Just across the creek is the trail camp, set on little flats and shaded by tall cedars, firs and pines. Dobbs' old cabin site is at the lower edge of the camp; only log foundations remain. To continue up the main trail, go left at the junction. The trail climbs through open forest along the west slope of Falls Creek, fords the west fork, and reaches Saxton Trail Camp, 2 more miles. Water is available from the west fork, 1/5 mile down the trail. Your trail now climbs northeastward, passes the sloping bog of Plummer Meadow (camping no longer permitted), fords the east fork of Falls Creek, and climbs steeply up through a lodgepole forest to Dollar Lake Saddle, 7 miles from the start. Two small trail camps are just west of the saddle: Red Rock Flat (no water) and, ½ mile farther west, just south of the main divide trail, High Meadow Springs (always water).

You now have a number of options. You can return the way you came. You can turn right (southeast) and ascend San Gorgonio Mountain (see trip 41), then descend via the Vivian Creek Trail (see trip 52). You can turn left (northwest) and follow the San Bernardino Peak Divide Trail (see trip 47), then descend either the Momyer Creek Trail back to Mill Creek Canyon (see trip 48) or continue on to Angelus Oaks (trips 46, 47). Or you can turn northeast and descend to South Fork Meadows and Jenks Lake Road (see trips 38, 41).

TRIP: Mill Creek Canyon to Big Falls

51 1 mile round trip; **200′** elevation gain
Classification: **Easy**
Season: **April-October**
Topo map: *Forest Falls* (7.5′)

FEATURES

Falls Creek churns and somersaults from high on the shoulders of San Bernardino Peak Divide into a narrow hanging valley, then plunges headlong into the canyon of Mill Creek. The place where it makes this final drop is known as Big Falls. Author-naturalist Charles Francis Saunders described it best: "Looking upward, you see the little creek, a couple of hundred feet above, leap out of a patch of blue sky and drop by a succession of precipitous pitches down a narrow, shadowy gorge, to be shattered at the bottom into a series of musical cascades." Waterfalls are infrequent in the San Bernardinos; it seems a slight upon the beauty of this one that it should have been given no more fanciful name than Big Falls.

These spectacular falls are but a short walk from the Mill Creek road. Visit them in the springtime, when the melting mountain snowpack is filling Falls Creek, and canyonsides are aroar with the thunder of plunging waters.

DESCRIPTION

From Redlands drive 14 miles east on State Route 38 to its junction with Valley of Falls Drive. Continue on the latter east up Mill Creek Canyon to the Big Falls parking area on your left, 4⅓ miles.

Follow the trail down across the broad boulder wash of Mill Creek, then up to the left and into the lower end of Falls Creek. The trail climbs up the east slope to a viewpoint some 200 yards below the falls. **Note:** As of late 1987 the Big Falls Trail is open but the signs have been removed. Hikers have been injured trying to climb the falls, so do not venture beyond trail's end.

TRIP: Mill Creek Canyon to Vivian Creek Trail Camp,
Halfway Camp, High Creek Trail Camp, San
Gorgonio Mountain **14 miles** round trip; **5300'**
elevation gain

52

Classification: **Strenuous** (1 day), mod. (2 days)

Season: **June-October**

Topo maps: *Forest Falls, San Gorgonio Mtn.*
(both 7.5')

FEATURES

The Vivian Creek Trail is the shortest way to climb San
Gorgonio Mountain, but also one of the steepest. You start
from near the head of Mill Creek Canyon, climb into the
verdant hanging valley of Vivian Creek, cross a high ridge
into High Creek, and finally ascend gravelly slopes to the
barren summit. En route you pass three beautiful trail
camps — Vivian Creek, Halfway Camp, and High Creek.
Any one of the three makes a pleasant overnight stop if you
are doing the mountain in two days.

The Vivian Creek Trail was the first one up the mountain, built shortly after the creation of the San Bernardino
Forest Reserve in 1893. For years it was known as "The
Government Trail" and was the only one to San Gorgonio's
summit. Today it is just one of many but, in the opinion of
many hikers, it remains one of the best.

DESCRIPTION

From Redlands drive 14 miles east on State Route 38 to
its junction with Valley of Falls Drive. Turn onto the latter
and continue east up Mill Creek Canyon to a new parking
area on your left, just before reaching closed Big Falls
Campground, 4½ miles. Walk on up the dirt road, through
the closed campground, to the old trail head parking area,
about ¾ mile.

Follow the trail down across the boulder wash of Mill
Creek, then up the mountainside. The first mile is a sharp
pull through oak woodlands — unpleasant going if the day
is hot — to the secluded hanging recess of Vivian Creek.
Here, nestled in a green forest of cedar, fir and pine, is
Vivian Creek Trail Camp, 1¼ miles from the start. The
welcome campsites are spread out for several hundred

yards along the bubbling creek. Beyond, the trail follows the creek, switching from bank to bank, for another 1¼ miles through miniature meadows spotted with wild-flowers and shaded by tall ponderosa pines and incense cedars, to Halfway Camp, 2½ miles out. This new trail camp has year-round water and many little flats for sleeping. Beyond, your trail climbs across a ridge to a high-perched, grassy cienega threaded by a small stream of cold, tumbling water. Here is a High Creek Trail Camp, 4 miles out, a favorite with knapsackers, but the altitude is 9000' and nights are apt to be cold. The pines, cedars and firs have been left below, and the slopes are covered with almost pure stands of weather-resistant lodgepole pines. The view across the head of Mill Creek Canyon to the saw-toothed wall of Yucaipa Ridge is reminiscent of the Sierra Nevada. Above High Creek, the trail winds up through silent lodgepoles to timberline at about 11000'. Ahead looms the massive crown of San Gorgonio, stark against the deep blue sky. Just below the summit you meet the main trail from Dollar Lake Saddle; turn right (east) and cross gravelly slopes, passing a few wind-flattened limber pines and diminutive alpine flowers, to the 11502-foot summit, 7 miles from the start.

Return the way you came. A popular option is to take the trail west to Dollar Lake Saddle, then descend the Falls Creek Trail back to Mill Creek Canyon (see trip 50).

Important Note:

All of the fire roads and trails that ascend the Mill Creek-Oak Glen Divide cross small segments of private property. Recently, some property owners have been voicing objections to hikers crossing their lands. This affects trips 53, 57, 58, 59, and 60. Before attempting any of these trips, check with the Mill Creek Ranger Station (714) 794-1123.

TRIP: Oak Glen to Oak Glen Divide Trail, Wilshire Peak

53

19 miles round trip; 4200' elevation gain
Classification: **Strenuous**
Season: **June-October**
Topo map: *Forest Falls* (7.5')

FEATURES

The Yucaipa Ridge — also known as Oak Glen Divide — forms the south wall of Mill Creek Canyon and the north wall of the Oak Glen apple country. It rises in gentle hills just east of Mill Creek Ranger Station, becomes progressively higher and more welted as it leads eastward, and climaxes in a steep rampart of jagged pinnacles before joining the San Gorgonio massif at the head of Mill Creek. This is the most rugged mountain ridge in the San Bernardinos, and although it lies close above the well-attended resorts in Mill Creek Canyon, few are the hikers who walk along its crest.

Traversing the middle portion of the ridge from the Yucaipa Ridge fire road to Wilshire Peak is the Oak Glen Divide Trail. This trip takes the fire road up to the ridge then follows the length of this trail as it snakes over crests and across saddles, through rich stands of pine, fir, cedar and oak, with panoramic vistas north into the San Gorgonio Wilderness and south over the apple country. The round trip is very long, and there are no springs or trail camps en route to lessen the severity. But since you return the same way, you can shorten the hike to suit your taste.

DESCRIPTION

The traditional approach to the Oak Glen Divide Trail is from the north, via the fire road from Mill Creek. But this route goes through private property, and it is virtually impossible to get permission to pass from the new owner. So the only legal approach is from Oak Glen Road, to the south. This approach is closed in summer by the Forest Service due to high fire hazard. The hiking distance is the same, and no permission to pass is necessary.

For the Oak Glen Road approach, drive north from Yucaipa on Bryant Street 1 mile, then east on Oak Glen Road 4⅔ miles. Just past McFarland's Apple Ranch, on your left, is a sign denoting *Yucaipa Ridge Road*. Park outside the locked gate and walk north, up the winding fire road, to its junction with the Oak Glen Divide Trail at the top of the ridge, 4 miles.

Leave the Yucaipa Ridge fire road and climb eastward, up the signed *Oak Glen Divide Trail*. The trail follows up the ridge, switchbacks through thick chaparral up the west slope of Birch Mountain, and traverses around to the north side of the mountain into a forest of Jeffrey pine, white fir and incense cedar. You then drop to a saddle and climb the next bump eastward, known as Cedar Mountain. Just before the summit, you pass a small clearing and reach a hard-to-spot junction with the Ford Canyon Trail, which drops down the south slope to Oak Glen (see trip 58). The trail then descends to another saddle, climbs and passes just south of an unnamed bump, and switchbacks to the summit of Wilshire Peak (8707'; named for Joe Wilshire, pioneer apple grower in Oak Glen Valley), 9½ long miles from the start.

TRIP: Highway 38 to Santa Ana River, Big Meadows,

54 Forest Road 1N02
9 miles round trip; **800′** elev. gain
Classification: **Easy**
Season: **April-October**
Topo map: *Moonridge* (7.5′)

FEATURES

For most of its length from the mountains to the sea, the Santa Ana River is not particularly appealing. Fortunately for hikers and nature lovers, the headwaters of the Santa Ana, close under the forested and gravelly ridges of the San Gorgonio high country, are a delight to behold. The

sparkling waters of the new-born river flow through verdant meadows and luxuriant streamside growth, amid a
mixed forest of Jeffrey and ponderosa pine, white fir and
black oak.

DESCRIPTION

From Redlands drive 30 miles east on State Route 38 to
a trailhead parking area on your left, just 100 feet before
the South Fork Campground turnoff to the right.

Your signed trail drops immediately to the river, passes
under the highway bridge, and reaches a second trailhead
just below the entrance to South Fork Campground. You
switchback up the slope and turn east. In ½ mile you reach
a junction with the Lost Creek Trail, which branches right
and climbs around the west slope of Grinnell Mountain to
South Fork Meadows, 5.5 miles. You go left and continue
eastward, through the forest, with the Santa Ana River
down to your left. Continuing east, you enjoy views of
9952-foot Sugarloaf Peak on the northern skyline, pass
several sidepaths leading down to the river, and look down
upon the vast expanse of Big Meadows. You pass an un-
signed side trail leading down to Big Meadows and on to
Heart Bar Campground, but your trail continues east to its
end at Forest Road 1N02.

Return the way you came, or arrange for someone to
pick you up at Heart Bar Campground or Forest Road
1N02.

TRIP: Mill Creek Canyon to Mill Creek Jumpoff

55   **9 miles** round trip; **3200'** elevation gain
Classification: **Strenuous**
Season: **May–October**
Topo Maps: *Forest Falls, San Gorgonio Mtn.* (both 7.5´)

FEATURES

9330´ Galena Peak rises in precipitous fashion above the head of Mill Creek Canyon. It is the most rugged-appearing peak in the San Bernardinos, standing in marked contrast to the higher but rounded summits of the nearby San Gorgonio Wilderness. No trails approach its rugged upper ramparts, and you must scramble high over loose boulders and steep rock slopes to stand on its crown.

Part of the Mill Creek headwall has slid away recently, making the trip more tedious than it was a few years ago. You must make a trailless, loose uphill scramble from the head of Mill Creek to the saddle that divides the headwaters of Mill Creek from those of the Whitewater River — known by the curious name of Mill Creek Jumpoff. You need cross-country experience and must wear lug-soled boots.

DESCRIPTION

Follow the driving directions of trip 52.

Hike up the poor dirt road that heads east up-canyon. When it ends, continue up the streambed to the headwall at the end of Mill Creek. Climb a small ridge just left of center, then bear right across loose rock slopes to Mill Creek Jumpoff, 4 miles. Turn right (south) and climb up the steep ridge, following a faint climbers' trail part way. Where the trail gets too close to the crumbling headwall, veer left and work your way through manzanita. Approaching the ridgetop, your route veers southwest and divides. The left path climbs to the eastern summit — Galena Peak (9324´). The right path climbs to the western summit, slightly higher but unnamed.

Return the same way. Do *not* try to descend directly into Mill Creek Canyon; it is steep, loose, and dangerous.

TRIP: Santa Ana River to Cram Peak, Morton Peak Lookout, State Highway 38

56

9 miles one way; 2800′ elevation gain

Classification: **Moderate**

Season: **Nov.-April** (fire closure 7/1 to winter rain)

Topo map: *Yucaipa* (7½′)

FEATURES

In winter, when the air is crisp and clear and the nearby high country is sparkling white, take this ridgetop walk to Morton Peak Lookout for a rewarding experience. From the 4624′ summit you get a grandstand vista of the snowy south slope of the San Bernardinos, with 2-mile-high San Bernardino Peak looming massively a few miles to the east. Below, you can trace the course of the great San Andreas Fault straight as a beeline, which forms the southwest and south boundary of the San Bernardinos.

This is a chaparral walk all the way, partly on fire road, but mostly on the ridgetop trail. A car shuttle is required. If you drive the steep 3 miles up the Morton Peak Lookout fire road — sometimes open to the public in winter — the hiking distance is cut to 6 miles. Never, never take this trip on a hot day.

DESCRIPTION

From Redlands drive 5 miles east on State Route 38 to Greenspot (2 miles past Mentone). Turn left (north) on Carnet Street, which later becomes Greenspot Road. Drive 2½ miles to the Front Line fire road, on your right (east), so indicated by a sign. Park here outside the locked gate. You will come out on the Morton Peak Lookout fire road, 1¼ miles east of Mill Creek Ranger Station on Highway 38, so arranged to be picked up there.

Walk up the fire road, which turns north, paralleling the Santa Ana River, then east again, to a junction, ½ mile. Take the right fork and continue ¼ mile to the beginning of the Morton Ridge Trail on the left (north), marked by a sign (*2W15*). Follow the trail as it climbs north to the top of the bare ridge, then east along the ridgetop. A recent fire burned away much of the chaparral along this ridge, and it is just beginning to grow back. In 2½ miles of steady climbing you round the south side of Cram Peak, just below the 4162′ summit. The trail then drops 200′ and continues east along the long ridgetop, rounding the north side of an unnamed bump to a spur road, 5 miles from the start. Follow the fire road 1 mile to the summit of Morton Peak. The fire lookout is permanently closed. After taking in the all-encompassing panorama, descend the Morton Peak Lookout Road 3 miles to Highway 38.

Big Falls in Mill Creek Canyon

TRIP: Yucaipa Gun Club to Wilson Creek, Yucaipa Ridge

57 5½ **miles** round trip; **1200′** elevation gain
Classification: **Moderate**
Season: **Nov.-June** (fire closure 7/1 to winter rain)
Topo map: *Forest Falls* (7.5′)

FEATURES

This little known, seldom used trail climbs from Oak Glen Creek up the narrow, forested recess of Wilson Creek to the Yucaipa Ridge fire road. The middle part is a delightful walk along a trickling stream, shaded by live oak and bigcone spruces. Farther up, the whitish cliffs of Allen Peak form a spectacular backdrop. Do this trip in spring, when the creek runs strong and the forest and chaparral are damp and blooming.

DESCRIPTION

From Yucaipa, drive 2 miles north on Bryant Street, then east on Carter Street 3 miles, through land belonging to the Yucaipa Gun Club (private property; permission to pass revokable at any time), to a junction just before an abandoned white building. Go left (northeast) and follow the dirt road ½ mile farther to a sign on your left, *Wilson Creek Trail*. Park here.

Follow the trail northwest up and around the slope into the narrow canyon of Wilson Creek. The trail is overgrown and eroded in spots, but readily passable. The trail follows the creek for a mile, shaded by live oak, willow, bigcone spruce and incense cedar. Then it turns right and climbs chaparral slopes to a junction with the Yucaipa Ridge fire road, 2¾ miles from the start.

Return the way you came. An option, adding 2½ miles to the round trip, is to turn west and follow the fire road 1 mile to the fire break on the north slope of Allen Peak, then climb the fire break south to the 5800′ summit. (Allen Peak dominates the western end of Yucaipa Ridge; it was named for an early-day ranger stationed in Mill Creek.) For another option, see trip 53.

TRIP: State Highway 38 to Glen Martin Creek, Moun-
58
tain Home Flats
5 miles round trip; **1100′** elevation gain
Classification: **Moderate**
Season: **May-October**
Topo map: *Big Bear Lake* (7.5′)

FEATURES

This hike, just outside the western boundary of the San
Gorgonio Wilderness, is relatively short, steep in places,
and a real wilderness experience. You follow a long-estab-
lished cross-country route, or "track," recently upgraded
to a trail, up trickling Glen Martin Creek, then hike over
the ridge to the turbulent East Fork Mountain Home Creek
and up to Mountain Home Flats, a beautiful forested bench
unknown to most hikers. The trail is steep and traverses
unstable terrain in places, so wear lug-soled boots. This
trip is not recommended for beginning hikers.

No Wilderness Permit is required, but you must obtain a
"Remote Area Camping Permit," available at the Mill
Creek Ranger Station, if you plan an overnight stay. A fire
is permitted only in the single fire ring.

DESCRIPTION

From Redlands, drive 17.5 miles east on Highway 38
(3.4 miles beyond the Forest Falls turnoff) to a very small
parking area next to Glen Martin Creek. If space is un-
available, drive another ¼ mile up the highway to a small
turnout on the right (east) side of the road.

Follow the trail as it contours and climbs above the south
bank of Glen Martin Creek, then ascends a branch of the
now-dry creek before switchbacking steeply up to the
ridgetop to the south. The trail then traverses a steep and
unstable slope to East Fork Mountain Home Creek. Cross
the creek and follow the trail as it climbs to a forested bench
and reaches Mountain Home Flats trail camp. Water is always available in the creek 60 feet below, reached by a
steep use trail.

Return the same way.

TRIP: Oak Glen Conservation Camp to Wilshire Peak

59 8 **miles** round trip; **3150′** elevation gain
Classification: **Moderate**
Season: **Nov.-June** (fire closure 7/1 to winter rain)
Topo map: *Forest Falls* (7.5′)

FEATURES

It is said that Joe Wilshire staked his claim in Potato Canyon back in 1876, and soon afterward planted his first apple trees, probably Rome Beauties. Later he married and raised a family. The story goes that, with the birth of each new baby, he planted a new orchard of apple trees. Later, Isaac Ford came into the little mile-high valley, changed the name to Oak Glen, and planted his own apple trees. Today the descendants of Wilshire and Ford still tend the orchards here. And the little green valley of Oak Glen on the south front of the San Bernardinos is nationally famous for its apples — Gravensteins, Rome Beauties, Winesaps, Jonathans, McIntoshes, Red Golds, Red Delicious, Golden Delicious, and others.

This trail trip climbs from the Oak Glen apple country to the mountain peak that honors the man who started it all. Do it in the fall, when the Red Golds and Golden Delicious are ripe on the trees and the valley is filled with a fragrant aroma. And when you return, hungry and thirsty from your mountain walk, stop in Oak Glen village and sample the delicious apples or a cold glass of cider.

Unfortunately this trip begins on the property of the Oak Glen Conservation Camp, amid a multitude of *No Trespassing* signs. The Forest Service insists that this trail is open to public use (except during fire-closure season), but it is best to state your intentions to conservation-camp officials before starting your hike. Armed guards take a dim view of persons wandering through camp property; several hikers have been stopped and hassled.

DESCRIPTION

From Yucaipa drive 1 mile north on Bryant Street, then 7 miles east on Oak Glen Road to its junction with the road to Oak Glen Conservation Camp. Turn left (northeast) and drive 2¼ miles to a sharp bend in the road just before you reach the conservation camp. Warning signs say *No Trespassing*, but hikers are allowed providing they stay on road and trail.

The trailhead is not marked. From the before-mentioned bend, head up the draw (northeast) and in 100 yards you will pick up the trail leading north up the mountainside. The trail makes several long switchbacks and enters a beautiful forest of pine and cedar. You then climb steeply up forested slopes to the crest of Yucaipa Ridge just west of a 8847′ point that climbers call "Wilshire Mountain" (higher than Wilshire Peak but unnamed on Forest Service and topo maps). A short ½ mile west along the ridgetop gets you to the forested summit of Wilshire Peak (8707′).

Return the way you came. Options include going west on the Oak Glen Divide Trail to Cedar Mountain (see trip 53), then descending the steep Ford Canyon Trail to Oak Glen (trip 58); or turning east and traversing the ridgetop (no trail) to Little San Gorgonio Peak, then descending the Little San Gorgonio Trail to Banning Canyon (see trip 60).

Note: All of the fire roads and trails that ascend the Mill Creek-Oak Glen Divide cross small segments of private property. Recently, some property owners have been voicing objections to hikers crossing their lands. This affects trips 53, 57, 58, 59, and 60. Before attempting any of these trips, check with the Mill Creek Ranger Station (714) 794-1123.

TRIP: Banning Canyon to Little San Gorgonio Peak

60 14 miles round trip; **4200′** elevation gain
Classification: **Strenuous**
Season: **Nov.-June** (fire closure 7/1 to winter rain)
Topo maps: *Forest Falls, San Gorgonio Mtn.*
(both 7.5′)

FEATURES

This is a long, steep haul up the south front of the San Bernardinos. The trail is brushy in spots, and the last mile to the summit is trailless ridge scrambling. It's tough, but the superb view from the top of 9140′ Little San Gorgonio Peak is worth the effort, particularly in early spring when the nearby San Gorgonio high country is coated dazzling white. If there's been a recent storm, chances are good you will be climbing the final 2 or 3 miles in snow; bring an ice axe. (If it weren't for fire closure, this would be best as a summer or fall trip.) Banning Canyon, where you start, is the property of the City of Banning Water Department. To drive past their locked gate, 3 miles short of the trailhead, you must obtain their permission. Otherwise, add 6 miles walking to the trip.

DESCRIPTION

From Banning turn north on San Gorgonio Avenue and follow it 7 miles up Banning Canyon to the locked gate on Banning Bench. Without permission and the key from the Banning Water Department, you must start walking here — 20 miles round trip. With permission drive 3 more miles to the trailhead, on your left (north), marked by a small Forest Service route marker (*1E11*).

The trail ascends the broad, chaparral-covered north slope of Banning Canyon, then begins steep switchbacks up the mountainside. This first stretch is exposed to the sun — not very pleasant walking on a hot day. In 2 miles you round the slope into the east fork of Gilman Canyon (water during rainy season). The trail then climbs steeply up the ridgetop and fades out just below the crest. You're in forest now, so the going is cooler. Continue upward, veering left, to the crest of Yucaipa Ridge, then climb west ½ mile to the summit.

Return the same way. Or continue west along the crest 2 miles, then descend the Wilshire Peak Trail to Oak Glen (trip 59).

Winter—Greyback ridge   *Cliff Youngquist*

TRIP: Millard Canyon to Deer Spring, Raywood Flat

61   **8½ miles** round trip; **3500′** elevation gain
Classification: **Moderate to strenuous**
Season: **All year**

Topo map: *San Gorgonio Mtn.* (7.5′)

FEATURES

Raywood Flat lies in a low, forested gap in the rugged mountain divide separating Banning Canyon from the South Fork of the Whitewater River. The flat has been the scene of lumbering ventures dating back a full century. According to Banning historian Tom Hughes, Sam Black and Jack Morrison built the first sawmill here back in the 1870s. They planned to build a 5-mile flume that would divert the headwaters of the Whitewater across the flat and down into Banning Canyon, a grandiose project in which they failed, but others later succeeded. You can still find pieces of the old wooden flume scattered around the area.

There is a road up Banning Canyon to Raywood Flat, but it is permanently closed to the public by the City of Banning Water Department. This trip uses the Millard Canyon approach from the southeast, and an old trail over the ridge to the flat. The trail has not been maintained in recent years and is quite brushy for the first two miles. In spite of brush, the hike is well worth the effort; the scenery in this relatively wild southeast corner of the San Bernardinos is superb, particularly in springtime. A wilderness permit is required to enter this newly added section of the San Gorgonio Wilderness.

DESCRIPTION

From Interstate 10 2 miles east of Banning, take the Fields Road offramp and drive north 1.3 miles, then east on Forest Road 2S05. Follow the latter as it jogs north, then east into Millard Canyon. Continue on 2S05 up the canyon, passing a ranger station on your left, to a locked gate 10¾ miles from Banning. Park off the road here.

Walk up the last 1¼ miles of dirt road to Deer Springs, a water seepage with the remains of a wooden tank. Here you pick up an unmarked trail heading northwest, through scrub oak, whitethorn and a few young pines. This first section is brushy and difficult to follow in spots. From near the head of the canyon, it climbs the ridge to your left, then continues steeply up around the east slope of a 7922' unnamed mountain, with fine views down into the San Gorgonio Pass country. You enter an open forest of pine and fir. The trail contours along the north slope of Peak 7922', with vistas into the South and East forks of the Whitewater. You then drop to the dirt Water Department road just south of Raywood Flat; turn right (north) and follow the road a short distance down to the flat, 3 miles hiking from Deer Spring. Here you can inspect the flume and, if you search carefully perhaps find relics from water-seeking ventures of past years.

If you have plenty of time and energy, you can take the trail that follows the flume north around the slope, then drops into the South Fork, 1½ miles, then over the ridge into the East Fork, ¾ mile farther. One trailless mile up the East Fork is Silverwood Falls, where the waters plunge off the San Gorgonio massif. This would add up to a very long day. Overnight camping is not allowed in the South Fork of the Whitewater due to fire danger. (There are no trail camps in the area.)

Return the same way.

This southeastern end of the San Gorgonio Wilderness is sometimes closed because of high fire danger. You'll find out whether you can do this trip when you apply for your wilderness permit.

IMPORTANT NOTICE!

The Tribal Council of the Morongo Indian Reservation has closed the access road to Trips 61 and 62. As of this writing (June 1999) there are no plans to reopen it anytime in the foreseeable future. For the latest information on these trips, check with the Mill Creek Ranger Station (909) 794-1123.

TRIP: Millard Canyon (East Branch) to Kitching Peak

62 9½ **miles** round trip; **2400′** elevation gain
Classification: **Moderate**
Season: **November-May**
Topo maps: *Banning, Morongo Valley* (both 15′),
San Gorgonio Mtn. (7.5′)

FEATURES

Kitching Peak is the southeastern sentinel of the San
Bernardinos. From its 6598′ summit you gaze out over the
Coachella Valley and San Gorgonio Pass, with the mighty
ramparts of San Jacinto Peak seemingly just a stone's throw
across the gap.

This trip, on trail all the way, climbs up the East Branch
of Millard Canyon to the mountain divide, then traverses
the ridgetop to the summit. You pass through clusters of
live oak, bigcone spruce in sheltered recesses, and dense
chaparral on sun-drenched slopes. The vista from the top
is a reward in itself, particularly on a clear winter day
when San Jacinto glistens in its snowy mantle and you can
see down the trough of Coachella Valley to the Salton Sea.

The Kitching Peak area was added to the San Gorgonio
Wilderness by the California Wilderness Act of 1984. A
wilderness permit is now required.

DESCRIPTION

Driving directions: follow trip 61 to a junction just beyond Millard Canyon Ranger Station. Turn right onto
Forest Road 2S03A and follow it up the East Branch to the
parking area under an immense bigcone spruce tree, 10½
miles from Banning.

Follow the trail up the East Branch, through live oak,
spruce and chaparral. In 3¾ miles you climb to the divide
between Millard Canyon and the Whitewater River. Here
you reach a junction. The main footpath continues over
the ridge and down to the Whitewater. You turn sharp
right (southeast) and follow the ill-defined trail 1 mile up
the ridge to the summit of Kitching Peak.

Return the same way.

Round Valley

W. R. C. Shedenhelm

PART 2

The San Jacinto Mountains

The San Jacinto Mountains

On clear days, travellers driving through San Gorgonio Pass toward the desert are treated to an awesome panorama. To their left, dominating the northern skyline, is the abrupt south slope of the San Bernardinos, crowned by the long gray hogback of San Gorgonio Mountain. To their right, and ahead, towers a stupendous rock escarpment, soaring in jagged ridgelines and scoured avalanche troughs almost 10000 vertical feet in five horizontal miles. This mountain wall is the northeast face of 10804' San Jacinto Peak, as rugged a precipice as exists in the United States. Somber gray in summer and fall, gleaming white in winter, snow-streaked by late spring, San Jacinto's vaulting desert face has fired the imagination and artistry of many a painter and photographer, and awed thousands of desert visitors.

San Jacinto, as is true with most mountains, has its gentle as well as its rugged features. The southwest side of the mountain is made up of rolling hills that rise from the San Jacinto Valley and become progressively higher and steeper until they culminate at the summit. Scenic paved highways traverse this gentle slope, winding through verdant woods, crossing streams that here and there are dammed to provide fishing lakes, giving access to rustic resorts. Idyllwild is the largest and best known of these resort communities, nestled in secluded, mile-high Strawberry Valley.

But it is the summit country of the San Jacintos that is most alluring. Here, well above the highways and byways that penetrate the lower slopes, is a sky island of delectable alpine wilderness, unsurpassed in Southern California. Under white granite summits and boulder-stacked ridges

145

lie little hanging valleys and tapered benches lush with forest and meadow. A multitude of bubbling springs nourish icy-cold streams that tumble and cascade down the mountain. In season, alpine wild-flowers add a beautiful dash of color. The thin atmosphere is cool, clean and refreshing.

Those who confine their mountain exploration to places they can reach by automobile will never see this unspoiled mountain roof-garden. Riders of the spectacular Palm Springs Aerial Tramway can witness a small portion of it. But it is only the hiker or horseback rider who can really know the San Jacinto high country. Summer and fall weekends find hundreds of these outing enthusiasts following the wilderness trails that lace the region, lingering overnight at one of the many secluded trail camps, and climbing to the summit of "San Jack" for a view that is unsurpassed in magnificence. Their numbers are increasing every year.

The top of the San Jacintos are protected from civilization's encroachment by two adjacent wild areas. The heart of the region, including San Jacinto Peak, is included within Mount San Jacinto State Wilderness, under the jurisdiction of the state of California. On both sides of it, north and south, is the San Jacinto Wilderness, part of the San Bernardino National Forest.

Geographers disagree over the extent of the San Jacinto Mountains. Some include only the great bulk of San Jacinto Peak and its surrounding ridges and valleys. Others say the San Jacintos take in the whole mountain mass from, roughly speaking, State Route 79, south of Beaumont, southeast some 40 miles to the Palms-to-Pines Highway, beyond which are the Santa Rosas. Most do not include the isolated ridges of Thomas and Cahuilla mountains, southwest of the main mountain mass, although both of these regions are part of the San Jacinto Mountain District of San Bernardino National Forest. For the purposes of this book, all of the areas mentioned above (except the Santa Rosas) are included in the San Jacinto Mountains.

The geologist looks at the San Jacintos and sees a strong

resemblance to the Sierra Nevada. Both are uplifted, westward-tilting blocks, essentially granitic in composition, bounded by major fault zones. He places the San Jacintos in the Peninsular Range province, a line of mountain ranges extending from the Santa Ana Mountains southward to the tip of Baja California. The Peninsular Ranges are generally low mountains, seldom topping 6000′ in elevation. Only the San Jacintos and the Sierra de San Pedro Martir in Baja California rise above 10000 feet. San Jacinto Peak is the loftiest summit in the entire 800-mile-long province. The San Jacintos are bounded on the west by the San Jacinto Fault, one of the most active in California, the source of many earthquakes in recent years. North and east of the range is a complicated network of relatively short-length faults, offshoots of the great San Andreas Fault. Although not all these desert-side faults have been charted, the stupendous mountain escarpment on this flank bears obvious testimony to their existence.

The botanist studies the San Jacintos and is amazed at the varieties and extremes of plant life. According to Harvey Monroe Hall, whose 1902 botanical survey is still an authoritative source on the flora of the range, "There is probably no place in North America where the alpine and Sonoran floras are in such proximity as they are on San Jacinto Mountain." Between the palm-lined desert canyons at the mountain base and the top of San Jacinto Peak, a horizontal distance of five miles, are stacked all the climatic and vegetation changes one would encounter on a journey from northern Mexico to Canada. Within this short distance are six distinctive life zones, five of which completely encircle the mountain.

At the northeast base, part of the Colorado Desert, is Lower Sonoran vegetation, the most common plants being creosote bush, burro brush, desert willow and ironwood tree. Above this, in a wide belt extending completely around the mountain, is the Upper Sonoran zone, the principal shrubs being chamise, manzanita, several species of ceanothus and scrub oak, and the main trees being canyon live oak, interior live oak, Palmer oak on the seaward side and pinyon pine and California juniper on the desert side. The Transition zone embraces the main mountain forest of the San Jacintos, the principal trees being ponderosa pine, Jeffrey pine, Coulter pine, sugar pine, incense cedar, California black oak and, higher up, white fir. The Canadian and Hudsonian Zones form narrow belts around the higher summits, and are so intermixed that the line between them cannot be definitely drawn. The principal trees — in fact the only trees — of these two zones are lodgepole pine and limber pine, and the main shrub is chinquapin. On the summit of San Jacinto Peak is a small island of Arctic-Alpine flora, the southernmost limit of this zone in the United States. There are some who question whether the summit is truly Arctic-Alpine, because of the handful of stunted limber pines, Hudsonian zone trees, just below the top. But botanist Hall found several small plants here that definitely are Arctic-Alpine species. Most notable is alpine sorrel, which grows along snow banks just north of the summit.

The climatic extremes are most striking to those living in the Coachella Valley just below the mountain. Winter storms often rage on the cloud-enveloped heights while desert foothills are bathed in sunlight. In early summer, it is not at all uncommon to look up from the sweltering valley floor, with temperatures well over 100 degrees, to see the long fingers of snow glistening in the upper ravines. From the opposite perspective, one can stand high on the northeastern escarpment, shivering from icy blasts of alpine wind, and gaze down on shimmering heat waves rising from the sun-scorched desert.

The wildlife of the San Jacintos is similar to that of the San Bernardinos, and just as timid. Here too, man has pre-empted most of the range. The most common large mammal is the California mule deer, which summers on the higher slopes and winters at lower elevations. A handful of mountain lions prowl the eastern high country. Bighorn sheep wander on the southern, desert-facing slopes. Bears, once abundant here, are never seen now. On rare occasions, the fortunate hiker glimpses a golden eagle soaring over San Jacinto Peak or a high ridge.

Every hiker has his own favorite mountains that never wear out their appeal. To a great many Southern Californians, the San Jacintos are such a range. There are those who return time and time again to sample the rich wilderness offerings of this granite-ribbed island in the sky. And nothing will cure an aggravated case of urbanitis quicker or more thoroughly than a weekend dose of the San Jacintos.

Between Long Valley and Round Valley   *W.R.C. Shedenhelm*

Man in the San Jacintos

> From this day Ramona never knew an instant's peace or
> rest till she stood on the rim of the refuge valley, high on
> San Jacinto. Then, gazing around, looking up at the lofty
> pinnacles above, which seemed to pierce the sky, . . . feel-
> ing that infinite unspeakable sense of nearness to heaven,
> remoteness from earth which comes only on mountain
> heights, she drew in a long breath of delight, and cried:
> 'At last! At last, Alessandro! Here we are safe!'
> —Helen Hunt Jackson, *Ramona* (1884)

This passage, from Miss Jackson's wondrous California
classic of romance and tragedy, reflects the aurora of reverence and mysticism that has so often been a part of man's
relationship with the San Jacintos. In the novel, the San
Jacintos served as a foreboding last refuge for Ramona and
Alessandro, Indian lovers, fleeing from the white man's
callousness and greed. Mrs. Jackson was not the only
famous author to see in these mountains something awesome, enchanting and mysterious. George Wharton James,
Charles Francis Saunders, and J. Smeaton Chase all
treated the San Jacintos with a degree of reverence unac-
corded any other mountains in the Southwest. From their
widely read works — and particularly from Helen Hunt
Jackson's *Ramona* — the San Jacintos have achieved
world-wide fame.

The Cahuilla Indians, the original inhabitants of the
San Jacinto country, were the first to weave a web of
mythical lore around the mountains. To the Cahuillas, the
San Jacinto Mountains were a sacred place, the home of
Dakush, a large, low-flying meteor, legendary founder of
the Cahuilla people. They were also the dwelling place of
Tahquitz, an evil and powerful demon with an insatiable
appetite for beautiful maidens and human flesh. The tales

Left: Grant L. Taggart, first Supervisor of the San Jacinto
Forest Reserve, and Con Silvas, first ranger, above Wellman Cabin

about Tahquitz are many and they vary greatly, but all of them agree that he was a terror to the Indians. Hunters and food-gatherers who disappeared in the mountains were said to have been carried off by the evil demon to his lair underneath Tahquitz Peak and eaten. When thunder and lightning rumbled across the mountains, it was said that Tahquitz was angry. At such times, no Indian would dare venture onto the mountain. The Tahquitz legend was known not just to the Cahuillas; it was part of the folklore of almost every Indian people in Southern California.

The Cahuillas were a hardy, independent and generally peaceful people. They lived in a number of small villages in a territory stretching from San Gorgonio Pass to the Borrego Desert, on both sides of the San Jacintos. Communities of Western (or Pass) Cahuilla were located in lower Snow Creek, Blaisdell Canyon, Andreas Canyon, Chino Canyon, Tahquitz Canyon and at the oasis of Palm Springs. The Mountain Cahuilla lived primarily in the southwestern foothills of the San Jacintos and Santa Rosas. The Desert Cahuilla were further south in the Coachella Valley.

The primary concern of these peoples was the search for food, in which they ranged far and wide. From the desert came such staples as mesquite and screwbean; slightly higher, agave and yucca were collected; and on mountain slopes, acorns and pinyon nuts provided a dependable source of food. Animals hunted by the Cahuillas included the rabbit, wood rat, quail, antelope, mountain sheep and deer.

It was the abundance of deer on the San Jacintos that lured the Western Cahuillas into the high country. Strong hunters climbed the desert face of the mountain to the area where the deer were grazing, killed and dressed them on the spot, and descended with their kill slung over their shoulders.

It was through the CahuillaValley and Bautista Canyon, below the southwestern foothills of the San Jacintos, that the white man came. First on the scene was the Spanish soldier Pedro Fages, pursuing army deserters from San Diego. Not much is known about the Fages trip, and he left us no descriptions of the San Jacinto country. Two years later, in 1774, came Captain Juan Bautista de Anza, leading a party of 34 from Mexico to Monterey in the most famous overland expedition in California history.

Anza had set out from Tubac, Sonora, to find a route across the desert to California. He and his men almost perished in the burning sands of the Colorado and Borrego deserts, but on their second attempt they managed to find water and locate a gap in the mountain barrier — today's Coyote Canyon. Up this boulder-strewn canyon they struggled until they reached the broad Cahuilla Valley. "Right here there is a pass which I named the Royal Pass of San Carlos. From it are seen most beautiful green and flower-strewn prairies, and snow-covered mountains with pines, oaks, and other trees which grow in cold countries," Anza wrote in his diary. This is the earliest description of the San Jacinto Mountains we have. In the Cahuilla Valley Anza met 200 peaceful Indians — his first encounter with the Cahuillas. Then he descended Bautista Canyon, crossed the San Jacinto Valley, "keeping on our right a high, snow-covered mountain," and continued on to Monterey. Anza passed this way once again in 1776.

Not for many years did the Spaniards or their Mexican Californio successors settle in the San Jacinto country. Just when they did come to stay is unknown — sometime before 1821 is as close as historians can pin it down. Around this time Mission San Luis Rey established an outlying cattle ranch in the flatlands west of the mountains. This they named Rancho San Jacinto, in honor of Saint Hyacinth of Silesia (1185–1231), a Dominican missionary credited with many conversions in Tibet and China. Thus the name *San Jacinto* was born, first used for the stock rancho, later extended to the San Jacinto Valley, the San Jacinto River, and finally the San Jacinto Mountains.

Except for occasional ventures to search for strayed stock or to hunt grizzlies, the early Spaniards and Californios stayed clear of the mountains. Even with their thick leather chaps, the rancheros found the dense chaparral that coated the lower slopes of the San Jacintos uninviting. There was enough feed for cattle on the plains.

The mountains existed mainly as a source of water. There is no evidence that these early Californians ever reached the high country.

With the coming of the Anglos — from the 1840s onward — the San Jacintos began to receive more attention. As far as is known, the first to leave his mark on the mountains was Tennessee-born Paulino Weaver. Weaver had come to California, perhaps with the Ewing Young trapping party, in the early 1830s. He apparently became a Mexican citizen, for he was granted land in the area of San Gorgonio Pass by Governor Pio Pico in 1845. According to Banning historian Tom Hughes, Weaver was cutting timber from both sides of San Gorgonio Pass — including the northern foothills of the San Jacintos — as early as 1846. He also is said to have hunted bear and deer in the mountains. Weaver later served as a U.S. Army scout during the Civil War, and moved to Arizona, where he died in 1867.

Lt. Robert S. Williamson's Pacific Railroad Survey party came through San Gorgonio Pass in 1853. William Blake, geologist of the expedition, crossed to the south side of the pass to investigate the rocks of San Jacinto Peak (which he mistakenly called "San Gorgonio"). His report contains the first scientific description of the mountain.

Lt. Williamson's official map, published by the War Department, showed San Jacinto Peak as "San Gorgonio" and San Gorgonio Mountain as "San Bernardino," which for a short time caused confusion among surveyors and new settlers.* However, the mistake was rectified two years later (1855) when Lt. John G. Parke's Pacific Railroad Survey party passed through the area. Dr. Thomas Antisell, geologist of the Parke expedition, correctly labelled the mountain south of the pass as "San Jacinto," and it has

*Some writers claim that at the same time San Jacinto Peak was called "San Gorgonio", San Gorgonio Mountain was known as "San Jacinto." The writer, after extensive research, was unable to find any evidence of this. As far as can be documented, San Gorgonio Mountain was never known as "San Jacinto."

Right: Portion of Williamsons map. Dark line is proposed railroad route.

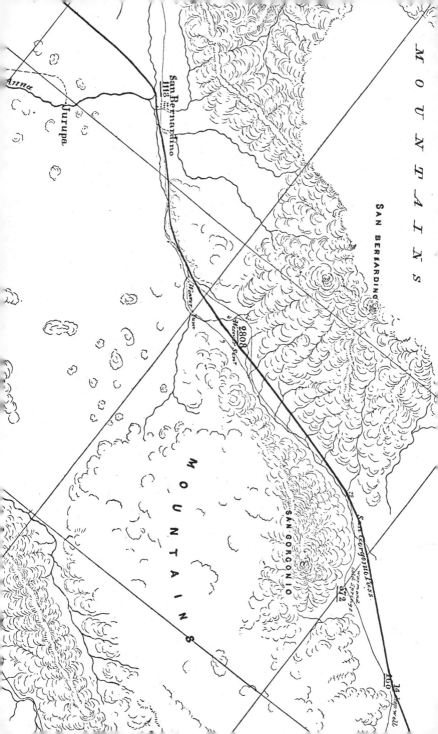

' been known singularly by this name ever since.

The 1860s saw pioneer settlers establish isolated homes in the San Jacinto Mountains. Most historians give Charles Thomas credit for being first. Thomas ran away from his New York home at the age of 12, sailed around Cape Horn, landed in San Francisco and drifted south in the 1850s. He took a young Californio bride at Santa Barbara and settled on a ranch near Temecula to raise cattle. The story goes that he was led into the beautiful Garner Valley (then unnamed), high on the south slope of the San Jacintos, by his Cahuilla Indian friends. Thomas fell in love with the mountain-rimmed basin and decided to make it his home. In 1861 he filed on 480 acres in the heart of the valley, brought up his wife and children, and began raising Mexican longhorn cattle there. In 1876 Thomas purchased 4,300 more acres of surrounding mountain land from the Southern Pacific Company. In later years, besides raising cattle, he bred race horses in partnership with Lucky Baldwin. The Thomas Ranch became a well-known Southern California landmark.

To obtain lumber for the ranch buildings and fences, he sent his ranch hands high into the lush forests of the San Jacintos — probably as far as Strawberry Valley — to cut and haul timber. Bears, grizzly and otherwise, abounded in the mountains then. A man named Herkey, cutting timber for Thomas, was attacked and severely mauled while drinking from a creek; he made it back to the ranch, where he died from his wounds. Herkey Creek commemorates him today. Deer were thick in the mountains too. Thomas and his men frequently made hunting trips into the high country. One story tells of deer coming into camp in Round Valley "so tame that six were shot before the herd took fright." Thomas and his family remained on the ranch until 1905, when they sold out to San Bernardino stockman Robert F. Garner.

Others followed Thomas into the San Jacintos — ranchers, herders, hunters, prospectors and lumbermen. As early as 1875, sheepmen and cattlemen herded their hungry livestock into the lush mountain grasslands around Strawberry Valley, some even climbing over the difficult Devil's

Slide into upper Tahquitz Valley. Hunters soon decimated the large herds of deer. Prospectors searched for mineral wealth in the mountains, but found little to reward their efforts. Henry Hamilton discovered a few valuable tourmaline gemstones on Thomas Mountain in 1872. An Englishman named Harold Kenworthy poured a fortune into a gold-mining operation near the southern end of Garner Valley in the 1880s, but no great amounts of gold were ever uncovered. Emil Chilsen developed the Hemet Belle Mine near Kenworthy around the turn of the century. No one ever made much off the Hemet Belle, and it changed hands so often that it became known as the "Grubstake Mine." Salting mines with gold became a regular procedure: "All you did was load up a shotgun with gold dust, fire it into the rock, and you had a mine for sale," mountain pioneer Lincoln Hamilton recalled.

It was the commercial loggers who really opened up the San Jacintos. Rich stands of sugar and ponderosa pine had long been known to exist in the mountains, but the difficulty of hauling out timber over rugged slopes had prevented all but insignificant logging efforts by local settlers. To bring out this timber, wagon roads would need to be hacked up the steep mountainsides. Two such projects were begun in 1875–76 — one up the north slopes from San Gorgonio Pass, the other up the west side from the San Jacinto Valley.

It was the Southern Pacific Railroad that got things started on the north side. The Southern Pacific was constructing its main east-west line through San Gorgonio Pass and needed lumber for construction camps and railroad ties. To obtain this timber, Colonel Milton S. Hall, a promoter and grading contractor who was commissioned by the Southern Pacific to grade the right-of-way between Spadra and Indio, built a very steep wagon road — known as Hall's Grade — up the mountainside from "Hall City" (near today's Cabezon) to a point above the present Lake Fulmor. Here he had a man named Fuller set up a small sawmill. Shortly afterward, Fuller moved the sawmill over the ridge and down to a new site above the present Fuller Mill Creek. The enterprise was none too successful. For one thing, the road was too precipitous for heavy loads, and at least two men were killed and several teams and loaded wagons smashed when they broke loose on the grade. After a frustrating year, the road was abandoned and the sawmill machinery hauled piece by piece down into lower Snow Creek Canyon. Here, at the bottom end of a dizzy skidway, it was set up to await the logs that never reached it. They either jumped the track or broke into splinters in their mad rush from high on the mountain. By 1877 the Southern Pacific had its railroad through the pass and the costly logging efforts were abandoned. But Hall's Grade remained, later to become the springboard for other road-making projects in the mountains.

Much more successful were the logging enterprises on the west slope of the San Jacintos. In 1875, Joseph Crawford, Union Army veteran and homesteader at Oak Cliff in the San Jacinto Valley, secured a 50-year franchise from the San Diego County Board of Supervisors (San Diego County included the San Jacintos until 1893) to build a toll road from Oak Cliff up the west side of the mountains to Alvin Meadow and Strawberry Valley. Crawford spent $5,500 building his road into the timber belt, and even before it was finished loggers swarmed into the mountains. The road was narrow and just about as precipitous as Hall's Grade, and it elicited comments such as, "Steep? Why in places it leans over backwards!" There was a welcome water stop at Halfway House Spring, where teamsters and animals often collapsed.

Shortly after Crawford finished his toll road, large-scale logging efforts began on the western slopes. A number of sawmills were built along the North Fork of the San Jacinto River, in the vicinity of Dutch Flat, and in Strawberry Valley. Who built the first mill is not known for certain. Bradley and Stafford are believed to have erected the pioneer sawmill in Strawberry Valley, then sold out around 1881 to Amasa Saunders, who built a spectacular overhead flume leading to a large waterwheel to operate his saws. Saunders Meadow near Idyllwild honors him today. Anton Scherman had a number of mills in and around Strawberry Valley and at the peak of his operations was said to have

cut 25,000 board feet per day. George B. Hannahs purchased 4500 acres of timberland from the Southern Pacific
Railroad* and erected two mills — one at Dutch Flat, the
other in Strawberry Valley. Hannah is credited with starting the first settlement in Strawberry Valley, which he
named Raynetta after his infant son Raymond. His store
was the focal point for "outers, ranchers, cowboys, lumbermen, and everyone else attached to the mountains by
either business or pleasure." Here also was the first post
office in the San Jacinto Mountains, established in 1893.
Hannahs was an explorer too, and knew every foot of the
mountains. He is credited with having named Round Valley and Long Valley and with discovering Hidden Lake,
which he called "Lake Surprise."

By the early 1890s, the timberlands of the western San
Jacintos vibrated to the thunder of falling trees, the swear-
ing of tough woodsmen, the creaking of wagons, and the
whine of steel saws. Tall pines were cut from the mountainside, hauled to mill by "bull teams," sliced into lumber,
then wagoned down Crawford's toll road — the toll-keeper
collected 75¢ per wagonload — to San Jacinto. Most of
the lumber was sold and used in the San Jacinto Valley;
some was shipped to San Bernardino and Los Angeles.

Water-seekers came into the mountains, too. Ranchers
in the San Jacinto Valley needed water for their lands and
saw in the San Jacinto Mountains a ready source. In 1887,
E. L. Mayberry, W.F. Whittier and other valley pioneers
formed the Lake Hemet Water Company to bring water
down from the mountains. A site was selected at the
northwest end of Garner Valley, where the South Fork of
the San Jacinto River drops into a deep gorge. At the top
of this narrow canyon, a masonry dam was constructed.
When the dam was completed in 1893, it rose 122 feet
above the canyon floor and formed a lake of 600 acres. It
was said to have been, at the time, the largest masonry dam

*In 1876 the Southern Pacific Railroad was given every other section
of land for 11 miles on both sides of their right-of-way, part of the
federal government's huge subsidy program for American big business during the later decades of the 19th century. Most of the San
Jacinto Mountains fell within this checkerboard pattern.

in the world. Water from the reservoir was carried to valley farms via a network of large wooden flumes.

Acre by acre, the lumber monster was eating away at the
mountain forest, each year relentlessly cutting farther up
the western slopes of the San Jacintos. Sheep and cattle
by the thousands were being herded to summer pasture
in the high-country meadows, stripping them of their rich
green cover. Wagon roads were being hacked higher and
higher into the mountains. As with the San Gabriel and
San Bernardino mountains, even those with myopic vision
could see that reckless land-use practices were destroying
both the beauty of the mountains and — more important to
the practical-minded — the mountain watershed. Federal
protection was called for. As a result of strong pressure
from those who wanted the mountains saved, for either
esthetic or practical reasons, President Grover Cleveland
signed a bill creating the San Jacinto Forest Reserve on
February 22, 1897. At first it was a forest reserve in name
only, and not much was done to stop the continuing depre-
dation. As with the San Bernardinos, much of the mountain lands were already in private hands — particularly the
hands of the Southern Pacific Railroad — and outside Forest Service jurisdiction. In 1898 the first forest rangers
were assigned to the reserve and a patrol system established. These early rangers of the old San Jacinto Forest
Reserve — Charley Van Deventer, Theodore Olds, John
Oloan, "Sulphur Springs" Thompson — did their job zealously, guarding against further timber cutting on public
lands, chasing herders and their herds out of the high
country, fighting brush fires, locating lost and injured persons. They set the standards followed by today's Forest
Service in the San Jacintos. In 1907 the name was changed
to San Jacinto National Forest, and the following year the
San Jacinto was joined with the smaller Trabuco to create
Cleveland National Forest. In 1925, the San Jacinto District was cut from the Cleveland and joined to San Bernardino National Forest. So it remains today.

Around the turn of the century, recreation replaced
logging as the major activity in the San Jacinto Mountains.
In 1893 or thereabouts, John and Mary Keen built their

one-story Strawberry Valley Hotel, and a few years later started Keen Camp. In 1898 a group of Los Angeles doctors, headed by Dr. Walter Lindley and Dr. W.W. Becket, formed the California Health Resort Company and purchased 3500 acres in Strawberry Valley. Here they built a 3-story hotel and surrounding cottages for the treatment of TB patients. Around this sanitarium hotel a small resort community grew. In 1899 the federal government decided to relocate the post office in the hotel, at the time managed by Mrs. Laura Rutledge and her husband. Mrs. Rutledge suggested the name "Idyllwild" for the new post office and community. So it is known today. The first hotel, known as the Idyllwild Sanitarium, burned to the ground in 1904 and was replaced a few years later by the Idyllwild Inn, which became a popular summer resort. The Idyllwild Inn burned in 1945 and was replaced by the present structure. Through the years, particularly after World War II, Idyllwild has grown into a well-known resort community with a population today over 3000. It stands at the gateway to the San Jacinto Wilderness.

With the people came new roads. Crawford's old toll road was superseded in 1891 by the Mayberry Road, which followed basically today's Highway 74 from the San Jacinto Valley to Keen Camp. Built by C.L. Mayberry, its original function was to transport materials for construction of Hemet Dam. From Keen Camp, Charley Thomas's old cattle trail to Strawberry Valley was improved into a road to Idyllwild. In 1909 the famous Idyllwild Control Road — one-way traffic only, alternating up and down every two hours — was constructed approximately along the route of Crawford's 1876 road. 1911 saw the first primitive road from Banning to Idyllwild. In recent years, many of these roads have been improved and new ones built, allowing easy, high-gear access to the mountain communities.

Visiting the spectacular and beautiful San Jacinto high country — on foot or by horseback — has long been a favorite pastime of outdoor-minded Southern Californians. As early as 1885, parties camped in Round Valley and climbed to the top of San Jacinto Peak. After 1900, visits became much more frequent. Many of these early mountain visitors realized the need for safeguarding this unique alpine wilderness from the perils of unrestricted overuse and possible exploitation. First with a concrete proposal was A.C. Lovekin of Riverside, who in 1919 advocated setting aside the higher altitudes of the San Jacintos as a great wilderness memorial park in memory of those who gave their lives in World War I. Lovekin's plan met with general public approval, but nothing came of it for eight years. Then, in 1927, the California Legislature created the State Park System, and attention was once again focused on the Mount San Jacinto wilderness park proposal. In 1928 the San Jacinto State Park Association was formed, Lovekin as president, with the express purpose of including San Jacinto Peak and the surrounding high country in the State Park system. At the time, the main stumbling block was land ownership: the odd-numbered sections of land, including San Jacinto Peak itself, were owned by the Southern Pacific Company, while the even-numbered sections were federally owned lands administered by the Forest Service. The State Park Bond Act, passed by the California voters in 1928, and the pledge of matching funds from the Riverside County Board of Supervisors and private citizens, along with land purchase and exchange proposals acceptable to all involved parties, overcame this hurdle. In 1929 the State Park Commission formally adopted plans to acquire the lands and create Mount San Jacinto State Park, and by 1935 all the land atop the range was in state ownership. The valuation of the 12,695 acres within the park, acquired in a 3-way deal with the Southern Pacific Land Company, the U.S. Forest Service and the State of California, was $84,218.75. Half of this sum was contributed by Riverside County and friends of the park project. The federal government aided greatly in the development of the park through the CCC program. In 1935-36, gangs of young CCC workers camped in Round Valley, Tahquitz Valley and near Idyllwild, built 26 miles of trail, developed 29 campsites, and erected the stone refuge cabin on San Jacinto Peak. June 19, 1937 was a memorable day to conservationists and lovers of the San Jacinto high country; Mount San Jacinto State Park was formally dedicated.

Since then, parcels of land have been added, and in 1963 the name was expanded to Mount San Jacinto Wilderness State Park.

In 1931 the Forest Service designated the mountain regions immediately north and south of the state park as the San Jacinto Wild Area. In 1964 the name was changed to San Jacinto Wilderness. The entire top country of the range, from Fuller Ridge on the north side to the Desert Divide south of Tahquitz Peak is now protected by the state and federal wilderness systems.

The story of the San Jacinto high country would end here if it were not for the determined efforts of two Palm Springs businessmen. In 1935 Francis F. Crocker of the California Electric Power Company and Carl Barkow of the Desert Sun newspaper presented the idea of a tramway from Palm Springs up the north face of San Jacinto Mountain to the Palm Springs Chamber of Commerce. The idea quickly caught on, particularly because it was felt that a spectacular mountain tramway would be a boon to the Palm Springs tourist industry. In 1939 a bill was introduced in the State Legislature to establish a "Palm Springs Winter Parks Authority" to build the tramway. It passed the legislature but was vetoed by Governor Olson. Similar bills, slightly changed, were introduced in 1941 and 1943, but both met the same fate. In 1945 a fourth bill was drawn up, this time with considerable change of language. The proposed agency was now called the "Mount San Jacinto Winter Park Authority" and benefits to all Californians, including skiers, were advertised. The appeal to skiers was a brazen smokescreen: the Far West Ski Association pointed out that, because of the craggy nature of the mountain, skiing here was highly unsuitable. But conservationists were caught with their guard down, and the bill sailed through the legislature and was signed by Governor Warren. The undisguised purpose of the Winter Park Authority was to build a tramway up the north wall of the mountain for the benefit of Palm Springs, and it quickly set about to achieve this goal. But it was a long time reaching it.

For the next 15 years — until actual construction began in 1961 — one of the most bitter battles between conservationists and business developers ever fought in California raged over the tramway proposal. Charges and counter-charges flew back, and both sides used every weapon in their legal arsenal to advance or defeat the project. A residue of bitterness remains to this day. Finally the last legal obstruction was batted down, $7,700,000 in revenue bonds to finance construction were sold, construction was commenced, and the spectacular aerial tramway became a reality in 1963. The Mount San Jacinto Winter Park Authority threw off any vestige of disguise for its true motive when it named the completed project the "Palm Springs Aerial Tramway." From Valley Station in Chino Canyon at an elevation of 2643', two gondolas suspended on wires supported by five towers whisk visitors over a mile in elevation gain to Mountain Station, located at 8516' on the edge of Long Valley. It is a steep and breathtaking rise for the 80 passengers on each gondola. And it gives almost instant access to a part of the high wilderness that once required several hours of strenuous hiking to reach. Such is the form of "progress."

The San Jacinto high country is a priceless heirloom of the people of Southern California. Sheer numbers of visitors, increasing every year, constitute what is perhaps the biggest threat to the wilderness character of the mountains. (Unless you take seriously the hare-brained schemes, voiced now and then, to build an extension of the tramway to the top of San Jacinto Peak.) To counter the weight of numbers, the state and the U.S. Forest Service instituted the wilderness permit system in 1971, which developed the present quotas for overnight use. Only with wisdom and restraint will Southern California's best mountain wilderness be preserved.

Just below the high country, battles are being fought too. In a landmark citizen-action campaign, the San Jacinto Mountain Conservation League (Box 1872, Hemet Calif. 92343) recently defeated a developer's proposal to urbanize Garner Valley before a land-use plan and zoning regulations were worked out. With zoning now accomplished, the league's next aim is to get the valley preserved as national forest through federal land exchanges. The future of the San Jacinto Mountains is at stake now.

TRIP
63
State Highway 243 to Black Mountain
7 miles round trip; **2600′** elevation gain
Classification: **Moderate**
Season: **All year**
Topo map: *Lake Fulmor* (7.5′)

FEATURES

7772′ Black Mountain dominates the northern end of the San Jacintos. From the fire lookout on top, you are rewarded with a superb vista over miles of mountain, valley and desert country, with the jagged ramparts of San Jacinto Peak looming high in the southeast.

The Soboba fire of August 1974 burned over the lower half of this trail. The vegetation has largely grown back, although you still pass many blackened stumps.

DESCRIPTION

From Banning drive up State Highway 243 12¾ miles to the beginning of the Black Mountain Trail, 1¼ miles beyond Vista Grande Ranger Station, marked by a large wooden sign. Turn left and drive 100 yards on a dirt road to the parking area.

Proceed up the trail through charred remains of Jeffrey pine, oak and chaparral. The trail climbs 2½ miles up the ridge, passing through the heart of the burned forest, crosses a divide, leaves the burned area, and contours into a shady forest to Indian Creek (water in spring only). You then climb steeply up to a pine-shaded flat on the ridgetop known as Shake camp (no overnight camping) and switchback up the forested slope to a spur of the Black Mountain lookout road, 3½ miles out. Turn right and walk the short distance to the summit lookout tower.

Return the same way. An option, with a 12-mile car shuttle, is to descend the lookout road (4S68), going right at the before-mentioned junction, passing Boulder Basin Public Campground, to Black Mountain Road (4S01), 1 mile. To reach this junction, drive up State Highway 243, passing Lake Fulmor, to Black Mountain Road, 4½ miles from the Black Mountain trailhead. Turn left (north) and drive up Black Mountain Road (4S01) to its junction with the side road to Boulder Basin Campground, 5¼ miles. Park here, or pay the campground fee at Boulder Basin, ¼ mile farther.

TRIP: State Highway 243 to Indian Mountain

64

5 miles round trip; **800´** elevation gain
Classification: **Easy**
Season: **Nov.–June** (fire closure 7/1 to winter rain)
Topo map: *Lake Fulmor* (7.5´)

FEATURES

5790´ Indian Mountain stands high over the western
foothills of the range, offering a splendid panorama over chaparral-coated hillsides and the flat expanse of San Jacinto
Valley. This trip is a fire-road walk most of the way, best done
on a cool, clear winter or spring day.

The south slopes of Indian Mountain were blackened by the
1997 Bee Canyon fire, but fortunately the chaparral is quickly
growing back tall and verdant.

DESCRIPTION

From Banning, drive up State Highway 243 to the Indian
Vista overlook parking area, 15½ miles. The Indian Mountain
fire road (4S21) begins just west of the overlook parking area.

Walk through the gate (usually open for ORVs) and down
the fire road to a saddle, then up and around the east and south
slopes of Indian Mountain — mostly through chaparral country, with clumps of Jeffrey pine and oak offering occasional
shade. The fire road climbs almost to the summit on the south
side before beginning its 6-mile descent to Highway 74. When
it reaches its high point, turn right and follow the old, partly
overgrown fire break to the boulder-strewn summit.

Return the same way.

TRIP: North Fork, San Jacinto River

65   **1-4 miles** round trip; **200´** elevation gain
Classification: **Easy** to **moderate**
Season: **May–Oct.**
Topo map: *Lake Fulmor* (7.5´)

FEATURES

There is no better place to experience the riparian delights of
the San Jacintos than along the North Fork of the San Jacinto
River. The musical waters of the creek exhibit a delightful
variety of moods — now splashing merrily over boulder, now
pausing in limpid pool, only to plunge headlong over miniature
waterfall and cascade. Along its banks sprout western azalea,
its sweet-smelling gold and white flowers often growing under
western dogwood, splendid in spring with flower-like clusters
of white bracts and just as glorious in fall when its leaves turn
burgundy-red. Scarlet monkeyflower and pale columbine
cheer these shady thickets with colorful blooms, all under a
verdant canopy of alder, willow, and bay. On the slopes above
is a mixed forest of live oak, incense cedar, ponderosa and
Jeffrey pine, all contributing to nature's soft picture of ele-
gance.

This trip is more of a saunter than a hike, a place to contemplate the gifts of the natural world and briefly forget civilization's tribulations. You can go as far as you want — a few hundred yards beside the dancing waters, or a mile or more over
and around the streamside boulders into hidden recesses.

DESCRIPTION

From Banning, drive up State Highway 243 to its crossing of
the signed North Fork of the San Jacinto River, 18 miles. There
is a large parking area on the south side of the highway about
50 yards west of the North Fork crossing and a small parking
area on the north side adjacent to the creek.

Just west of the highway bridge, on the north side, follow a
use trail that drops steeply down to the creek. The trail soon
disappears and you must scramble over boulders alongside the
stream. Farther up, there are places where you must climb
away from the creek to get around rock obstructions, small
waterfalls and cascades. Here and there you come across a use

trail, which soon disappears among the boulders. If you are a beginner, a half mile is about as far as you should go. It is possible to follow the North Fork all the way up to Dark Canyon Public Campground, but this is for experienced hikers only. Lug-soled boots should be worn.

TRIP: Forest Road 5S10 to North Fork of the San Jacinto

66 River

5 miles round trip; 1900′ elevation loss and gain

Classification: **Moderate**

Season: **October–June**

Topo map: *Lake Fulmor* (7.5′)

FEATURES

The North Fork of the San Jacinto River cuts a deep swath down the west slope of the range. Melting snows and gushing springs high on the western ramparts of San Jacinto Peak nourish the several streams that join to become the North Fork; then the united waters tumble down the broad, V-shaped chasm to join with the South Fork, just above the San Jacinto Valley. A green canopy of fir, pine, cedar and oak shades the stream for most of its length.

This trip drops into the lonely middle reaches of the North Fork via the old Webster Trail, named for David G. Webster, pioneer rancher at Valle Vista in the San Jacinto Valley, who drove cattle up to high pasture on this path in the 1870s and '80s. Helen Hunt Jackson patterned her character Merrill in *Ramona* after Webster, whom she met while researching Indian conditions in the San Jacinto Valley.

This is an ideal outing for a cool winter or spring day. You start under Jeffrey pines and live oaks, drop down slopes covered with chaparral, swiftly growing back after a fire, and reach a secluded part of the creek, spotted with tall pines, oaks and alders. Try it after a rain, when the streams run full and the aroma of damp chaparral perfumes the air. Allow plenty of time for the return trip — it's all uphill.

DESCRIPTION

From Pine Cove on State Highway 243, 3 miles from Idyllwild, turn west on Pine Cove Road and follow it for 1 mile as it curves north to a junction with Forest Roads 5S09 and 5S10. Turn sharp left (southwest) on 5S10 and con-

tinue ½ mile past Lia Hona Lodge to the beginning of the
Webster Trail, indicated by a wooden sign. Park in the adjacent
clearing.

Follow the trail west as it descends the ridge, first
through an open forest of Jeffrey pine and oak, then
through dense chaparral. Your view is superb if the day
is clear — across velvet-coated foothills to the flat expanse
of the San Jacinto Valley. The dirt road you see climbing
the next ridge south is part of the old Hemet-Idyllwild
control road, used from 1910 to 1929, one-way traffic only.
Where the slope begins to descend more steeply as it nears
the gorge, the trail makes one long switchback south and
reaches the cool waters of the North Fork, 2½ miles from
the start.

After your streamside rest amid sylvan greenery, return
the way you came — all uphill now.

TRIP: Black Mountain Road via Fuller Ridge to Deer
67 Springs, Little Round Valley, San Jacinto Peak
12 miles round trip; **3000´** elevation gain
Classification: **Strenuous** (1 day), **mod.** (2 days)
Season: **June–October**
Topo maps: *Lake Fulmor, San Jacinto Peak* (both 7.5´)

FEATURES

From Black Mountain, the craggy spine of Fuller Ridge
dips downward and then soars upward, like a long kite
string, to Folly Peak. Broken gendarmes and huge granite
outcroppings make it one of the most rugged mountain
backbones in Southern California. Weather-toughened
pines and firs cling to its precipitous slopes.

The Fuller Ridge Trail, completed in 1970, threads its
way around these gray-white gendarmes, first on the north
side of the ridge, then on the south, from the Black Mountain Road to the Deer Springs Trail below San Jacinto
Peak. Views are magnificent, particularly down into the
wild and beautiful gorge of upper Snow Creek and beyond
to the desert. Once this new footpath becomes known, it
should be one of the most popular trails in the San Jacinto
Wilderness.

This trip takes the Fuller Ridge Trail to Deer Springs,
then uses the Deer Springs Trail to ascend San Jacinto
Peak. You can do it in one very long day, or make it more
leisurely by staying the night at Little Round Valley Trail
Camp. (Note: Deer Springs Trail Camp and the summit
camping area have been closed because of overuse.)

DESCRIPTION

From State Highway 243 (17 miles from Banning or 8
miles from Idyllwild), drive up the Black Mountain Road 8
miles (1½ miles past Black Mountain Campground) to a
junction with the Fuller Ridge Trail access road; turn right
and continue ¼ mile to the parking area.

The trail rounds the north side of the slope and climbs
through pine, cedar and fir to a notch in Fuller Ridge, 2

miles. You then drop, climb and contour around granite outcroppings on both sides of the ridge, with spectacular views through "windows" in the rocky spine. You can peer down into the extremely rugged upper reaches of Snow Creek's west fork, where there are the remains of the flume in which Colonel Hall tried to drop timber from the mountain forest to the desert in 1876. Southward, you look down into the forested bowl of Fuller Mill Creek, once the scene of large-scale logging. After another mile you begin to contour, then climb along the southwest slope of the San Jacinto massif, passing two small springs of icy-cold water, to a junction with the Deer Springs Trail, 5 miles from the start.

Go left (northeast) up the slope, and follow the Deer Springs Trail past small Boggy Meadow to Little Round Valley Trail Camp, 1½ miles above the junction (see trip 72 for a full description of the Deer Springs Trail). You are in lodgepole forest now. From Little Round Valley, continue up the trail to a junction with the San Jacinto Peak Trail, 1¼ miles. Turn left and climb past the stone shelter cabin to the summit, 300 yards. Camping is not allowed on the peak.

Return the same way—or, with a car shuttle, take one of the numerous options that are open to you (see trips 68, 69, 72, 74). Climbers have traveled cross-country over to Folly Peak, then down the brush-spotted ridge to the Fuller Ridge Trail halfway between the Deer Springs Trail junction and the roadhead, but don't attempt this unless you are experienced in cross-country travel.

TRIP: Forest Road 4S02 via Seven Pines Trail to Deer

68 Springs
7½ **miles** round trip; **2600´** elevation gain
Classification: **Moderate**
Season: **June–October**
Topo maps: *Lake Fulmor, San Jacinto Peak* (both 7.5´)

FEATURES

The Seven Pines Trail climbs the ridge between Fuller Mill Creek and Dark Canyon and continues up to Deer Springs. You wind through granite outcroppings and beautiful forest country, with views now and then toward the rugged headwall of Fuller Ridge. It is a steep but pleasant walk on a good trail, crossing and recrossing the tumbling North Fork, with several options for the return.

DESCRIPTION

200 yards east of Alandale Ranger Station on State Highway 243 (19 miles from Banning, 6 miles from Idyllwild), drive up Marion Mtn. Road (4S02), going left at a junction in 100 yards and left again in 1 mile, to Dark Canyon Public Campground. Follow the one-way loop road right through the campground to rejoin 4S02 just past the top of the loop. Turn right and follow 4S02, passing Azalea Trails Girl Scout Camp, to the signed Seven Pines trailhead, on your right, 4½ miles out.

Follow the trail as it climbs up the boulder-stacked, forested ridge between Fuller Mill Creek and Dark Canyon. In 1¼ miles you cross the ridgecrest and drop to the North Fork, where you enter San Jacinto State Park Wilderness. The trail fords the creek and climbs east, crossing and recrossing the North Fork, to a junction with Deer Springs Trail, 3½ miles. Turn left (east) and follow the latter to Deer Springs, ¼ mile. There is water here but overnight camping is not allowed.

Return the way you came. Options are to descend the Marion Mountain Trail (Trip 69), the Deer Springs Trail to Idyllwild (Trip 72), or the Fuller Ridge Trail to Black Mountain Road (Trip 67). All require car shuttles.

TRIP: Forest Road 4S71 via Marion Mountain Trail to
Deer Springs, Little Round Valley, San Jacinto Peak.

69

11 miles round trip; **4600´** elevation gain
Classification: **Strenuous** (1 day), **mod.** (2 days)
Season: **June–October**
Topo map: *San Jacinto Peak* (7.5´)

FEATURES

This is the shortest way to climb San Jacinto Peak from the
southwest slope; it is also very steep in places. Old-timers call
this a no-nonsense route — right up the mountainside in short,
steep zigzags. The first 2¼ miles are the most strenuous; you
gain 2200´ from the new trailhead just below Marion
Mountain Campground to Deer Springs. The remainder of the
route is only slightly less precipitous — 2400´ more gain in 3¼
miles via the Deer Springs Trail. You can do it in one exhaust-
ing pull, or make it more enjoyable by spending the night at
Little Round Valley Trail Camp. This trip is a living demonstration of forest change with altitude — you start up in Jeffrey
pine and oak, climb through a belt of sugar pine and white fir,
then into lodgepole pine interspersed with thickets of manzanita, snow brush and chinquapin, and finally emerge above
timberline at the summit.

DESCRIPTION

From 200 yards east of Alandale Ranger Station on State
Highway 243 (19 miles from Banning or 6 miles from
Idyllwild), drive up Marion Mountain Road (4S02), going left
at a junction in 100 yards, to a junction with Marion Mountain
Campground Road (4S71), 1 mile. Go right and follow the lat-
ter, passing the entrance to Fern Basin Campground, to the
Marion Mountain trailhead, just short of Marion Mountain
Campground, 1½ miles above the highway. The parking area
on your left has space for 10–12 vehicles.

Cross 4S71 to the signed Marion Mountain Trail. You climb
through pines and cedars, passing a short access trail coming
up from Marion Mountain Campground, then ascend steeply
up the northwest flank of forested Marion Ridge to a junction
with the Deer Springs Trail, 2¼ miles. Turn left and follow the
latter footpath ¼ mile to Deer Springs. Water is available here

but no camping. Continue up the Deer Springs Trail past Boggy Meadows to Little Round Valley Trail Camp, nestled snugly in a small, sandy basin just below the peak. Water is available here though late summer but should be purified before drinking. Continue up the trail to a junction with the short San Jacinto Peak trail, 1 mile. Turn left and climb the latter, passing the stone shelter cabin built by the CCC in 1936, to the 10,804´ summit, less than ¼ mile. Camping is not allowed in the summit area.

Return the same way. Another way down, requiring a 3-mile car shuttle, is via the Seven Pines Trail (Trip 68). With much longer car shuttles, you can descend the Fuller Ridge Trail to Black Mountain Road (Trip 67), the Deer Springs Trail to Idyllwild (Trip 72), the Wellmans Cienega Trail to Humber Park (Trip 74), or — with a very lengthy car shuttle, via Round and Long valleys to the Palm Springs Aerial Tramway (Trip 78).

Summit block of Marion Mountain

TRIP: Idyllwild to Suicide Rock

70   8 miles round trip; **1900′** elevation gain
Classification: **Moderate**
Season: **May-October**
Topo map: *San Jacinto Peak* (7.5′)

FEATURES

Suicide Rock is an outcropping of white granite that juts from the south slope of Marion Ridge, high above Strawberry Valley. Legend says that Suicide Rock was so named after an Indian maiden and her lover jumped to their deaths from its rim rather than live without each other as had been decreed by the tribal chief. A splendid panorama of the valley floor covered with dense forest, the village of Idyllwild, and the rugged granite cliffs of Lily Rock and Tahquitz Peak awaits the hiker who reaches this viewpoint. This relatively short trip takes the Deer Springs Trail to Suicide Junction, then a side trail over to the rock.

DESCRIPTION

From Idyllwild Ranger Station drive west 1 mile on the Banning-Idyllwild Highway (Highway 243) to the Idyllwild County Park Visitor Center parking area, just south of the highway. Park here, then cross the highway to the new beginning of the Deer Springs Trail, marked by a wooden sign.

Your trail follows an abandoned dirt road about 200 yards, then turns right (north) and climbs steadily through an open forest of oak, Jeffrey pine and king-sized manzanita to the ridgetop. You switchback up the ridge to a signed junction with the Suicide Rock Trail, 3 miles from the start. Here you leave the Deer Springs Trail and turn east, following the lateral trail as it contours across slopes clothed with pine and fir, crosses the trickle of Marion Creek, and climbs the back side of Suicide Rock to the abrupt rim overlooking Strawberry Valley, 1 mile from the junction. The white dome you see directly across the valley is Lily Rock; the steepled granite summit on the skyline is Tahquitz Peak.

Return the same way.

TRIP: Idyllwild to Strawberry Junction, Strawberry
71 Cienaga, Saddle Junction, Devils Slide Trail to
Humber Park
12½ miles round trip; **3100′** elevation gain
Classification: **Moderate**
Season: **June-October**
Topo map: *San Jacinto Peak* (7.5′)

FEATURES

Although bordered by desert and semi-arid hill country,
the San Jacintos are a particularly lush mountain range.
Nowhere is this more evident than at the numerous springs
and marshy cienagas that dot the upper slopes. The abundant rain and snow that fall at the high elevations seep into
the porous granite, which acts as a natural storage reservoir. Water from this rock reservoir flows out at many
points high in the mountains, forming emerald-green and
flowery marshes threaded by clear, gurgling streamlets.
One of the lushest of these sloping mountainside gardens
is Strawberry Cienaga, high on the south face of Marion
Mountain.

This loop trip — requiring a short car shuttle between
Idyllwild and Humber Park — climbs the Deer Springs
Trail to Strawberry Junction, contours across the steep
south slope of Marion Mountain to Strawberry Cienaga,
then descends the Wellman Trail to Saddle Junction and
the Devils Slide to Humber Park. It is a delightful day-
long hike on good trail all the way, passing through rich
forest and meadow country, with continuous views of the
Yosemite-like cliffs and ridges of Tahquitz Peak and Lily
Rock.

DESCRIPTION

From Idyllwild Ranger Station drive 1 mile west on the
Banning-Idyllwild Highway (Highway 243) to Idyllwild
County Park Visitor parking area, just south of the high-
way.

Cross the highway to the new beginning of the Deer
Springs Trail, marked by a wooden sign. Follow the trail

as it climbs northward to a junction with the Strawberry Cienaga Trail, 4½ miles from the start (1½ miles beyond the Suicide Rock Trail junction). Turn right (east) and follow the Strawberry Cienaga lateral trail across the south face of Marion Mountain, through open stands of lodgepole pine and white fir, to Strawberry Cienaga, 2¼ miles. There is no overnight camping here, but there are nice picnic spots alongside clear, cold rivulets. Your view across the valley to the rugged spurs of Tahquitz Peak is breathtaking.

Continue east along the trail to a junction with the Wellman Cienaga Trail, 1 mile. Turn right (south) and descend the boulder-stacked ridge, through scattered Jeffrey pines, to Saddle Junction. Turn right again (west) and descend the Devils Slide Trail to Humber Park, 2½ miles (see trip 73 for full description).

You should be tired but well satisfied after this long loop through some of the most beautiful mountain country in Southern California.

Tahquitz Ridge from Wellman Cienaga Trail

TRIP: Idyllwild to Deer Springs, Little Round Valley,
72 San Jacinto Peak
18 miles round trip; **5000′** elevation gain
Classification: **Moderate** (2 days)
Season: **June-October**
Topo map: *San Jacinto Peak* (7.5′)

FEATURES

The western slopes of San Jacinto Peak and the long, sinuous ridge of Marion Mountain are blanketed with dense stands of pine, fir and cedar, interspaced here and there with manzanita and chinquapin thickets and, where water seeps to the surface, verdant meadows. The Deer Springs Trail, a popular hikers' route built by the CCC during the 1930s, threads most of the length of this slope, then climbs steeply to within a stone's throw of the summit.

This trip makes use of the Deer Springs Trail to ascend San Jacinto Peak, then loops around and back through Wellmans and Strawberry cienagas on the return. Enroute you pass two trail camps—Strawberry Junction, 3 miles up the trail where the Strawberry Cienaga Trail meets your route, and Little Round Valley, high on a lodgepole-pine-shaded bench under San Jacinto Peak. Water at Little Round Valley until late summer, should be purified before drinking. Choose one for your overnight stay; the next day, climb to the summit for a panorama unsurpassed in Southern California, and circle back via the two cienagas.

DESCRIPTION

From Idyllwild Ranger Station drive west 1 mile on the Banning-Idyllwild Highway (Highway 243) to Idyllwild County Park Visitor Center parking area, just south of the highway.

Cross the highway to the new beginning of the Deer Springs Trail, marked by a wooden sign. Proceed northward up the new section of trail, through alternate stands of oak, Jeffrey pine and manzanita, passing junctions with the Suicide Rock and Strawberry Cienaga trails, to the top of Marion Ridge, 5 miles. Your path now contours and climbs through a dense forest of pine and fir and crosses several trickling streamlets of icy-cold water. You pass junctions with the Marion Mountain Trail (trip 69) and the Seven Pines Trail (trip 68), both leading down to your left, and continue to Deer Springs, 7 miles from the start. There is water here but the trail camp has been closed because of severe overuse. From Deer Springs, the trail climbs 200 yards to a junction with the Fuller Ridge Trail (trip 67). Go right (northeast), up a steep slope covered with manzanita, snow brush and chinquapin, across a marshy bench known as Boggy Meadows, and up to Little Round Valley, 1½ miles from Deer Springs. Here also are plentiful campsites amid lodgepole pine under granite spurs. Water here until late summer, should be purified before drinking. From Little Round Valley, the trail climbs steeply through lodgepoles to a junction with the San Jacinto Peak trail, 1 mile. Turn left and climb past the stone shelter building to the boulder-stacked summit, 300 yards.

After taking in the fabulous view, descend back to the before-mentioned junction. Turn left (southeast) and descend the main trail (see trip 74 for a full description) past Wellmans Cienaga to a junction with the Strawberry Cienaga lateral trail, 3 miles. Turn right (west) on the latter and follow it 2¼ miles through Strawberry Cienaga (see trip 71) to its junction with the Deer Springs Trail. Strawberry Junction Trail Camp is here, with water available from Stone Creek about 100 yards up the Deer Springs Trail. Turn left (south) and descend the Deer Springs Trail to Idyllwild.

TRIP: Humber Park to Saddle Junction, Skunk Cabbage
73 Meadow
6 miles round trip; **1600'** elevation gain
Classification: **Easy**
Season: **June-October**
Topo maps: *San Jacinto Peak, Palm Springs* (both 7.5´)

FEATURES

The Devils Slide Trail is the hikers' main gateway into
the San Jacinto Wilderness. The trail climbs the steep
mountain wall above the head of Strawberry Valley in
long, easy-graded switchbacks, then abruptly crosses the
crest to Saddle Junction, the takeoff point for footpaths
leading in five directions. En route you pass through beautiful stands of oak, pine, cedar and fir, with patches of
manzanita and snow brush just below the top. Three trickling rills — Jolley Spring, Middle Spring and Powderbox
Spring — offer trailside refreshment in early season, but
dry up one by one as summer fades into fall.

The Devils Slide Trail today is a gradual uphill climb, cer-
tainly undeserving of its notorious name. But once it
was quite different. In pioneer days, when Charley Thomas and later Frank Wellman drove cattle up the mountain
to feed on the rich grasses of Tahquitz Valley, it was a
frightful climb. No switchbacks then, just right up the
mountainside, over loose boulders and fallen trees, through
thorny chaparral thickets. Many a cow and even a few
cowboys took a neck-breaking spill on this treacherous
slope, and anyone who knew the Devils Slide then always
remembered it. Since then, the Devils Slide Trail has
been worked and reworked many times, until today it in
no way resembles its historical namesake. In fact, it has
become so gentle now that one wiseacre has suggested the
name be changed to "Angels' Walk."

This rather short trip uses the Devils Slide Trail to offer
a small sampling of the beautiful San Jacinto Wilderness.
You climb to Saddle Junction, then continue a slight
distance to Skunk Cabbage Meadow, an emerald-green
oasis set amid the dark forest. Here is Skunk Cabbage Trail

Camp, with spring water, stoves, and toilet. An overnight stay here is guaranteed to please.

DESCRIPTION

From Idyllwild drive 2 miles up Fern Valley Road to the large parking area in Humber Park.

The trail starts from the top of the parking area, under the shadow of towering Lily Rock. You zigzag up the mountainside through a varied forest of Jeffrey pine, incense cedar, white fir and several species of oak. As you gain elevation, the views south over Strawberry Valley and north across the canyon to the precipitous south slope of Marion Mountain become impressive. In 1¼ miles, a small rivulet coming down from Jolley Spring is passed. The trail then makes a long switchback out across oak- and manzanita-covered slopes and passes minute Middle Spring. The trail then re-enters the pine and fir forest, passes Powderbox Spring, and crosses a low point in the rim to Saddle Junction, 2½ miles. Here, on the heavily-forested tableland, is a 5-way trail fork (see Trips 74, 76, 80 and 81 for particulars). A sign points to the northeast fork as leading to Skunk Cabbage Meadow. Proceed this way, through a lush forest of tall Jeffrey pines with ferns matting the floor, to another junction, ¼ mile. Turn right (south) as indicated by the sign and walk ¼ mile farther to the verdant clearing of Skunk Cabbage Meadow. (Note: take particular care here on this part of the tableland — trails criss-cross in all directions. Fortunately most of them are well marked.)

From Skunk Cabbage Meadow, short exploratory trips are possible to Willow Creek (see trip 76), Tahquitz Valley and Tahquitz Creek (see trip 79). Longer sidetrips are possible to points too numerous to mention here (see trips 74, 80 and 81). Because of its central location, Skunk Cabbage makes an ideal campsite.

Return the way you came.

TRIP: Humber Park to Saddle Junction, Wellmans
74 Cienaga, San Jacinto Peak
15½ **miles** round trip; 4400′ elevation gain
Classification: **Strenuous** (1 day), **mod.** (2 days)
Season: **June-October**
Topo map: *San Jacinto Peak* (7.5′)

FEATURES

When naturalist John Muir stood on the summit and watched the sunrise in 1896, he is said to have exclaimed: "The view from San Jacinto is the most sublime spectacle to be found anywhere on this earth!" Since then, countless others have experienced Muir's inspiration. The vista is utterly magnificent, extending over hundreds of square miles of mountains, foothills, valleys and desert. On the western horizon, beyond row after row of misty-purple ranges, is the glimmering Pacific. Northwest, the gray hogback of San Gorgonio rises grandly across the deep trough of San Gorgonio Pass. Eastward sprawls the drab tawniness of the Colorado Desert and its debris-strewn hills. Southeast lies the shining platter of the Salton Sea and beyond, in the distant haze, is Mexico. But what gives the panorama a final touch of grandeur is the gigantic north rampart, plunging in sheer cliffs and castellated ridges to Coachella Valley, nearly two miles below. It is truly the altar of the Gods!

To the early Indian peoples of Southern California, San Jacinto was a sacred mountain. The Cahuillas knew it as "Aya Kaich," meaning "smooth cliffs," the home of the meteor Dakush, legendary founder of the Cahuilla people. The Luisenos called it "Yamiwa," the Serranos "Sovovo." Even the far-away Gabrielinos revered it as "Jamiwu." The Spanish padres supposedly gave it the name "San Jacinto," after an outlying stock ranch of Mission San Luis Rey, which in turn was named for the 15th century martyr Saint Hyacinth of Silesia. Lt. Robert S. Williamson's Pacific Railroad Survey party passed under its towering face in 1853, mistakenly calling it "San Gorgonio" and misjudging its heights as 6000–7000′. Two years later, Dr. Thomas Antisell of Lt. John G. Parke's railroad survey party corrected

Williamson's error. Antisell's report of 1855 contains the first written reference to the peak as "San Jacinto."

Who made the first ascent of San Jacinto Peak will probably never be known. Most likely it was a Cahuilla hunter, centuries before the arrival of the white man. The earliest climb on record was made in 1874 by a person identified only as "F. of Riverside" (story in San Diego Union of Sep. 16, 1874), who rode a horse up most of the way and scrambled the last 1000 feet on foot. In 1878 the peak was climbed by Lt. George M. Wheeler's U.S. Army survey party, which used the summit for a triangulation station and calculated its height at 10,987' above sea level.

In 1897 Edmund T. Perkins of the United States Geological Survey lugged a 60-pound plane table and theodolite to the top without benefit of trail, and corrected the elevation to 10805'. Perkins' work was amazingly accurate — today's official height, determined by instruments far superior to those he used, is 10804'. The first trail to the summit was forged by the U.S. Coast and Geodetic Survey in 1898 in order to install a heliograph for signaling to parties on other Southern California peaks. This trail was the forerunner of the present Devils Slide-Round Valley-San Jacinto Peak route. Since then, thousands have made the ascent via this trail and other footpaths constructed by the CCC during the mid-1930s. The stone shelter cabin just below the summit was built by the CCC in 1936.

This trip takes the most direct and the most traveled route from Idyllwild to the summit. It is an arduous 7¾-mile pull, but one of the most scenic and rewarding mountain paths in Southern California. You climb rock-ribbed slopes, cross chaparral thickets, pass through dense forest, and pause at bubbling springs. The higher you climb, the more glorious the vista. Half way up, high on the mountainside, you pass a spot of lush grasses ribboned with trickling rills of icy water. This is Wellmans Cienaga, named for Frank Wellman, a part Irish and part English character who herded cattle on the mountain in the 1890s. Beyond Wellmans you enter a world of weather-toughened lodgepole, sky-piercing granite crests, and thin cold air — the alpine rooftop of Southern California.

DESCRIPTION

From Idyllwild drive 2 miles up Fern Valley Road to the large parking area in Humber Park.

Climb the Devils Slide Trail, which starts at the top of the parking area, to Saddle Junction, 2½ miles (see Trip 73 for details). At Saddle Junction, take the leftmost trail, leading north and marked by a sign indicating *San Jacinto Peak*. You climb, through a forest of Jeffrey pine and white fir, up the bouldered ridge that forms the northeast wall of the Strawberry Valley amphitheater. Views into the valley and across to Lily Rock and Tahquitz Peak are impressive. The trail then winds along the mountainside to a junction with the lateral trail to Strawberry Cienaga (see Trip 71), 2 miles from Saddle Junction.

Continue straight ahead (north), through lodgepole pine and white fir. The footpath rounds the head of Willow Creek to the grassy patch of Wellmans Cienaga, ⅔ mile. Here is the last running water before the summit. Beyond Wellmans, you climb through thickets of manzanita and chinquapin to Wellman Divide, ½ mile, high on the ridge between Round and Tahquitz valleys. Here is a trail junction — left to the summit, right to Round Valley. If you're doing the climb in one day, go left. (If it's a two-day venture, your best overnight camp is in Round Valley — go right and descend to Round Valley Trail Camp, 1 mile.) Going the summit route (left), the trail climbs through a silent forest of lodgepole pine, then makes a long switchback up the southeast slope of San Jacinto Peak, through dense chinquapin and manzanita, to the ridgetop between Jean and San Jacinto peaks, 2 miles. Here you meet the abandoned trail coming up from the Tamarack and Round valleys. Go left, continuing up the mountain. You now make a long switchback up the southeast slope of San Jacinto Peak, through dense chinquapin and manzanita, to the ridgetop between Jean and San Jacinto peaks, 1 mile. Here you meet the San Jacinto Peak trail. (The main trail continues down to Little Round Valley and Deer Springs — see trip 72). Turn right and climb through an open lodgepole forest, past the stone shelter cabin, to the boulder-strewn summit, 1/5 mile.

Return the same way. Or take the roundabout route back through Round Valley and across Hidden Lake Divide (see trip 76). With a 2-mile car shuttle, descend the Deer Springs Trail to Idyllwild (see trip 72). Or take the aerial tramway down to Palm Springs with an across-the-range car shuttle (see trip 77).

Old Greyback from Mt. San Jacinto

TRIP: Humber Park to Saddle Junction, Wellmans
75 Cienaga, Jean Peak, Marion Mountain, Idyllwild
16 miles round trip; **4600′** elevation gain
Classification: **Strenuous**
Season: **June-October**
Topo map: *San Jacinto Peak* (7.5′)

FEATURES

Edmund Taylor Perkins had a special way of immortalizing the women in his life. He named mountains for them. When the tall, good-looking topographer came into the San Jacintos in 1897 to map the range for the U.S. Geological Survey, he met a young school teacher camped with friends near today's Pine Cove. She was Marion Kelly of White Cloud, Michigan, described as "a wonderful woman, blue eyes, and a gentle nature." She was employed by the Indian Bureau at the Morongo Valley Reservation. The story goes that Miss Kelly fell deeply in love with Perkins, but he kept putting her off by saying he was married to his work. But he did think enough of the young woman to place her name on a nearby mountain peak — Marion Mountain. Another young lady was in Perkins' mind too, one he had met previously while surveying in northern California. She was Jean Waters of Plumas County, California. He put her name on the neighboring mountain — Jean Peak. Marion was destined to be disappointed. Jean was more fortunate; she and Edmund Perkins were married in 1903.

No trails reach to the twin summits of white granite that eternalize the memory of these two young women. To reach them, you must scramble across jumbo boulders and, in the case of Marion, climb a short but rather precipitous summit block. This loop trip is only for those in top condition and experienced in cross-country travel.

DESCRIPTION

Leave one car at the beginning of the Deer Springs Trail, at the entrance to Idyllwild County Park Visitor Center, on State

Highway 243 1 mile west of Idyllwild. Drive the other car to
Humber Park, 2 miles up Fern Valley Road from Idyllwild.

Take the Devils Slide Trail to Saddle Junction, then the
San Jacinto Peak Trail to the point where it reaches the
ridge-top just south of San Jacinto Peak, 7½ miles (see
trip 74 for details). Leave the trail here and scramble across
boulders, south along the ridge, through an open lodgepole
forest. You drop 100' to a saddle, then ascend 300' to the
pile of white granite that marks the 10560' summit of Jean
Peak. After signing the Sierra Club summit register, continue down the ridge, south, then southwest, over an inter-
mediate unnamed bump to the granite outcropping that
is the summit of 10332' Marion Mountain. The granite
block is not difficult, but climb with care. After signing
in here, continue down the ridge, curving west, through
some brush, to the Deer Springs Trail. (Note: do not try
to descend southeast to Wellmans Cienaga or south to the
Strawberry Cienaga Trail from Marion Mountain — you
will become tangled in dense, thorny chaparral.) Follow
the Deer Springs Trail 4 miles south to Idyllwild County Park
Visitor Center.

Alternatives to avoid a car shuttle are two: climb back
over Jean Peak to the San Jacinto Peak Trail and descend
the way you came; or drop southwest down the ridge from
Marion Mountain to the Deer Springs Trail, then take the
Strawberry Cienaga lateral trail (see trip 71) back to the
San Jacinto Peak Trail below Wellmans Cienaga. Both of
these options add about 4 miles to the total hiking mileage.

Hidden Lake

TRIP: Humber Park to Saddle Junction, Willow Creek,
Round Valley, Wellmans Cienaga

76

15 miles round trip; **3600′** elevation gain
Classification: **Moderate** (2 days)
Season: **June-October**
Topo map: *San Jacinto Peak* (7.5′)

FEATURES

Southeast from San Jacinto's lofty crown, nestled in high hanging valleys ringed by jagged spurs of white granite, is an enchanting wonderland of green. Here, suspended 8000′ above the desert, pines and firs grow tall and sturdy, lush meadows are waist-high with fern and azalea, lupines spot hillsides in their late-summer bloom of purple and pale mauve, and little singing streams flow clear and cold. In the heart of this high sylvan wilderness is Round Valley, an oval meadow of verdant grass, threaded by an icy-cold brook, surrounded by a dense forest of lodgepole pine. Here is the most popular trail camp in the San Jacinto high country, frequented by dozens of knapsackers almost ever summer and early fall weekend.

This trip makes a broad loop through this inviting wilderness beneath the high peaks, with an overnight stop in Round Valley. The entire hike is on good trail and can be done in one long day, if you're in a monumental hurry. But it's a much more enjoyable trip if you take the full two days and savor this superb bit of sylvan grandeur high on the rugged shoulder of the San Jacintos.

DESCRIPTION

From Idyllwild drive 2 miles up Fern Valley Road to the large parking area in Humber Park.

Climb the Devils Slide Trail, which starts at the top of the parking area, to Saddle Junction, 2½ miles (see trip 73 for details). At Saddle Junction take the trail fork leading northeast, marked *Willow Creek* and *Long Valley.* The 1½-mile walk to Willow Creek Trail Camp passes through a forest garden of ferns shaded by tall Jeffrey pines, passing a side trail leading south to Skunk Cabbage Meadow. Here, on a forested bench above the stream, is Willow Creek Trail Camp. Beyond, the trail starts climbing northeastward, and in ½ mile it reaches a junction with a new lateral trail down to Laws Camp and Tahquitz Valley. Continue straight ahead and within minutes arrive at the boundary of Mount San Jacinto State Wilderness, marked by a handsome sign. (California State Park signs are usually done in a more artistic manner than Forest Service signs.)

The trail continues to climb higher on the south slope of the rocky divide overlooking Tahquitz Creek, with splendid vistas over the latter and beyond to the desert and the Santa Rosa Mountains. About 2¼ miles from Willow Creek, the trail makes several switchbacks and reaches Hidden Lake Divide. Just beyond, leading east, is the presently closed lateral trail to Hidden Lake and Desert View. The little lake, just above the escarpment, has suffered from overuse and needs time to recuperate, so please do not visit it. Continue north on the main trail. In ¼ mile you reach a junction with the trail leading northeast to Long Valley and the upper tramway terminal, 1 mile. Go left (northwest)—the sign indicates *Round Valley 2 miles.* The trail contours through lodgepole pines, along the north slope of the divide overlooking Long Valley, passes a junction with the other end of the loop trail from Long Valley and the tramway, and reaches the lush green meadow of Round Valley. Here, on both sides of the valley, are many lodgepole-shaded camping spots.

For the return trip, take the trail that leads west, upstream; a sign indicates *Wellmans Junction 1 mile.* You climb 1 mile through lodgepoles, verdant grasses and lupine to a junction with the San Jacinto Peak Trail. Turn left (southwest) and descend the trail through Wellmans Cienaga to Saddle Junction, 3⅓ miles (see trip 74 for details). Then take the Devils Slide Trail down to Humber Park.

TRIP: Palm Springs Aerial Tramway to Long, Round and
77 Tamarack Valleys
5 miles round trip; **600'** elevation gain
Classification: **Easy**
Season: **May-October**
Topo map: *San Jacinto Peak* (7.5')

FEATURES

From lower Chino Canyon, just above Palm Springs, the spectacular Palm Springs Aerial Tramway hauls visitors from palms to pines in a matter of a few short minutes. For hikers, this is the easy way to enter Mount San Jacinto State Park. From 8516' Mountain Station, the tramway's upper terminus, trails lead into the heart of the high wilderness.

This pleasant trip takes the wooded trail through upper Long Valley to the beautiful, though overused, green oasis of Round Valley. You can enjoy a picnic lunch along the crystal stream in Round Valley or under the tamarack (really lodgepole pines) in Tamarack Valley.

DESCRIPTION

From State Highway 111 at the northern edge of Palm Springs, turn west up Tramway Road and drive 2 miles to Valley Station, the lower terminus of the tramway. The tramway operates daily, starting at 10 a.m. M-F, 8 a.m. Sat., Sun. and holidays. Check for time of last return. Ride the tramway to Mountain Station, the upper terminus just above Long Valley.

From Mountain Station, proceed down the cement walkway into the Long Valley picnic area, then take the trail leading west, next to the ranger station, marked *Round Valley 2 miles.* Follow the well-graded footpath as it leads up Long Valley Creek, through a rich forest of sugar pine and white fir. After a mile the trail veers left (southwest) and climbs into a lodgepole forest. In another ¾ mile, you junction with the Hidden Lake Divide-Willow Creek-Saddle Junction Trail (see trip 76); continue west ¼ mile to Round Valley. Here is a well-used campground and a three-way trail junction. Turn right (north)—the sign indicates *Tamarack Valley*. You pass the trail camp and wind through a lodgepole forest to the grassy clearing of Tamarack Valley and its small trail camp, ½ mile. Across the valley, dominating the skyline, is the needlelike summit of Cornell Peak (named for Cornell University of Ithaca, New York, alma mater of Robert T. Hill, geologist for the USGS mapping party of 1897–98). Don't climb it unless you're an experienced mountaineer.

Return the way you came. (Note: The old trail from Tamarack Valley northwest to San Jacinto Peak has been closed to travel to protect a sensitive deer fawning area.)

TRIP: Palm Springs Aerial Tramway to Long Valley,
78 Round Valley, San Jacinto Peak
11½ miles round trip; **2300′** elevation gain
Classification: **Moderate**
Season: **June-October**
Topo map: *San Jacinto Peak* (7.5′)

FEATURES

The Palm Springs Aerial Tramway gives the hiker a 6000′ head start on this desert-side route to San Jacinto Peak, leaving him just 2300′ to gain on foot. And this route climbs through some of the most verdant and inviting high country in the range—all on good, well-marked trail. You visit lush Round Valley, then ascend granite slopes dotted with lodgepole pines to the summit with the best view in southern California.

DESCRIPTION

From State Highway 111 at the northern edge of Palm Springs, turn west up Tramway Road and drive 2 miles to Valley Station, the lower terminus of the tramway. The tram is now open daily starting at 10 a.m. Monday through Friday, and at 8 a.m. Saturdays, Sundays and holidays. It runs every half hour. Check to find out time of last return, usually shortly after sundown. Ride the tramway to Mountain Station, the upper terminus just above Long Valley.

From Mountain Station, proceed to Round Valley, 2 miles (see Trip 77 for details). From Round Valley, your last dependable water, ascend the trail west—the sign indicates *San Jacinto Peak*. You climb steadily through an open lodgepole forest to a junction with the Saddle Junction–San Jacinto Peak Trail, 1 mile. Turn right (north) and follow the well-used trail through the silent lodgepoles, then up a long switchback through dense manzanita and chinquapin, to the south ridge of San Jacinto Peak. Here you intersect the summit trail. Go right (north) and climb past the stone shelter building to the top, 300 yards.

Return the same way.

Note: The old trail, which cut a good 2 miles off the round trip from Long Valley to San Jacinto Peak, went from Round Valley north through Tamarack Valley and then up to a junction with the Saddle Junction-San Jacinto Peak Trail at what was once known as Wellman's Junction, a mile short of the peak. The section of the old trail from Round Valley to Tamarack Valley is now open, and camping is again permitted at the latter. However, the section from Tamarack Valley to Wellman's Junction is overgrown with chinquapin, and State Park authorities have not yet removed the brush debris blocking both ends. Whether that section of historic trail will ever be officially reopened remains to be seen. (Check with San Jacinto State Park authorities.)

TRIP: Humber Park to Saddle Junction, Tahquitz Val-
ley, Little Tahquitz Valley
79
9 miles round trip; **1700′** elevation gain
Classification: **Moderate**
Season: **June-October**
Topo maps: *San Jacinto Peak, Palm Springs* (both 7.5′)

FEATURES

Close under the granite spurs of Tahquitz Peak, nestled
in a shallow bowl floored with forest and lush green meadow, is Tahquitz Valley. For the lover of pure sylvan beauty,
this is the best the San Jacintos have to offer. Ferns and
azaleas grow waist-high amid emerald grassland. Lemon
liles, crimson penstemon, purple lupine and creamy but-
tercups add an enchanting dash of brilliance during early-
summer bloom. Springs bubble up cool clear water, and a
musical creek threads the valley floor. Surrounding this
mountain garden are dense stands of pine and fir.

Years ago, cowboys herded cattle up the notorious
Devils Slide and into Tahquitz Valley to feed on the rich
grasses. Frank Wellman is said to have built the first cabin
here back in the 1890s. But the cattle have been gone for
half a century and the old cabin has been removed, and
nature's pristine beauty once again reigns in this lovely
mountain basin.

This trip climbs the Devils Slide Trail and drops into this
sylvan sanctuary. You can do it in one day, picnicking in the
green, flower-bedecked turf, or make it a leisurely two-day
jaunt, staying the night in one of the camping zones,
indicated by yellow posts, in Tahquitz Valley.

DESCRIPTION

From Idyllwild drive 2 miles up Fern Valley Road to the
large parking area in Humber Park.

Climb the Devils Slide Trail, which starts at the top of the
parking area, to Saddle Junction, 2½ miles (see trip 73 for
details). At Saddle Junction, take the trail leading right
(southeast), marked by a sign indicating *Tahquitz Valley*.
Proceed ¾ mile through the forest of Jeffrey pine and

white fir to Tahquitz Valley. Here is the Tahquitz Valley camping zone, with yellow posts indicating where you may camp. Water is always available here. Stop here or proceed ¼ mile farther south, going right at a trail fork, to Little Tahquitz Valley and its camping zone. There's water here also. A left turn at the before-mentioned junction takes you to Reeds Meadow camping zone, with water from the stream. The water needs to be purified before drinking.

If you are making Tahquitz Valley your base camp and staying awhile, several interesting sidetrips are possible. You can climb by good trail to Tahquitz Peak Lookout (see trip 81). You can descend Tahquitz Creek to Laws Camp and Caramba (see trip 80), also on good trail. You can walk a short distance north to Skunk Cabbage Meadow (see trip 73). Or you can scramble cross-country up Red Tahquitz for a breathtaking view of the Desert Divide country (see trip 85).

Return the same way. An option is to take the trail to the roadhead above Saunders Meadow (see trip 83).

Lily Rock

TRIP: Humber Park to Saddle Junction, Tahquitz Valley,

80

Laws Camp, Caramba
13½ miles round trip; **3300′** elevation gain
Classification: **Moderate**
Season: **June-October**
Topo maps: *San Jacinto Peak, Palm Springs* (both 7.5′)

FEATURES

Eastward from Tahquitz Valley, Tahquitz Creek descends in little tumbling cascades and swirling rapids for three meandering miles, then plunges abruptly off the eastern precipice to die in the thirsty sands of the desert. As the creek loses elevation, the character of the vegetation changes. Emerald grasses, ferns and flowering herbs gradually give way to willow thickets and clumps of bitter cherry and nettle. The adjacent forest cover changes too, from dense stands of white fir and Jeffrey pine to sparse Jeffreys and finally to hardy pinyon pine.

Winding through the Tahquitz Creek basin, from Tahquitz Valley through Laws Camp to the sudden dropoff just past Caramba, is a well-beaten trail, a pathway through some of the wildest high country in the range.

Laws Camp, near the junction of Willow and Tahquitz creeks, commemorates writer George Law, who built a cabin of shale rock with a ramada-type roof near here about 1916. Every summer for years, Law and his "little donkeys with their tinkering bells" would pack in to enjoy nature's solitude and find inspiration for his newspaper and magazine articles. The remains of his old cabin are still here, hidden on a rocky spur several hundred yards above Willow Creek.

Caramba is a little-used Spanish word meaning strange or unusual. The story goes that many years ago some cowboys camping here were terrified by weird sounds during the night and gave the place this unusual name.

This trip climbs over the Devils Slide and drops down Tahquitz Creek to the small trail camps at Laws and Caramba. Just past the latter, you are rewarded with a breathtaking vista over the desert. If you like your mountains primitive and unpeopled, this outing should suit your taste.

DESCRIPTION

From Idyllwild drive 2 miles up Fern Valley Road to the large parking area in Humber Park.

Climb the Devils Slide Trail, which starts at the top of the parking area, to Saddle Junction, 2½ miles (see trip 73 for details). At Saddle Junction take the trail leading right (southeast), marked *Tahquitz Valley* and *Laws-Caramba*. Proceed ¾ mile through forests of pine and fir to Tahquitz Valley. In the valley take the trail forking left (northeast), marked *Laws* and *Caramba*. The trail proceeds above the north bank of Tahquitz Creek, dropping 400′ in 1½ miles to Laws Camp, a small forested camping zone alongside Willow Creek. A lateral trail leads north from here to connect with the main Humber Park-Round Valley Trail (Trip 76), 1 mile. Beyond Laws, your trail follows the north slope high above Tahquitz Creek, then drops to Caramba, another small camping zone just above the eastern precipice—1000′ loss in 2 miles from Laws. Just east of Caramba, you can scramble onto some large rock outcroppings for superb views over the desert face of the San Jacintos. But do not try to descend the precipice or Tahquitz Creek to the desert—many have become lost or injured trying. The Gordon Trail once went this way (see Appendix II), but it has not been maintained for 40 years, and is almost impossible to follow now.

Return the way you came.

Laws Cabin, 1920s   *Charles Van Fleet*

TRIP: Humber Park to Saddle Junction, Chinquapin Flat,
81   Tahquitz Peak Lookout
         8½ miles round trip; **2400′** elevation gain
         Classification: **Moderate**
         Season: **June-October**
         Topo maps: *San Jacinto Peak, Palm Springs* (both 7.5′)

FEATURES

8828′ Tahquitz Peak is the southern citadel of the San
Jacinto high country. Its granite spurs and steep battlements rise impressively above Strawberry Valley on one
side and Tahquitz Valley on the other. From the Forest
Service lookout on its summit, you are rewarded with
breathtaking panoramas over the southern half of the San
Jacintos, with the Santa Rosas on the distant skyline.

Tahquitz Peak is named for the powerful evil demon
of Cahuilla legend, who allegedly lived in a cave below
the peak and came out at night to terrorize and devour
Indians who ventured too close to his sacred mountain.
The summit lookout tower, held up by steel beams, was
built in 1938 to replace a more primitive wooden structure
built around 1918. It is manned during fire season, usually
June-November.

As of this writing (June 1999), however, the lookout tower
is closed.

DESCRIPTION

From Idyllwild drive 2 miles up Fern Valley Road to the
large parking area in Humber Park.

Climb the Devils Slide Trail 2½ miles to Saddle Junction (see trip 73). At Saddle Junction take the far-right trail
leading south, marked *Tahquitz Peak*. In 1¼ miles through
the forest, you reach Chinquapin Flat junction — covered,
as the name implies, with a thick mantle of bush chinquapin. Go right again (southwest) and follow the trail up
through chinquapin, lodgepole pine and a few limber pine
to the summit lookout, ½ mile.

Return the same way, or take the South Ridge Trail
down (trip 84).

TRIP: Humber Park to Lily Rock

82
2 miles round trip; **1500'** elevation gain
Classification: **Moderate**
Season: **May-October**
Topo map: *San Jacinto Peak* (7.5´)

FEATURES

If you're starting up the Devils Slide Trail some summer weekend, chances are good that you'll hear faint shouts such as "On belay," "Climbing," "Off belay," and sometimes, "Falling." If you glance upward, you may be able to spot tiny, antlike figures clinging to vertical walls, now and then inching ahead with patience and care. These are rock-climbers testing their skill on the Yosemitelike dome of Lily Rock. Climbers prefer to call it by the more masculine-sounding name of Tahquitz Rock, but whatever you use, there is no doubt that this sheer-walled granite monolith offers the best technical climbing in Southern California. Almost every rock-climber in this part of the state has, at one time or other, improved his skill here.

The front walls of Lily Rock are no place for anyone not trained in climbing techniques. But for hikers who want to climb this striking natural feature, there is an easy route up the back side. This trip follows a very steep trail from Humber Park up and around to a saddle between Lily Rock and the serrated ridge leading to Tahquitz Peak; from here it is a short scramble to the summit. Lug-soled boots should be worn.

DESCRIPTION

From Idyllwild drive 2 miles up Fern Valley Road to the bottom of the parking area in Humber Park.

Take the prominent footpath marked *Scenic Trail* that leaves the southeast edge of the parking area and runs directly below Lily Rock. In ¼ mile turn left on a narrow, unmarked trail that leads steeply up the slope towards the rock. The trail zigzags up the hillside, keeping just to the right of the prominent rockslide that extends down from the center of the rock. After 700' of climbing, you reach what climbers call Lunch Rock, at the foot of many of the climbing routes. To your right (southeast) notice a worn pathway leading around the bottom of Lily Rock. Follow this trail — used by climbers descending from the rock — around the west face and steeply up the back side to the saddle between Lily Rock and the broken ridge leading up to Tahquitz Peak. From this saddle, scramble up easy granite ledges and slopes to the bald summit.

After taking in the fabulous view of Strawberry Valley and the high surrounding ridges, descend exactly the same way. Any other route is very dangerous.

Lily Rock, climbers' playground   *Louise Werner*

TRIP: Saunders Meadow to Humber Park

83 2½ miles one way; 300' elevation gain
Classification: **Easy**
Season: **May-October**
Topo maps: *Idyllwild, San Jacinto Peak* (both 7.5´)

FEATURES

This is an ideal family trip — level most of the way. The Ernie Maxwell Scenic Trail, named for the late Idyllwild conservationist and former editor of the *Town Crier*, contours along the mountainside above Strawberry Valley from Saunders Meadow to Humber Park. This easygoing footpath lives up to its name, winding through rich stands of pine, fir and oak, with superb vistas over the densely wooded valley to the granite spurs of Marion Ridge. In spring wildflowers add a beautiful sprinkling of color, It is a fitting introduction to the Idyllwild country.

DESCRIPTION

From the south edge of Idyllwild, drive up Saunders Meadow Road past Desert Sun School, turning left on Pine Avenue, then right on Tahquitz View Drive, passing the South Fork Trail road junction, to the beginning of the *Ernie Maxwell Scenic Trail*, so marked by a small sign to the right of the road, 1½ miles. Parking is limited to a few wide spots along the road. You finish at Humber Park, so have someone meet you there or employ a car shuttle.

Follow the well-built trail as it winds along the slope through beautiful forest. It is mostly level going, with gentle ups and downs here and there. The prominent feature ahead is Lily Rock, which looms more massively as you get nearer. The final ½ mile is gentle uphill, with 2 switchbacks just before reaching Humber Park.

You can do this trail the other way — from Humber Park to Tahquitz View Drive — even more easily.

TRIP: South Ridge Road to Tahquitz Peak Lookout

84

8 miles round trip; **2000'** elevation gain
Classification: **Moderate**
Season: **June-October**
Topo maps: *Idyllwild, San Jacinto Peak* (both 7.5´)

FEATURES

This trail trip climbs the steep south ridge to Tahquitz Peak, zigzagging up through stands of Jeffrey pine, white fir and live oak, with chinquapin thickets and lodgepole pine near the top. Various points along the trail offer far-reaching vistas south over the Desert Divide country, and northwest over Strawberry Valley to Marion Mountain and its rocky spurs. The trail has been recently rebuilt with easy grades, replacing the old, steep footpath up from Keen Camp. Old-timers would hardly recognize it now.

DESCRIPTION

From the south edge of Idyllwild, drive up Saunders Meadow Road past Desert Sun School. Turn left on Pine Avenue, right on Tahquitz View Drive, and then right again up South Ridge Road to the South Ridge Trail, marked by a wooden sign, 2½ miles from Idyllwild.

Follow the trail as it climbs to the ridge crest, then zigzags up the divide through rich forest. In 1¼ miles you reach a flat area laced with jumbo boulders — halfway, a good rest stop. Beyond, you climb steeply through chinquapin thickets and scattered lodgepoles, between granite gendarmes, to the summit lookout, 2½ miles from the start.

After taking in the fabulous panorama over the southern half of the San Jacintos, descend the way you came. An option, with car shuttle, is to descend the Tahquitz Peak Trail to Saddle Junction, then go down the Devils Slide Trail to Humber Park (see trip 81).

TRIP: Humber Park to Tahquitz Valley, Pacific Crest
Trail over Desert Divide to Apple Canyon
85 **16.6 miles** one way; **2800'** elevation gain
Classification: **Strenuous** (1 day), **Mod.** (2 days)
Season: **May-October**
Topo maps: *San Jacinto Peak, Palm Springs, Palm View Peak* (all 7.5´)

FEATURES

South from Red Tahquitz Peak runs an extremely rugged mountain backbone known as the Desert Divide, separating the high basin of Garner Valley from the desert-draining palm canyons to the east. The northern part of this backbone — from Red Tahquitz south to Antsell Rock — contains some of the wildest, most inaccessible mountain terrain in Southern California. Until the Pacific Crest Trail was carved through here in 1977, only the crude Sam Fink route penetrated this wall of granite spurs and saddles, brush-choked slopes and forested ledges.

The late Sam Fink, former Santa Ana fire captain whose avocation was mountaineering, was a living legend among Southern California hikers. One of his exploits was to build a trail along this forboding mountain ridge. In 1967 Sam went up, by himself, with a saw and pruner and spent three days on the ridge, cutting brush and marking a route with red tags. This became known as "The Sam Fink Trail" and remained a hikers' route until the new stretch of the Pacific Crest Trail was cut and blasted through in 1977.

According to the Idyllwild district ranger, this stretch of Pacific Crest Trail over the Desert Divide was the most difficult route to survey and construct in all of Southern California. Parts of it had to literally be carved out of granite walls by tedious drilling and blasting. The job required three years of strenuous effort.

The result is one of the best engineered trails in California. A broad pathway and gentle switchbacks take the place of the steep, sometimes exposed, tedious scrambling of the old Sam Fink route. This trail trip takes the hiker over the northern, more spectacular section of the new footpath, from Tahquitz Valley to the Apache Peak-Spitler Peak saddle.

You can do it in one long, strenuous day, or, better, stay the night in Tahquitz or Little Tahquitz Valley and enjoy two days in this premier mountain wilderness country.

DESCRIPTION

The trip requires a car shuttle. Drive one car to the Humber Park parking area, 2 miles up Fern Valley Road from Idyllwild. Either park another car or arrange to be picked up at the Spitler Peak trailhead in Apple Canyon. To reach the latter, drive south on State Highway 74 3½ miles from Mountain Center to Apple Canyon Road; turn left and go 2½ miles to a parking area on your right, just south of the signed trailhead.

From Humber Park, take the Devils Slide Trail to Saddle Junction (see Trip 73 for details). Here you reach a 5-way trail junction. Follow the Caramba Trail southeast (2nd from the right) to the edge of Tahquitz Valley to a second trail junction, then right (south) across Tahquitz Meadow and Creek to Little Tahquitz Valley, 1¼ miles from Saddle Junction. If you are making this a two-day trip, there are camping zones in both Tahquitz Meadow and Little Tahquitz valleys, with water that needs to be treated. To continue, proceed south up the Little Tahquitz Trail to its junction with the Pacific Crest Trail. Be certain to fill your canteens in Tahquitz or Little Tahquitz Creek; this is the last water until Apache Spring, 8½ miles south.

Turn left (east) and follow the broad, well-graded PCT as it contours and climbs along the north slope of Red Tahquitz, through an open forest of lodgepole pine and white fir, then abruptly turns south around the east shoulder of the peak. Panoramic views open to the east, down over Andreas and Murray canyons to the deep trench of Palm Canyon and the desert beyond. Although much of the vegetation here was burned in the 1980 Palm Canyon Fire, it is steadily growing back. Your trail gradually descends southward along the east slope of what is known as the Desert Divide, reaching a saddle between Red Tahquitz and South peaks, where you pass among the jagged granite crags with alternating views west to Garner Valley and Lake Hemet and east to the desert. The trail then climbs around the east flank of South Peak and drops in long, majestic switchbacks to the precipitous rock ridge north of Antsell Rock. Except for the fire-scarred areas, the scenery here is more befitting the Sierra Nevada than Southern California. You pass well below the crags, traverse under the east face of Antsell Rock, and contour through a charred forest of bigcone spruce, white fir, and black oak to Apple Canyon Saddle. An old trail drops down Apple Canyon from here, but you don't take it; it has been closed because it traverses private property. Staying on the PCT, you climb the blackened slopes of Apache Peak, traverse around the east flanks a few hundred feet below the bare summit, and reach a junction with the Apache Spring Trail. The spring, which usually has water, is 1 mile down to your left (east). Continue south on the PCT down to the saddle between Apache and Spitler peaks. Here you can leave the PCT and turn west, descending the Spitler Peak Trail to Apple Canyon Road (see Trip 86 for full description), where your transportation should be waiting.

An option is to continue south on the PCT to Fobes Saddle, then right, down the Fobes Trail (4E02), to the Fobes Canyon Roadhead (see Trip 88). This option adds 1¼ miles to the trip.

TRIP: Apple Canyon to Desert Divide, Antsell Rock

86
12 miles round trip; **2600'** elevation gain
Classification: **Strenuous**
Season: **All year**
Topo maps: *Idyllwild, Palm View Peak* (both 7.5´)

FEATURES

7720' Antsell Rock is the crowning feature of the Desert
Divide. Its imposing knob of multicolored rock can be
seen from almost anywhere in Garner Valley. Antsell Rock
is one of the very few peaks in the San Jacintos whose
ascent involves more than a plodding walk up. Its nearly
vertical upper ramparts give you a taste of the alpinist's
exhilaration. It's what climbers call a "fun peak."

The peak was named by U.S.G.S. topographer Edmund
Perkins in 1897–98. The story goes that Perkins ran across
an artist painting mountain scenes at Keen Camp, an early-
day resort just east of Mountain Center. The artist's name
was Antsell and the mountain he was painting was this
imposing rock knob, so Perkins labeled the knob "Antsell
Rock" on his survey map.

The climb is not particularly difficult for those in good
physical condition who have had experience on Class 3
rock. Lug-soled boots for traction on rock are strongly
recommended. Take extra care on the descent, for that is
when most accidents occur.

The old direct route up Apple Canyon to the Desert
Divide, so long the nemesis of property owners in the
upper canyon, is no longer open to hikers. You must now
use the newly rerouted Spitler Peak Trail (3E22) from
lower Apple Canyon, making the trip 2 miles longer each
way.

The terrible Palm Canyon fire of 1980 burned right up
Andreas and Murray canyons to the Desert Divide.
Fortunately, the brush is growing high and green again, but
for part of the way from Apache Peak to Antsell Rock you
walk through a ghost forest of blackened trunks.

DESCRIPTION

From State Highway 74, 3½ miles south of Mountain Center, turn left (northeast) onto Apple Canyon Road and follow it 2½ miles to the Spitler Peak trailhead, marked by a small wooden sign, on your right. A large parking area is just south of the trailhead. (Note: do not continue to the private ranches at road's end.)

Follow the newly rerouted trail east, through oak and high chaparral, then northeast up the rock-ribbed slopes of Apple Canyon's east fork. You pass through open groves of Jeffrey and Coulter pine and the ubiquitous live oak as you climb steadily to the Apache Peak-Spitler Peak saddle on the Desert Divide and a junction with the Pacific Crest Trail, 4 miles.

Turn left (north) and follow the PCT up and around the east and north flanks of bare Apache Peak, passing a side trail that drops down the desert slope to Apache Spring, and then down 200 vertical feet to Apple Canyon saddle. (The old trail down Apple Canyon joins the PCT here.) Continue north on the PCT through a forest of black oak, white fir and Jeffrey pine until it traverses the slope almost directly underneath and east of Antsell Rock. Here you must look carefully for a small duck and a climber's rough path leading steeply up the gully to your left. Leave the PCT and follow this route up unstable slopes to the top of the divide immediately southeast of Antsell Rock's summit block. The final 100 feet to the top is class 3 and not recommended for inexperienced hikers. To continue, scramble to the top of the large rock outcropping to your right, then step across and friction-climb the sloping granite to a steep, narrow gully. Follow the gully to the summit ridge, and on to the summit. Some may desire a rope belay on these final pitches.

Return the same way.

TRIP: Apple Canyon to Desert Divide, Apache Peak,
87 Apache Spring
12.2 miles round trip; **2600′** elevation gain
Classification: **Moderate**
Season: **All year**
Topo maps: *Idyllwild, Palm View Peak* (both 7.5′)

FEATURES

This trip climbs Apache Peak (7567′) for a superb vista over the southern end of the San Jacintos and the desert canyons, then drops over the desert side to secluded Apache Spring. You follow the newly rerouted Spitler Peak Trail to the Desert Divide, then ascend the Pacific Crest Trail to the southeast slope of Apache Peak. Steep but clearly discernible lateral trails take you first up to the summit of Apache Peak and then down to Apache Spring, both recovering from the 1980 Palm Canyon fire.

DESCRIPTION

Follow the driving directions for Trip 86.

Take the Spitler Peak Trail from lower Apple Canyon up to the Desert Divide and a junction with the Pacific Crest Trail (see Trip 86 for details). Turn left (north) and follow the PCT up to an unmarked but clearly discernible trail junction, ¾ mile. Here you leave the PCT and scramble up a steep, rocky path to the bare summit of Apache Peak and its far-reaching vistas, ¼ mile. Return the same way to the PCT, then take the lateral trail leading east and then northeast 500 vertical feet down the desert slope to Apache Spring. The little wooded spring (burned over in 1980 but growing back) always flows cold and clear, although in dry months it's reduced to a trickle.

Return the same way.

TRIP: Fobes Canyon to Fobes Saddle, Palm View Peak

88   **7 miles** round trip; **2200´** elevation gain
Classification: **Moderate**
Season: **all year**
Topo map: *Palm View Peak* (7.5´)

FEATURES

South from Apache Peak the Desert Divide gradually
descends and loses its rugged character. Following along the
crest of the long backbone from Apache south 13 miles to the
head of Bull Canyon is the Desert Divide Trail, a hiker's
avenue through waist-high chaparral and occasional clusters of
fir and oak, with far-reaching views in all directions.

The Desert Divide country, particularly the southern half, is
not well known to hikers, partly because it is overshadowed by
the nearby San Jacinto Wilderness, partly because so many of
its access roads are blocked by locked gates. But it offers great
opportunities for hiking and knapsacking trips, particularly in
the fall-winter-spring season when the high country to the
north is closed by snow. Sample it sometime; you won't be disappointed.

This trip utilizes a new access to the Desert Divide Trail
(PCT) from Fobes Canyon, formerly blocked to public access
by a locked gate and the private property of Fobes Ranch. The
new trail (4E02) lies just east of the ranch boundary and offers
easy access to Fobes Saddle, a low gap on the long Desert
Divide. From the saddle, you climb southeast on the view-rich
PCT to Palm View Peak. The panoramas are magnificent in all
directions — the tawny Coachella Valley to the east, Garner
and Anza valleys to the west, and on the northern skyline the
San Jacinto high country, covered by its snowy mantle until
spring turns to summer.

DESCRIPTION

From State Highway 74, 7 miles south of Mountain Center,
turn left (northeast) onto Fobes Ranch Road (6S05) and follow
it across Garner Valley and up to a junction in 3½ miles. The
main road goes north to Fobes Ranch (private); you turn right
and proceed 0.4 mile to the signed Fobes trailhead, to your
right. Parking is limited to three or four vehicles; you may

have to park a short distance below the trailhead.

Proceed up the gently graded Fobes Trail (4E02), through waist-high chaparral and, higher up, through a small open grove of Jeffrey pines to a junction with the PCT at Fobes Saddle, 1½ miles. Turn right (southeast) and follow the PCT as it climbs to a grassy bench, 2 miles from the low saddle. Halfway across the grassy area, veer left, off trail, through a grove of black oak and white fir, to the hidden summit of Palm View Peak (7185´). (The peak is misnamed — there are no palms nearby and the view from the wooded top is nonexistent.)

Return the same way. Or, you have several options. If your desire is to bag more peaks, you can follow the PCT north from Fobes Saddle and scramble to the summit of Spitler Peak (7490´), and/or Apache Peak (7567´), adding 4 and 6 miles respectively to the round trip. With a car shuttle, you can descend via the Spitler Trail to Apple Canyon (see Trip 87) or the Morris Trail to Morris Ranch Road. Any way you do it, you're bound to enjoy this sample of the scenic Desert Divide country.

TRIP: Morris Ranch Road to Desert Divide, Cedar Spring

89

5½ **miles** round trip; **1700′** elevation gain
Classification: **Moderate**
Season: **All year**
Topo maps: *Palm View Peak, Butterfly Peak* (both 7.5´)

FEATURES

On both sides of the Desert Divide are a number of little springs trickling cold water. Cedar Spring, on the desert slope of the ridge, shaded by masterful incense cedars and black oaks, is one of the nicest of these water sources. Just below the spring, in a shaded recess, is a small campsite much favored by hunters and Boy Scout groups.

This short trail trip climbs over the Desert Divide from Morris Ranch Road and drops into this little sylvan sanctuary with its ribbon of running water. It's best as a spring trip, when the water flows abundantly and the hillside is damp from spring rains.

DESCRIPTION

From State Highway 74, 8½ miles south of Mountain Center in the Garner Valley, turn left (northeast) onto Morris Ranch Road (6S53) and follow it up to a locked gate on your right, just beyond the entrance to 101 Ranch, 4 miles from the Highway. (If you reach Morris Ranch, you've driven ¼ mile too far.) Park adjacent to the locked gate.

Proceed on foot past the locked gate (a sign says *No trespassing*, but hikers are o.k.) and follow the dirt road east to its end in an oak-dotted valley, ½ mile. At the head of the miniature valley, pick up a trail that switchbacks up the chaparral-coated slope to a saddle on the Desert Divide, 1 mile. Here is a 4-way junction. Go northeast on a trail marked *Cedar Spring* and drop down the desert-facing slope ¾ mile through chaparral, contouring north after ¼ mile, to Cedar Spring, located in a forested crease in the mountainside. 100´ below the spring, on a small shaded bench, is an unimproved campsite.

Return the same way. Or, from the 4-way trail junction, follow the PCT north to Palm View Peak and on to the Fobes Canyon roadhead (see Trip 88), adding 3 miles to the trip and requiring a car shuttle.

TRIP: Highway 74 via Ramona Trail to Tool Box Spring,
90 Thomas Mountain
12 miles round trip; **2100´** elevation gain
Classification: **Moderate**
Season: **all year**
Topo maps: *Idyllwild, Anza, Butterfly Peak* (all 7.5´)

FEATURES

The Ramona Trail climbs from Garner Valley over Thomas
Mountain and down to the Ramona Indian Reservation,
named, of course, after the beautiful Indian girl in Helen Hunt
Jackson's famous novel. This trip takes the Ramona Trail to
the crest of the divide, then follows the Thomas Mountain fire
road northwest to the summit. En route you climb slopes dense
with chaparral (mainly red shank) and reach into Jeffrey pine
forest that covers the crown of the mountain, passing little Tool
Box Spring and its primitive trail camp. There is water here
usually the year round.

DESCRIPTION

From State Highway 74, in Garner Valley 8 miles south of
Mountain Center, turn right and drive through the gate (usual-
ly open) to the Ramona Trail parking area. As of this writing
(June 1999), there is a sign on Highway 74 indicating *Ramona
Trail*.

Follow the well-marked trail (3E26) as it switchbacks and
climbs up the chaparral-coated mountainside.

As you climb higher, fine views open up over the Garner
Valley, with the San Jacintos and Desert Divide country
beyond. After 1½ miles, you begin encountering Jeffrey pines,
a welcome change from the shadeless red shank, manzanita
and mountain mahogany. In 2 miles your trail enters the forest
and, a short distance higher, reaches Tool Box Spring and its
welcome water seeping from the tank and the protruding pipe.
From the spring, continue up the trail to Tool Box Campground, 3½ miles from the highway. When you reach the crest
of Thomas Mountain's long hogback, turn right onto Forest
Road 6S13 and follow it northwest to primitive Thomas
Mountain Campground and the summit, 6 miles from the start.
The Forest Service has removed the fire lookout tower that

long stood on the summit.

Return the same way. Or someone could drive up Thomas Mountain Road (reached from Highway 74 1 mile south of Lake Hemet turn-off) to meet you on top. Another option is to descend the other half of the Ramona Trail southwest to the Indian Reservation. Obtain the Indians' permission before doing this.

The Pacific Crest Trail on the Desert Divide

TRIP: Juan Diego Flat to Cahuilla Mountain

91

5 miles round trip; **800′** elevation gain
Classification: **Moderate**
Season: **November-June**
Topo map: *Anza* (7.5′)

FEATURES

Cahuilla Mountain, its stony battlements facing southward, rises in lonely isolation above Cahuilla Valley, 10
miles southwest of the San Jacintos proper. The mountain
is seldom visited nowadays, yet it is the setting for the
climax of one of the most famous novels of early-day California. The novel, of course, is Helen Hunt Jackson's
Ramona, published in 1884.

High on the mountain, on a small flat between the summits of Cahuilla and Little Cahuilla, once lived Juan
Diego, his wife Ramona Lubo, and their small child. Juan
Diego, a Mountain Cahuilla who often did odd jobs for
nearby white settlers, had fashioned a small cabin, a garden and a few fruit trees alongside a spring here. He was
known to those in the valley as a friendly but "loco" Indian,
whose occasional mental lapses caused him to do erratic
things.

One day he returned home from sheep shearing in the
San Jacinto Valley riding a strange horse. His wife, afraid
he would be accused of stealing the horse, urged him to
return it at once and get his own, which he had apparently
left in the valley. Juan replied that he would as soon as he
had rested, and fell asleep. He was awakened a short time
later by the barking of dogs, and ran out to see what was
causing the noise. A white man, Sam Temple, the owner
of the horse which Juan had ridden home, rode up, and
on seeing Juan poured out a volley of oaths, levelled his
gun and shot him to death. After firing three more shots
into the prostrate body, Temple took his horse and rode
away. Ramona, who had witnessed the killing, ran with her
baby on her back to the Cahuilla village and told what had
happened. The next day the Indians went up to the flat,
brought Juan Diego's body to the village and buried it. Sam

Temple was later tried for murder in the court of Judge Samuel V. Tripp and acquitted.

Here the story would have ended, soon forgotten, if Helen Hunt Jackson had not heard of it. Mrs. Jackson was concerned with the plight of the Indians in the United States. In 1881 she had written *A Century of Dishonor,* a factual chronicle of the white man's cruelty to the red man, but this book had not really stirred the public conscience. Now, in 1883, she was investigating Indian conditions in California for the federal government, and in the back of her mind was an idea for a novel to dramatize the sad situation. In the course of her work, Mrs. Jackson came to San Jacinto and learned of the tragic killing of Juan Diego. Here at last was the long-looked-for episode around which could be crystalized the experiences and facts she had picked up in her studies. *Ramona* was conceived.

In the novel, the character Alessandro is patterned after Juan Diego. Jim Farrar is Sam Temple. (However, the beautiful Ramona of Mrs. Jackson's pen is in no way similar to Juan Diego's wife Ramona Lubo.) Although many of the episodes are pure fiction, the tragic climax where Farrar shoots down Alessandro with Ramona looking on is very close to what actually happened.

Ramona was an overnight success, and it achieved astounding popularity that has lasted to this day. The spotlight of public attention turned to the Cahuillas, and travelers came by the wagon-load into the Cahuilla Valley, some journeying up to lonely Juan Diego Flat, others seeking out Ramona Lubo. The plight of the Cahuillas, brought in sharp focus by *Ramona,* was lessened as the federal government stepped in to take a more active role in achieving justice for the Indians.

Ramona Lubo died in 1922 and was buried beside her husband Juan Diego in the old Cahuilla cemetery that lies in the shadow of Cahuilla Mountain. Juan Diego Flat has been almost forgotten and sees few visitors nowadays. The access road, a small section of which crosses private property, is now open to the public.

This trip relives these stirring events of the past as it visits Juan Diego Flat and climbs to the top of Cahuilla Mountain for a breathtaking view over the country of Ramona and the Cahuillas.

DESCRIPTION

From the town of Anza on State Highway 371, drive west 3.8 miles to Cary Road. Turn right (north) and proceed to a junction, where you turn left (west) to Tripp Flats Ranger Station, 5 miles. Take the road (6S22) left just outside the ranger station entrance and drive up to Juan Diego Flat, 2 miles, to the beginning of the Cahuilla Mountain Trail (2E45), on your left, close to phone lines overhead, and ¼ mile *before* a road junction. As of this writing (June 1999) the trail sign, burned in a 1996 fire, has not been replaced. Park in the small clearing on your right.

Follow the distinct, well-graded trail up the northeast slope of the mountain, through an elfin forest of burnt manzanita that is swiftly growing back, to the ridgetop. The trail then crosses to the west side of the mountain, drops about 200 feet, contours, climbs through an open forest of black oak and Jeffrey pine, and arcs back to the 5635´ summit, 2½ miles. Or is it the true summit? The trail ends here and there is a summit register, but a point about ½ mile to the south appears to be as high, or perhaps a few feet higher. About ¼ mile to the north there is another bump that looks equally high.

After taking in the superb vista east over the Anza Valley, the route taken by the great pathfinder Juan Bautista Anza two centuries ago, and the long hogback of Palomar Mountain to the southwest, return the way you came.

TRIP: Hermits Bench to Palm Canyon

92 4 miles round trip; 200′ elevation gain
Classification: **Easy**
Season: **November-April**
Topo maps: *Palm Springs, Palm View Peak* (both 7.5˝)

FEATURES

The splendid palm canyons at the desert foot of the San Jacintos and Santa Rosas are a delight to behold. Thousands of California fan palms (*Washingtonia filifera*), their bright green fronds swaying in the breeze, crowd the canyon bottoms, seeking the life-giving water that tumbles down all-year streams. Rushes and other verdant water plants grow dense alongside limpid pools, completing the oasis effect that is all the more striking because the adjacent slopes are bone-dry and drab.

The daddy of all these green oasis canyons is Palm Canyon, running almost due south from Palm Springs to the Palms-to-Pines Highway. Somewhere around 3000 California fan palms grace the lower half of this canyon, extending from just below Hermits Bench almost to Palm Canyon Falls, a distance of 7 miles. Other groves of these palms extend short distances up many of the lower tributaries of Palm Canyon — Andreas Canyon, Murray Canyon, Fern Canyon, the West and East forks of Palm Canyon.

For centuries before the white man arrived, the Cahuillas lived in these beautiful canyons. Relics of this Indian habitation are still found along the banks and up the dry slopes — grinding holes, stone tools, faint traces of red pictographs. Today, most of lower Palm Canyon is the property of the Agua Caliente band of Mission Indians. Funds derived from the nominal admission charges collected from visitors at the entrance *garita* go into the tribal treasury.

This trip follows a well-traveled trail that leads up Palm Canyon from the roadhead on Hermits Bench. It is a streamside walk through lush greenery, with arid canyon walls close on both sides. You have the option of extending the trip by wandering up some of the palm-filled tributary canyons. Do it in leisurely fashion to fully appreciate nature's unique contribution to the desert side of the mountains.

DESCRIPTION

From Palm Springs drive south on South Palm Canyon Drive to the Indian toll gate at the entrance to the canyon (open 7 a.m. to 5 p.m. every day; cost is under a dollar). After paying the entrance fee, proceed south 2½ miles to the end of the road on Hermits Bench.

Walk along the trail that drops into the canyon, then winds through the California fan palms, along the stream, up-canyon for about 2 miles. Beyond here, the trail follows the east slope before dropping back into the canyon farther up (see trip 93). But you stop at the 2-mile point and saunter back down-canyon to Hermits Bench.

If you wish to explore these beautiful palm canyons further, trails lead up Fern Canyon, east from Hermits Bench, and up the East Fork, east from Palm Canyon ½ mile south of Hermits Bench. Or you can drive over to Andreas Canyon on your way out and explore the palm greenery there — the road leads west ½ mile from just south of the toll gate. Just remember you must be out of the canyons by 5 p.m., when the toll gate closes.

Palm Canyon

TRIP: Ribbonwood to Palm Canyon, Hidden Falls, Agua
Bonita Spring, Hermits Bench

93

18 miles one way; **3200'** elevation loss
Classification: **Strenuous** (1 day), **mod.** (2 days)
Season: **November-April**
Topo maps: *Palm Springs, Palm View Peak* (both 7.5´)

FEATURES

This trip, best done as an overnight backpack, descends
the length of Palm Canyon from Ribbonwood on the
Palms-to-Pines Highway to Hermits Bench, 14 mostly
downhill miles. Besides some spectacular canyon scenery,
another highlight is the rich and varied desert flora. You
start down through Upper Sonoran vegetation — slopes
dense with red shank, mesquite, sage, yucca and scattered
junipers and pinyon pines. As you descend, Lower Sonoran
flora becomes predominant — bisnaga, cholla, buckthorn,
and hedgehog cacti; agave, ocotillo, goatnut, ephedra, and
scores of other arid-zone plants. Then, alongside the creek,
you meet the startling contrast of lush greenery — California fan palm, of course, supplemented by scattered cottonwoods, rushes, ferns and grasses. It's a different world
from the San Jacinto high country just a few miles above.
Florally speaking, it's as if you had traveled from Canada
to Mexico, the contrast is so pronounced.

A car shuttle is required for this one-way trip, made more
complicated by the fact that you cannot leave your car
at Hermits Bench or anywhere inside the toll gate (Indian
property) overnight. Unless someone picks you up at the
end, plan on hiking an extra 3½ miles to the south edge of
Palm Springs. But the rewards of this venture are so great
that it is worth the extra complications.

DESCRIPTION

From Palm Desert drive up State Route 74 (Palms-to-
Pines Highway) to Ribbonwood, 18¾ miles. Turn north on
Pine View Drive and proceed ¼ mile to its end over-
looking Palm Canyon. Park here.

Arrange to be picked up at Hermits Bench, 3½ miles
south of Palm Springs at the south end of Palm Canyon

Drive, between 7 a.m. and 5 p.m. the following day, or leave another car at the south edge of Palm Springs, outside Indian property, on South Palm Canyon Drive, and walk an extra 3½ miles at the end.

The trail—in reality jeep tracks—begins just before the end of the dirt section of Pine View Drive, to your right. Go right at the first junction. Shortly beyond is a second junction: you have a choice of staying on the ridge or descending into the canyon; both trails rejoin a mile down. After 1½ miles, the jeep tracks become a trail. A half mile farther, you drop into the canyon bottom and walk close to the trickling stream. For the next 3 miles you mostly follow the canyon bottom, with detours here and there to get around rocky obstructions. You pass the entrances of Live Oak and Oak canyons, coming down from the Desert Divide country. 300 yards up the latter, out of sight around a bend, is Hidden Falls. A short, trailless, side trip gets you to the foot of the falls.

About 5½ miles from the start you pass a junction with the Live Oak Trail coming down from the Desert Divide (see Trip 94). Continue north down canyon, 2½ miles farther is Agua Bonita Spring, shaded by cottonwoods, a good overnight campsite. A short distance below here you enter Indian property (overnight camping prohibited). Below Agua Bonita, the trail climbs southeast out of the canyon to get around the rocky gorge of Palm Canyon Falls. (There is no trail through this most spectacular section of Palm Canyon; hikers have reached the falls by scrambling up-canyon from below.) For the next 6 miles you follow the cactus-rich slopes above the east wall of the canyon, crossing several small tributary canyons. As you near Hermits Bench, you look down on splendid groves of *Washington filifera*, both in the main canyon and in tributary canyons to the west. The lush greenery amid the drab desert offers a scene of striking contrast. Finally you climb to Hermits Bench, where you either pick up your ride or walk a farther 3½ miles to Palm Springs.

TRIP: Morris Ranch Road to Desert Divide, Live Oak

94 Spring, Palm Canyon, Hidden Falls, Ribbonwood
17 miles one way; **2900'** elevation gain
Classification: **Moderate** (2 days)
Season: **November-May**
Topo map: *Palm View Peak* (7.5´)

FEATURES

This backpack trip traverses the semi-arid southern end of the San Jacintos, climbing from Garner Valley over the Desert Divide, then dropping into upper Palm Canyon and ascending the latter to Ribbonwood. You pass through some rich chaparral country, and enjoy far-reaching vistas of the snow-capped high mountains and the tawny desert foothills. It makes an ideal winter or early spring outing.

DESCRIPTION

Drive to Morris Ranch Road trailhead — see trip 88.

You will come out at Ribbonwood, 10 miles farther down Highway 74, so either shuttle a second car there or arrange to be picked up there upon completing your trip.

Proceed on foot past the locked gate (a sign says *No trespassing*, but hikers are o.k.) and follow the dirt road ½ mile east to its end, then pick up the trail that switchbacks up the chaparral-covered slope to a saddle on the Desert Divide, 1 mile farther. Here is a 4-way junction (see trips 88, 89). Go right (southeast) and follow the Pacific Crest Trail past Pyramid and Lion peaks, mostly through chaparral, with scattered groves of pine and oak, to a four-way trail junction, 4 miles. You leave the Pacific Crest Trail here and turn sharp left (northeast), descending the Live Oak Trail to Live Oak Spring, 1 mile. There is usually water running out of a pipe here, and primitive camping facilities under the oaks. About ½ mile below Live Oak Spring the trail forks: the right branch is shorter and better maintained, reaching Palm Canyon in 2 miles. The left fork descends the ridge between Live Oak and Oak canyons, drops into the latter, and reaches the floor of Palm Canyon near Hidden Falls, 4 miles. Hidden Falls, spectacular in spring but usually dry by early summer, can be reached by a ½-mile scramble up Oak Canyon from Palm Canyon. Proceed up the Palm Canyon Trail (south) to Ribbonwood on Highway 74, 5 miles via the shorter route, 7 miles via the longer. (See trip 93 for Ribbonwood trailhead details.)

Palm Canyon Falls   *Louise Werner*

PART 3

The Santa Rosa Mountains

The Santa Rosa Mountains

South from the Palms-to-Pines Highway, the Santa Rosas rise as a sky island out of the desert foothills. Reaching elevations in excess of 8000′ at Toro Peak and Santa Rosa Mountain, the high mountain backbone supports a rich forest of Jeffrey and ponderosa pine, white fir and incense cedar. A multitude of springs seep cold water down the slopes to the thirsty regions below. In summer, when the surrounding desert country swelters under the burning sun, this green oasis in the sky is cool and refreshing.

There are really two Santa Rosas. South and east from the lofty Santa Rosa Mountain-Toro Peak backbone, the range is lower and shows the strong influence of the desert. Here on the slopes and benches above 4000′ Pinyon pine and California juniper are supreme, covering endless miles of mountainous terrain. On the north flank of the range is an ocean of chaparral, primarily shaggy-barked, olive-green red shank (also called ribbonwood). In the desert foothills and canyons to the east, west and south, lower Sonoran vegetation takes over — tall and spindly ocotillo, yucca, chamise, barrel and cholla cacti and waxy-green creosote. In some of the watered canyons are small oases of *Washingtonia filifera*, floral monarchs of the California desert. Except for the high backbone of Santa Rosa Mountain and Toro Peak, the Santa Rosas are primarily a desert range.

The desert Santa Rosas are the home of the largest herd of bighorn sheep in California, estimated at more than 500 head. These noble masters of the arid crags live mainly in the eastern and southern parts of the range, rocky regions where man seldom disturbs their living habits. Crucial to their survival are the handful of all-year springs that trickle

Left: Looking south from Toro Peak

from some of the pinyon flats and desert canyons. The easiest way to see and photograph bighorn sheep is to hide near one of these water holes and await their appearance. (The author has seen many in this manner.) Other large mammals common in the Santa Rosas are mule deer and mountain lion. The latter are seldom seen, but their large, unmistakable tracks betray their existence.

Perhaps the greatest appeal of the Santa Rosas is their relative isolation and primitiveness. Except for the Forest Service road climbing to Santa Rosa Mountain and Toro Peak and, at the other end of the range, jeep tracks leading into Rockhouse Canyon, the range is devoid of roads. Trails are few, and most of those that do exist are unmaintained, ancient relics of Indian days. You can have most of these mountains almost to yourself. They make for superb winter outings.

The California Wilderness Act of 1984 created the Santa Rosa Wilderness. Included within this new wilderness area is most of the northern Santa Rosas that are within San Bernardino National Forest, excluding only the Santa Rosa Mountain Road and Santa Rosa Peak. Trips within the Santa Rosa Wilderness are 96, 97 and 98. A wilderness permit is not required for these trips at present.

Man in the Santa Rosas

Like the San Jacinto country to the north, the Santa Rosas were the ancestral home of numerous Cahuilla Indian peoples. In Deep Canyon, on the northeastern slope of the range, were villages of the Western Cahuilla. Groups of Desert Cahuilla lived in spring-fed oases at the eastern foot of the mountains, above the shoreline of ancient Lake Cahuilla (today's Salton Sea). Mountain Cahuilla villages were numerous on the western slope of the range, particularly in Horse and Rockhouse canyons and on Vandeventer Flat. The Santa Rosas supplied these hardy peoples with the necessities of life — pinyon nuts, acorns, agave, yucca fibers, wild game, water. Indian footpaths crisscrossed the range, traveling from spring to spring. Many of these ancient trails are still traceable today. In summer, whole villages would migrate into the mountains to gather food and escape from the searing desert heat. About the only place in the Santa Rosas avoided by the Indians was Toro Peak; there are stories that this highest mountain in the range was taboo, the dwelling place of evil spirits.

Spanish trail-blazer Juan Bautista Anza was probably the first white man to get a good look at the Santa Rosas — in 1774 during his historic overland trek from Mexico to Monterey. Anza and his party rounded the southern tip of the range after crossing the Colorado Desert, then paralleled the Santa Rosas to the west as they ascended Coyote Canyon. There is no record that he took more than perfunctory notice of the range. In fact, the Spaniards and their Mexican Californio successors tended to avoid the mountains of California.

The Californios apparently supplied the name for the mountains, however. "Santa Rosa" was the name given to a Mexican land grant in western Riverside County, dated 1845. This name was apparently later transferred to the mountain range. The reason is a mystery, for the Santa Rosa Mountains lie many miles south of the original land grant. Early maps of San Diego County show the range as an extension of the San Jacintos. Not until 1901, when the U.S. Geological Survey completed its mapping of the mountains, did the name "Santa Rosa Mountains" come into general use.

Gold seekers were probably the first white men to penetrate the desert ramparts of the Santa Rosas. The earliest visitor may have been one-legged Thomas L. "Pegleg" Smith. In 1828 Smith, traveling from Yuma to Los Angeles via Warner's Ranch, left the standard route somewhere near the southern end of the Santa Rosas and sought a shortcut. The story goes that he picked up some black lumps of what he thought was native copper atop "one of three hills". In Los Angeles he showed his rocks to a friend, who suggested he have them assayed. The assayer's report: pure gold coated with "black desert varnish". Smith returned to the region where he found the rocks but was never able to locate the right spot. Ever since, an endless stream of prospectors have sought Pegleg Smith's fabled "black gold". The southern Santa Rosas have been "turned inside out" in a vain search that has lasted more than a century.

Pegleg's black gold may be nothing more than an elusive fable, but gold in small amounts has been brought out of the Santa Rosas. Around 1900 Nicholas Schwartz made a strike in upper Rockhouse Canyon on the southwest slope of the range. It is said that Schwartz took out $18,000 in several years work. He reportedly built and occupied one of the rock houses that gave the canyon its name. Old Nicholas Canyon, a tributary of Rockhouse Canyon, honors the old prospector today. Other prospectors have dug out minute amounts of gold from ledges in the Rockhouse Canyon area, but not enough to make their years of searching worthwhile. And there was Fig Tree John, the colorful Cahuilla Indian who lived above the shores of the Salton Sea and died, some say, at the ripe age of 136. Old Fig Tree often made his purchases with gold dust or small nuggets, giving rise to the belief that he had a secret gold mine somewhere in the Santa Rosas. Even today, an occasional prospector sets out to find the "lost" gold mine of Fig Tree John.

The largest commercial mine in the Santa Rosas was the Garnet Queen, located at 6000′ elevation on the northwest slope of the range. Tungsten and garnet were recovered from the Garnet Queen Mine on and off from its development in 1896 into the 1940s. The mine changed hands several time under false premises, and was a marginal success at best.

In 1897 the entire Santa Rosa Mountains were included within the newly created San Jacinto Forest Reserve. Charlie Vandeventer, who had a cabin on what is now Vandeventer Flat, was appointed forest ranger and assigned to patrol the Santa Rosas, which, according to all accounts, he did with vigor and relish. In 1908 the old San Jacinto Reserve was cut down in size and joined to the Trabuco Reserve in the Santa Ana Mountains to form Cleveland National Forest. Only the northern end of the Santa Rosas remained as part of the Cleveland. Since 1925, this north section has been in San Bernardino National Forest. The northwestern slope, including the summit of Toro Peak, is within the Santa Rosa Indian Reservation.

Until recent years, only a handful of settlers sought homes in the desert-tempered Santa Rosas. The Vandeventer family built a cattle ranch at the northwestern foot of the range in the 1890s, and herded their stock to high mountain pastures every summer. Charley Van Deventer was for years a familiar character in these parts. A.H. Nightingale came to Pinyon Flats early in this century and built a hunting cabin at Stump Spring, high on the forested slope of Santa Rosa Mountain. Desert Steve Ragsdale, long a gas-station operator at Desert Center and later the best known dweller of the Santa Rosas, came to the mountains in 1937. He bought 560 acres of timberland atop Santa Rosa Mountain and, right on the summit, built a sturdy log cabin and a spectacular tree ladder, and posted his mountain domain with placards advising visitors, among other things, that "Decent folks are welcome; Enjoy but don't destroy." Old Desert Steve died a few years ago, and his cabin burned down several years ago.

Until the 1940s the Santa Rosa Mountain-Toro Peak high country was reached only by steep trails. Since then, the road built by the Forest Service and Desert Steve Ragsdale to Santa Rosa Mountain and the later extension to Toro Peak have rendered this sylvan sky island accessible to less energetic campers and hunters. Public camp grounds have been constructed high in the forest at Santa Rosa Spring, Stump Spring and Cedar Spring.

On the lower northern slopes, subdividers are moving in. Pinyon Flat is now honeycombed with roads and new homes are springing up along the Palms-to-Pines Highway. The San Jacinto Mountain Conservation League is seeking some sort of protective classification before speculation and haphazard development overrun this high-desert northern end of the Santa Rosas.

But most of the range remains as wild as ever. South from Horsethief Creek and Toro Peak, the Santa Rosas are the lonely domain of desert bighorn sheep, coyotes and rattlesnakes. Here, often within sight of the tourist-infested Salton Sea and Anza-Borrego State Park, you can wander for days, with only the wind, the soft rustle of pinyon needles, and the occasional howl of a coyote to keep you company.

Desert Steve Ragsdale's cabin

TRIP: Santa Rosa Mountain Road to Toro Peak

95

3 miles round trip; **800'** elevation gain
Classification: **Easy**
Season: **May-November**
Topo map: *Toro Peak* (7.5´)

FEATURES

8716' Toro Peak is the crown of the Santa Rosas. From its summit you are rewarded with far-reaching views that take in the entire Santa Rosa range, the San Jacintos to the north, the Coachella Valley, the Salton Sea, Anza-Borrego State Park, and mile after mile of endless desert, stretching to Mexico.

Until a few years ago, Toro Peak had a nice summit block of jumbo granite boulders and gnarled Jeffrey pines. (The writer is fortunate enough to have climbed it then.) But today a steep dirt road has been bulldozed up, and the top has been flattened for a TV microwave relay station and a Marine Corps radio-relay outpost. Just below the top is a heliport.

Toro Peak is believed to have received its name from Los Torres (The Bulls), a Cahuilla Indian village once located in the Coachella Valley, due east of the peak. The peak lies within the boundary of the Santa Rosa Indian Reservation. The Indians have leased the summit to the Marine Corps.

This trip leaves the Santa Rosa Mountain Road at a locked gate and climbs the steep bulldozed path to the summit. The views are still superb of distant landmarks, if you don't let yourself be bothered by the destruction and uprooting close at hand.

DESCRIPTION

From Palm Desert drive up the Palms-to-Pines Highway (Highway 74) 19½ miles to a junction with the Santa Rosa Mountain Road, marked by a large wooden sign. Turn left (south) and proceed via the well-graded dirt road up the mountainside, past the turn-off to Santa Rosa's summit

(10 miles; on the return trip you may wish to turn off here and drive the mile up to Desert Steve Ragsdale's mountaintop cabin and tree ladder), to a locked gate 1 mile past Stump Springs, 12¼ miles from Highway 74. Park 50 yards along the road, at a widening where you won't block traffic.

Proceed on foot past the locked gate, continuing 1¼ miles up the road and going right at two forks, to a generator station just below the peak. Beyond, ascend the very steep bulldozed swath ¼ mile to the summit installations. Take care not to disturb the electronic equipment.

After taking in the wondrous vista, return the way you came, or descend directly down the northwest slope, through pine and fir, to the road, which you should intersect near the locked gate.

TRIP: Santa Rosa Mountain Road to Alta Seca Bench

96 8 miles round trip; 800′ elevation loss and gain
Classification: **Moderate**
Season: **May-November**
Topo map: *Toro Peak* (7.5′)

FEATURES

Southeast from Toro Peak, the sky island of the Santa Rosas extends three miles before plunging abruptly to desert canyons and foothills. This section of undisturbed high country is known to old-timers as Alta Seca Bench, although it is not so labeled on maps. Little shallow valleys filled with Jeffrey pine and live oak lie under rocky outcroppings and gentle, chaparral-spotted slopes. It is a place where you can find natural beauty and solitude, and, from its edge, gaze far out over the desert.

No maintained trails reach into the Alta Seca, and about the only visitors nowadays are occasional deer hunters during the fall. But you can find traces of the historic old Indian pathway that climbed out of Horsethief Canyon, crossed the bench, and descended to Old Santa Rosa, a long-abandoned Cahuilla village near the head of Rockhouse Canyon. This trail is too ancient and overgrown to follow with certainty today. You can read about it in Charles Francis Saunders' chapter "Old Santa Rosa" in his *Southern Sierras of California*; in George Wharton James' "Up Martinez Canyon" in *Wonders of the California Desert*, and, more recently, in Nina Paul Shumway's "Burro-ing in the Santa Rosas" in her *Your Desert and Mine*. These books offer delightful introductions to the Santa Rosa high country and the Indian trails that once crisscrossed it.

This cross-country trip leaves Santa Rosa Mountain Road below Toro Peak and drops to Alta Seca Bench, then crosses it to a delightful pine flat at the southeastern end. Here you can look down into Rockhouse Basin and see the route the Indians took to Old Santa Rosa. (Unless you're an experienced mountaineer and are equipped for a 2-day trip, don't try to descend the old pathway.) There is no water on Alta Seca (High Dry) Bench, so tote 2 canteens.

DESCRIPTION

Follow driving directions of trip 95.

Proceed on foot 1 mile past the locked gate, up the dirt road, to a fork just before the main road turns right to climb to the top of Toro Peak. Go left ¼ mile to a dead end. From here on it's cross-country. Descend southeast 1 mile over rocky terrain spotted with pines and chaparral to Alta Seca Bench. Then follow the bench southeast 2 more miles, staying to the right (southwest) of several boulder outcroppings, to a shallow bowl filled with Jeffrey pines and some live oaks. Here, in a parklike setting, is an ideal picnic spot. To look down, climb to the rocky rim immediately south of the shallow valley. The old Indian trail dropped south down a steep ridge to Old Santa Rosa, nestled at the head of the large desert basin you see below you.

Return the same way, with 800′ gain at the end. Crosscountry travel can be deceptive; if you're not certain of your return route, head up for the right (north) shoulder of Toro Peak, which looms high before you.

TRIP: Pinyon Flat to Horsethief Creek

97

5 miles round trip; **900'** elevation loss and gain
Classification: **Easy**
Season: **November-April**
Topo maps: *Toro Peak, Martinez Mtn.* (both 7.5´)

FEATURES

The northeastern end of the Santa Rosas is high desert country, ideal for winter hiking trips. Vast sloping benches and boulder-laced hills are dotted with pinyon pine, juniper, red shank, chamise, yucca, agave and prickly pear. Shady cottonwoods grow in stream-watered canyons and around seeping springs. The snow-crowned Santa Rosa Mountain-Toro Peak massif dominates the southwestern skyline, while white-capped San Jacinto glimmers on the northern horizon.

This leisurely trip samples a small bit of this delightful high desert region. You follow the Cactus Spring Trail, an old Indian pathway recently reworked by the Forest Service, from near the Palms-to-Pines Highway down into the shady gorge of Horsethief Creek. Here, amid tall cottonwoods and willows, alongside the trickling stream, you can picnic and enjoy nature's solitude.

Horsethief Creek is wrapped in the lore of the old West. A century ago, it is said, horse thieves used this canyon as a hideout and a place to rebrand stolen stock. Gangs of rustlers stole the horses in the San Diego region and drove them to Horsethief Creek where the animals were rebranded, then herded them to San Bernardino to sell. Before the horses could leave San Bernardino, the story goes, the bandits stole the animals back and went through the entire process in reverse.

DESCRIPTION

From Palm Desert drive 16 miles up the Palm-to-Pines Highway (Highway 74) to Pinyon Flat. Opposite the campground road, turn left (south) onto a paved side road (7S09). A new highway sign indicates the Ribbonwood Equestrian Park and the Sawmill Trail, a new footpath leading south. Drive 7S09 to the large parking area, ¼ mile. Notice the old Cactus Springs Trail sign on the left side of the parking area.

Proceed east on the Cactus Springs Trail. After 200 yards you enter the Santa Rosa Wilderness, indicated by a large sign. You follow the trail east, up and down over several small north-draining gullies, and drop to Horsethief Creek, 2 miles. Here is an all-year stream shaded by magnificent cottonwoods. You can explore up or down Horsethief Creek for quite some distance.

Return the same way.

Cottonwoods, Horsethief Creek

TRIP: Pinyon Flat to Horsethief Creek, Little Pinyon

98 Flat, Cactus Spring, Pinyon Alta Flat, Agua Alta
Spring

18 miles round trip; 2400′ elevation gain

Classification: **Mod.** (2 days), **strenuous** (1 day)

Season: **November-April**

Topo maps: *Toro Peak, Martinez Mtn.* (both 7.5′)

FEATURES

This trip follows the Cactus Spring Trail from near the Palms-to-Pines Highway down across Horsethief Creek, then up over miles of rolling plateau country covered by an elfin forest of pinyon and juniper, to Agua Alta Spring. Agua Alta (High Water) Spring, creased into the south slope of Martinez Mountain, flows sparingly over green slime among cat's-claw bushes and bunch grass — not much to look at, but a heaven-sent source of water for the bighorn sheep that roam this region. Keep a sharp lookout; you may spot some of these noble animals climbing the rocky slopes of Martinez Mountain or coming down for water.

DESCRIPTION

Drive to Cactus Springs trailhead, then proceed to Horsethief canyon (see trip 97).

The trail crosses the creek, climbs steeply east out of the canyon, follows a dry wash, and climbs through sloping, pinyon-dotted terrain to Cactus Spring, 2 miles from Horsethief Creek. The spring, 25 yards north of the trail, is often dry. Your trail continues east, turns left up a broad, sandy wash, curves southeast up a tributary wash, and climbs toward the ridge south of Martinez Mountain. You cross the ridge well above its low point and descend into a series of dry washes leading southeast. The path climbs and descends through rough pinyon-and-juniper terrain to Agua Alta Spring, marked by a wooden sign, 6 miles from Horsethief Creek. The trickling spring is about 100 yards up the draw to your left. Enough water is almost always available here for drinking and cooking. About ½ mile farther on is Pinyon Alta Flat and its campsites.

Return the same way. An option is to scramble north up the long slope to the rocky summit block of Martinez Mountain, 5 miles round trip from Aqua Alta Spring. A very interesting option, with a car shuttle, is to descend southeastward, following the Indian Trail, into Martinez Canyon, then follow the broad canyon around to the northeast all the way out to Highway 86 near Valerie Jean's Date Shop, 15 miles. A variation is to descend east from Pinyon Alta Flat into Aqua Alta Canyon, then follow this canyon to its junction with Martinez Canyon and on out to the highway. Old trails descend both of these desert canyons. For these last two options, you will need the *Valerie* (7.5′) quadrangle map as well as *Toro Peak* and *Martinez Mtn.*

Hidden Spring

TRIP: Rockhouse Canyon to Hidden Spring, Cottonwood
99 Spring, Old Santa Rosa (ruins)
14 miles round trip; **2200′** elevation gain
Classification: **Mod.** (2 days), **strenuous** (1 day)
Season: **November-April**
Topo maps: *Clark Lake, Clark Lake NE* (both 7.5′)

FEATURES

Charles Francis Saunders, writing in 1923, called Rockhouse Canyon "as wild a region, perhaps, as the Southern
California mountains afford, scantily watered, uninhabit-
ed and unvisited except by an occasional wandering en-
thusiast like ourselves or a cowman in search of his strayed
stock." Saunders' description holds true today. Only an
occasional visitor makes his lonely way up this narrow
desert canyon to the hidden alluvial plain immediately
above its head, nestled under the brooding shoulder of
the Santa Rosa massif.

Years ago, this naked sloping plain above Rockhouse
Canyon was the home of Mountain Cahuillas. Their vil-
lage, at the northwest edge of the plain, was Old Santa
Rosa. They gathered mescal from agave plants, acorns from
oaks and pinyon nuts from pines, and took water from the
seeping springs below the mountainside. Although the
Cahuillas have long departed and nothing remains of Old
Santa Rosa, signs of their former presence are numerous.
Potsherds, ollas and other artifacts can be seen by the
diligent searcher. The crumbling walls of rock houses near
Cottonwood Spring (dry), however, date from a later era
when Nicholas Schwarz and other prospectors combed the
region for mineral wealth. From these remains Rockhouse
Canyon received its name.

This wintertime trip ascends the narrow confines of
Rockhouse Canyon to the lonely plain at the foot of the
Santa Rosas. Chances are you will have this forgotten
corner of the Santa Rosas to yourself. The only sure water is
in Nicholias Canyon, just above the northwest corner of
the sloping plain. You will probably need a 4-wheel drive

vehicle to reach within 2 miles of Hidden Spring; the road is very poor.

DESCRIPTION

From Borrego Springs, follow San Diego County road S22 east, then north, then east again to the Pegleg Smith Monument, 9½ miles. Continue east ½ mile farther to an unmarked dirt road branching left (northeast) toward Clark Dry Lake. (You can also reach this junction from State Route 86 by turning west at Salton City on the Borrego-Salton Seaway and following the latter 22 miles.) 1½ miles north on the before-mentioned dirt road is another junction; go left (northwest), around the west edge of Clark Dry Lake and the strange protruding antennae of the U. of Maryland Radio Telescope. In 8 miles (from S22) your road enters a rocky wash; those with low-slung vehicles may wish to park here. Continue up the wash, on rocks and soft sand, 1½ miles farther, then turn sharp right, out of the wash, where a sign reads *Rockhouse Canyon.* Your "road" rounds a low ridge and enters the lower reaches of Rockhouse Canyon—the absolute limit for standard cars. Jeep tracks continue another mile up-canyon until they too become impassable for any type of vehicle. Continue up the canyon on foot to Hidden Spring, marked by a wooden sign (12½ miles from S22). Water is seldom available here.

Proceed northeast into the narrows of Rockhouse Canyon. After 3 miles, you round a bend to the north and reach the southern end of the broad, sloping plain, covered with xerophytic shrubs. Follow the dry creekbed 1 mile northwest to the remains of rock houses on your right, and ¼ mile farther to small Cottonwood Spring. The spring is now completely dry; except for one tough cottonwood, the trees are dead. To visit the ruins of Old Santa Rosa, continue 2½ miles to the valley's north edge, close under the abrupt wall of the Santa Rosa Mountains. The village site and its artifacts are protected by Antiquities Act of 1906. There are a few seeps at the foot of the mountain wall, but your only sure water is in Nicholias Canyon, a mile northwest.

TRIP: Coachella Valley to Rabbit Peak

100
16 miles round trip; 6700' elevation gain
Classification: **Strenuous**
Season: **November-April**
Topo map: *Rabbit Peak* (7½')

FEATURES

Rising high over the southern end of the Santa Rosas, overlooking Anza-Borrego Desert State Park on one side and the Salton Sea on the other, is the 6623' hogback of Rabbit Peak. Pinyon, juniper and mountain mahogany cover the higher parts of this desert mountain, while the arid lower slopes are spotted with ocotillo, agave, yucca, prickly pear and other Lower Sonoran types of plants.

Rabbit Peak is a long, tough climb. No trails reach above its desert foothills, and to reach its summit you must scramble up steep, cactus-infested slopes and traverse to the north end of its long hogback. Yet it seems to hold a strange attraction to climbers, and there are those who return to this dry, unspectacular mountain time and again. In fact, it seems somehow to inspire the grandest and most touching literary artistry — exemplified in the epic poem "Wild Rabbit" written by Los Angeles Sierra Clubber Chester Versteeg, placed in the summit register in 1948:

You sneak up on him, mile by mile,
Foot by foot, bit by bit.
Four jaws are grim, there's no smile;
Then a final lunge and you've captured it —
                              THE RABBIT!

For seasoning use sage or wild pea,
And, if you want to pep it up a bit,
Dip the meat yonder in the Salton Sea.
Yum yum, boys and girls, this is it —
                         THE WILD RABBIT!

Telescope, White Mountain, Boundary or New York
    Butte,*
You bet, we like 'em all a bit.
But today — no steak tough as a climber's boot;
Today, tender and sweet, this is it —
                           WILD RABBIT!

*Other popular desert peaks.

In 1950, a Sierra Club group led by Jerry Zagorites added the following verse after climbing through clouds and cold rain:

And for flavor add snow and fog,
Even worse than Los Angeles smog.
When it is so cold the fire freezes,
And snow and sleet come on icy breezes —
                    FROZEN WILD RABBIT!

The latest stanza is a lament by Parker Severson of Los Angeles, written in 1964:

Alas, what prompts we mortals so vain,
To pursue this mighty sore-muscle game.
Plodding with sweat and tears through storm and rain,
To crown these noble summits with our name?

Rabbit Peak can be climbed from almost any direction, a tough haul any way you do it. This trip starts from the Salton Sea side and utilizes an old prospectors' trail to gain the lower slopes. Take along a pen or pencil, and add your own stanza to the inspired poetry that this desert mountain seems to generate.

There is *no water* enroute; take a plentiful supply. (There is a spring in Sheep Canyon which usually flows into April or May.)

DESCRIPTION

From Indio drive south on State Route 86 15½ miles to the 74th Avenue junction. From here, drive south on Fillmore Avenue to its end at a levee, 2½ miles. Park here.

Walk south over the levee and down into the wash below it. Turn right and proceed west along the wash (quite sandy in places) to where a road crosses it, ½ mile. Turn left (south) on the road and go about 100 yards, passing a lemon grove on your right, to a poor jeep road. Follow this road southwest about ½ mile to the beginning of a well-ducked trail that leads across the open desert toward the mountains. (The trail is indistinct in places, so look for the ducks.) Your route climbs steadily southwest to the ridge between Sheep and Barton canyons, 3½ miles. You now follow a ducked climbers' path to the left, up to the ridgetop, across a saddle, and on up to a broad, undulating bench just below the steep ridge leading up to Rabbit's hogback, 6 miles and 3300' gain from the start. This is where most parties camp, but it is waterless.

Beyond, it is steep, trailless climbing. Climb up the ridge, around several big rock outcrops, to the top of the sloping hogback that is Rabbit Peak. You follow ducks most of the way. The register is in the summit rocks at far (northwest) end of the plateau.

Return the same way.

The Salton Sea from the eastern slope of Rabbit Peak

ORGANIZED TRAIL SYSTEMS

Pacific Crest Trail Traversing the crest of the Pacific states from Mexico to Canada, two-thirds of its 2400 miles complete, is the Pacific Crest Trail, the most ambitious footpath in the United States. The proposal to carve this wilderness path from border to border was conceived by a single individual in 1932 — Clinton C. Clarke of Pasadena. He urged the Forest Service and National Park System to knit together and extend the threads of high-country footpaths already existing, such as the Oregon Skyline Trail and California's John Muir Trail. Clarke achieved partial success before his death in 1957; he prevailed upon the Forest Service to call the footpaths in Oregon and Washington by the collective name "Pacific Crest Trail System." But not until 1968, when Congress, responding to pressure from outdoorsmen, created the Pacific Crest as a national scenic trail, did active work begin to join together a border-to-border system.

The Pacific Crest Trail through San Bernardino National Forest is incomplete, but most of the route has been charted out and some stretched of trail have been finished. Temporary detours have been marked around some of the incomplete sections. The route, south to north, including detours goes as follows.

From Anza Valley up and along the crest of Thomas Mountain, down Thomas Mountain Road to Highway 74, north from the east end of Lake Hemet through May Valley to the South Ridge of Tahquitz Peak, over Tahquitz Peak and down to Saddle Junction, up past Wellman's Cienega to San Jacinto Peak, down the Deer Springs Trail to the Fuller Ridge Trail, northwest on the latter to Black Mountain Road, down the north slope to Hurley Flat and on to San Gorgonio Pass. East to Whitewater Road, north up the Whitewater River, across the ridge to Mission Creek, up the North Fork of the latter to Heart Bar Creek, up Coon Creek and across Onyx Summit, northwest down to Big Bear City, up Van

Dusen Canyon to Holcomb Valley, west to Big Pine Flat, down Holcomb Creek to Deep Creek, west north of Lake Arrowhead to Grass Valley Creek, south on Tunnel 2 Ridge, west down the East Fork of the Mojave River to Summit Valley, west to Cajon Pass and up Lone Pine Canyon into the San Gabriels.

Golden Arrowhead Trail The Great Western Council of the Boy Scouts of America, located in Van Nuys (tel. 213-786-9500), offers scouts the challenge of . . . making the *Golden Arrowhead* hike across the San Bernardino Mountains (comparable to the *Silver Moccasin* hike in the San Gabriels). The 47-mile trail starts at Fallsvale in Mill Creek Canyon, crosses the San Gorgonio Wilderness to Barton Flats, drops down to Seven Oaks, then goes up the Radford fire road to Big Bear Lake, through Fawnskin Valley, along Butler Peak ridge to Green Valley Lake, down to Deep Creek and thence to the Big Horn Boy Scout camp complex out from Cedar Glen. Boy Scouts who complete the long trek receive the Golden Arrowhead award.

APPENDIX II

THE DESERT FACE OF SAN JACINTO

San Jacinto's northeast escarpment is one of the most precipitous mountain faces in the United States, dropping almost 10000′ in five horizontal miles. It has long fascinated mountaineers, who see in its jagged ridges and sheer granite cliffs a resemblance to the Sierra Nevada. To accomplish this most strenuous mountain climb in Southern California has been the goal of numerous experienced hikers and climbers.

There are four main routes used by those who make this desert-alpine ascent: the East Fork of Snow Creek directly to the summit of San Jacinto Peak, the old Chino Trail from Palm Springs to Long Valley, Tahquitz Creek, and the old Gordon route from Andreas Canyon to Caramba Camp and upper Tahquitz Creek. These routes are extremely strenuous, difficult to follow, and dangerous in places. They should be attempted only by experienced mountaineers in top physical condition. Following are brief route descriptions.

Snow Creek, East Fork: This is a steep, trailless rock scramble, with several class 4 pitches (rope required), from the end of Snow Creek Road directly up the north face of the summit, gaining 8,800′ in 6 miles. It is only for experienced mountaineers with rock-climbing knowledge. Since you start on the property of the Palm Springs Water Department, you must secure permission before the attempt by writing the Desert Water Agency, 1345 North Palm Canyon Drive, Palm Springs 92262. From the roadhead, ascend south onto the sloping plateau that parallels Snow Creek on the east, avoiding the brush and boulders of the creek bed. After 2 miles, you reach the Narrows, where climbing begins. From 3,500′ to 6,000′, the gorge of Snow Creek is punctuated with numerous granite waterfalls, ranging in height from 10 to 40 feet. On both sides of the narrow canyon are either abrupt granite walls or steep slopes choked with brush. For most of this section you can climb along the side of the falls, using a rope belay. In some places it's easier to thrash upward through the brush.

Right: Climbing waterfall, Snow Creek

At 6000' you are above the last waterfall and your technical problems are over. The next 4800' are simply an extremely steep trudge up the widened gully to the summit. If it's May or early June (the best time to make the climb), you climb up the snow tongue; later in the year you're on loose boulders or granite staircase. The climb from the roadhead to the summit takes from 10 to 13 hours for parties in top condition. With a predawn start, you should be able to make the summit by late afternoon, staying the night in the stone shelter just over the peak. Strong parties have made the climb and descended to Humber Park the same day. The first ascent of this North Face via Snow Creek was made by Howard J. Sloan, Morgan Leonard and Glenn Rickenbough of the Sierra Club, Los Angeles, on April 16, 1932. Since then, at least 40 parties (including the author in 1958) have made the climb.

Chino Trail: This footpath, originally an old Indian trail, last worked by the CCC in the 1930s, climbs up the northeast escarpment from Palm Springs to Long Valley, on the ridge south of Chino Canyon. It gains 7600' in 9 winding, switchbacking miles, from arid, cactus-infested slopes into lush pine-and-fir country at the top. Most of the old trail is still well-defined, although the middle portion has some brushy sections. Watch for rattlesnakes.

Tahquitz Creek: This route — trailless except for the first mile to Tahquitz Falls — follows the extremely rugged gorge of Tahquitz Creek from Palm Springs 6000' up to Caramba Camp. It involves difficult climbing around several waterfalls and cascades, and some bushwhacking higher up. You must obtain permission from the Agua Caliente Indian Reservation to do this; the lower canyon was closed to the public in 1969 after a hippie "invasion."

Gordon Trail: This is another ancient Indian path, reworked by Dr. M.S. Gordon of Palm Springs in 1915–16 and the CCC in the 1930s, but not touched since then and badly overgrown. It climbs from the mouth of Andreas Canyon northwest up and over the ridge to Caramba Camp in Tahquitz Creek, 6000' gain in about 8 miles of walking. Much of the trail is brush-infested and very difficult to follow. The route is definitely not recommended.

Right: On the snow tongue, Snow Creek

BIBLIOGRAPHY

General

Fletcher, Colin, *The Complete Walker*, Alfred A. Knopf, New York, 1968

Leadabrand, Russ, *A Guidebook to the San Bernardino Mountains of California*, Ward Ritchie Press, Los Angeles, 1964

Manning, Harvey (ed.), *Mountaineering: The Freedom of the Hills*, The Mountaineers, Seattle, 1967

Nature

Booth, Ernest S, *Mammals of Southern California*, U. of Calif. Press, Berkeley, 1968

Dawson, E. Yale, *Cacti of California*, U. of Calif. Press, Berkeley, 1966

DeLisle, Harold, *Common Plants of the Southern California Mountains*, Naturegraph Co., Healdsburg, 1961

DeLisle, Harold, *Wildlife of the Southern California Mountains*, Naturegraph Co., Healdsburg, 1963

Furtz, Francis, *The Elfin Forest*, Times-Mirror Press, Los Angeles, 1923

Grinnell, Joseph, *Biota of the San Bernardino Mountains*, U. of Calif. Publ. in Zoology, Berkeley, 1908

Grinnell, Joseph and H.S. Swarth, *Birds and Mammals of the San Jacinto Area*, U. of Calif. Publ. in Zoology, Berkeley, 1913

Hall, Harvey M., *A Botanical Survey of San Jacinto Mountain*, U. of Calif. Publ. in Botany, Berkeley, 1902

Kenline, George A., *Familiar Trees of the San Bernardino Mountains*, Grizzly Press, Big Bear Lake, 1971

Munz, Philip, *California Mountain Wildflowers*, U. of Calif. Press, Berkeley, 1963

Peterson, P. Victor, *Native Trees of Southern California*, U. of Calif. Press, Berkeley, 1966

Raven, Peter H., *Native Shrubs of Southern California*, U. of Calif. Press, Berkeley, 1966

Sudworth, George, *Forest Trees of the Pacific Slope*, Dover Publications, New York, 1967 (reprint of 1908 edition)

Vaughn, Francis E., *Geology of the San Bernardino Mountains North of San Gorgonio Pass*, U. of Calif. Publ. in Geology, Berkeley, 1922

History

Beattie, George William & Helen Pruitt, *Heritage of the Valley: San Bernardino's First Century*, San Pasqual Press, Pasadena, 1939

Beldon, Burr, "History in the Making", *San Bernardino Sun-Telegram,* various issues, 1953–1964

Big Bear Panorama, Big Bear High School, Big Bear, 1934

Brown, John, Jr., & James Boyd, *History of San Bernardino and Riverside Counties,* Lewis Publ. Co., Chicago, 1922

Drake, Austin, *Big Bear Valley: Its History, Legends and Tales,* Big Bear Historical Society, Big Bear, 1970 (reprint of 1949 ed.)

Holmes, Elmer W., *History of Riverside County, California,* Historic Record Co., Los Angeles, 1912

Hughes, Tom, *History of Banning and San Gorgonio Pass,* Banning Record, Banning, no date (1938?)

Ingersoll, Luther A., *Century Annals of San Bernardino County, 1769–1904,* Ingersoll, Los Angeles, 1904

Jackson, Helen Hunt, *Ramona,* Little, Brown & Co., Boston, 1884

James, George Wharton, *Through Ramona's Country,* Little, Brown & Co., Boston, 1909

James, George Wharton, *Wonders of the Colorado Desert,* Little, Brown & Co., Boston, 1906

James, Harry C., *The Cahuilla Indians,* Westernlore Press, Los Angeles, 1960 (reprinted 1969 by Malki Museum Press, Banning)

Johnson, Frank, *The Serrano Indians of Southern California,* Malki Museum Press, Banning, 1965

La Fuze, Pauliena, *Saga of the San Bernardinos,* San Bernardino County Museum Association, 1971.

Maxwell, Ernest (ed.), *The Town Crier* (newspaper), Idyllwild, various issues, 1946–1971

Patencio, Chief Francisco (told to Margaret Boynton), *Stories and Legends of the Palm Springs Indians,* Palm Springs Desert Museum, Palm Springs, 1970 (reprint of 1943 edition)

Ruby, Jay W., *Aboriginal Uses of Mt. San Jacinto State Park,* U.C.L.A. Dept. of Anthropology Annual Publ., Los Angeles, 1961–62

Saunders, Charles F., *The Southern Sierras of California,* Houghton-Mifflin Co., Boston, 1923

Williamson, Robert S., *Report of Explorations in California for Railroad Routes,* War Dept., Washington, 1853

Woodward, Lois Ann, *Mount San Jacinto,* W.P.A. Project, Berkeley, 1937 (typescript in Bancroft Library)

INDEX

Trail notes

READ THIS

Hiking in the backcountry entails unavoidable risk that every hiker assumes and must be aware of and respect. The fact that a trail is described in this book is not a representation that it will be safe for you. Trails vary greatly in difficulty and in the degree of conditioning and agility one needs to enjoy them safely. On some hikes routes may have changed or conditions may have deteriorated since the descriptions were written. Also trail conditions can change even from day to day, owing to weather and other factors. A trail that is safe on a dry day or for a highly conditioned, agile, properly equipped hiker may be completely unsafe for someone else or unsafe under adverse weather conditions.

You can minimize your risks on the trail by being knowledgeable, prepared and alert. There is not space in this book for a general treatise on safety in the mountains, but there are a number of good books and public courses on the subject and you should take advantage of them to increase your knowledge. Just as important, you should always be aware of your own limitations and of conditions existing when and where you are hiking. If conditions are dangerous, or if you're not prepared to deal with them safely, choose a different hike! It's better to have wasted a drive than to be the subject of a mountain rescue.

These warnings are not intended to scare you off the trails. Millions of people have safe and enjoyable hikes every year. However, one element of the beauty, freedom and excitement of the wilderness is the presence of risks that do not confront us at home. When you hike you assume those risks. They can be met safely, but only if you exercise your own independent judgement and common sense.

IMPORTANT NOTICE

The massive Willow Fire of September 1999 burned over 63,000 acres on the north slope of the San Bernardinos and the high desert. It was the largest fire in the San Bernardino National Forest in 80 years. Eleven trips in *San Bernardino Mountain Trails* are partly or wholly burned over: trips 4, 9, 10, 12, 13, 14, 15, 16, 17, 18, and 19. Although they are still hikeable, you will be walking through large areas of charred forest and chaparral until the vegetation can grow back. We suggest you call the Arrowhead Ranger District (909) 337-2444 or the Big Bear Ranger District (909) 866-3437 before you attempt any of these trips.